Frank Hatton

**North Borneo**

Explorations and Adventures on the Equator

Frank Hatton

**North Borneo**
*Explorations and Adventures on the Equator*

ISBN/EAN: 9783337244200

Printed in Europe, USA, Canada, Australia, Japan

Cover: Foto ©Andreas Hilbeck / pixelio.de

More available books at **www.hansebooks.com**

# NORTH BORNEO

## EXPLORATIONS AND ADVENTURES ON THE EQUATOR.

BY THE LATE

### FRANK HATTON,

*Fellow of the Chemical Society and Associate of the Institute of Chemistry, of London; Member of the Chemical Society of Berlin, and of the Straits Settlements Branch of the Asiatic Society; and Scientific Explorer in the Service of the British North Borneo Company.*

With Biographical Sketch and Notes by

JOSEPH HATTON,

AND

PREFACE BY SIR WALTER MEDHURST,

*Commissioner of Emigration to the British North Borneo Company, and late Her Majesty's Consul at Shanghai.*

ILLUSTRATED.

London:
SAMPSON LOW, MARSTON, SEARLE, & RIVINGTON,
CROWN BUILDINGS, 188, FLEET STREET.
1885.

LONDON:
PRINTED BY GILBERT AND RIVINGTON, LIMITED,
ST. JOHN'S SQUARE.

# PREFACE.

A LONG association with the East, an intimate acquaintance with the work which has been accomplished in North Borneo, and the fact that, during my official residence at Hong Kong, in connection with the British North Borneo Company, it fell to my lot to report home the death of Mr. Frank Hatton, may perhaps be thought to give appropriateness to the few prefatory words which I am glad to have the opportunity of addressing to the readers of the latest addition to the literature of biography and exploration.

This volume is an unpretentious record of useful and interesting work, and at the same time a tribute from a loving father to a devoted son; a tender *in memoriam* to a young life, rich in promise, but suddenly cut off by a sad mishap, ere youth had matured into manhood, and when distinction had already been achieved in the paths of science and research.

The straightforward, unaffected story which the young man's diaries tell, brings us face to face with life and adventure in British North Borneo, until lately as much a *terra incognita* as some parts of Central Africa. The island of Borneo was first brought

into notoriety some forty-five years ago by the late Sir
James Brooke, whose philanthropy and enterprise were
instrumental in rescuing from savagery a considerable
strip of country upon the eastern side of the island, now
represented by the flourishing State of Sarawak, under
the *quasi*-protection of the British Government. The
active trade which grew up as a consequence could
scarcely flourish, without inducing adventurous spirits
to test the practicability of turning to account other
tracts of an island so rich in material resources. Various
attempts, more or less abortive, by individuals followed
from time to time, culminating, not long ago, in the
*bonâ fide* acquisition, by a syndicate of British capi-
talists from the Sultans of Brunei and Sulu, of the
territory now known as British North Borneo. It is
the northern extremity of the island that has been thus
acquired. The new territory covers an area of 28,000
square miles, and over 600 miles of sea-coast, and it
boasts many navigable rivers and excellent harbours,
as well as numerous natural resources, the list of
which is being daily swelled by active research. Its
position, in a strategical point of view, is first-rate,
and it stands upon the high-road between our Australian possessions and China. The history of this
acquisition is now well known. It has been confirmed and consolidated under a charter from the
British Crown. A complete administrative apparatus
has been set on foot: whole tribes, once addicted
to head-hunting and such like savage practices, have
been won over to agricultural and other peaceful
pursuits: promising commercial relations have been

established with the prominent markets of the East, and, in spite of many discouraging difficulties and perplexing misfortunes, the enterprising originators of the project are slowly but steadily winning their way towards commercial and political success. The British North Borneo Company, moreover, have not confined their efforts to the selfish promotion of their own financial interests. With a comprehensive spirit worthy of praise, they have sought to render their acquisition geographically serviceable, by instituting extensive inland exploration, and general coast surveys, so that tracts of country formerly quite unknown, and seas which hitherto could only be cautiously traversed, are now rendered safe to travellers and mariners of all nations. The map which accompanies this work may be instanced as a remarkable evidence of what has been effected in this direction.

The settlement of a country so new, and peopled by savage races so hostile to the European, has, of course, not been accomplished without the sacrifice of much valuable life. Accident and climate have claimed their inevitable victims, and the names of Witti, Hatton, Collinson, Fraser, De Fontaine, and others will live in the early history of the colony, as those of men to whose pluck and endurance its opening successes may to a great extent be attributed.

The life of the explorer in savage lands is subject to many of the responsibilities and risks which attend the soldier's career, but without its glory and display. Military expeditions have their pageantry, their incidents of march, and their *camaraderie* on the battlefield and in the bivouac. The explorer, on the other hand, is denied the solace of physical diversion or mental companionship. His native followers, with rare exceptions, only weary and disgust him by their baffling, half-hearted ways. No bugle arouses him for his morning march. No band cheers him at his halt, or when the day is done. He has to press on alone, often despairing, his life in his hand, and with the discouraging reflection, that, after all, his efforts may prove without fruit, through mishap to himself or to his manuscripts. But the Englishman is born to the inheritance of possessions yet unexplored. The more tenderly he is nurtured, and the more happy his home, the readier he is to court privation and danger, in order to plant his country's flag in some hitherto untrodden tract, and add to the scientific, geographical, or commercial prestige of his native land.

It was this natural and heroic bent that fired the youthful Frank Hatton to aspire to win a place upon the honourable roll of explorers, amongst whom the indomitable Stanley had always been his favourite hero. Few though the relics recovered of his diaries, they show a culture of mind, an intelligence of aim, a singleness of purpose, an originality of thought, a decisiveness of action, and a fitness to lead, which were remarkable in one so young; whilst his letters exhibit throughout that touching love for home-ties and associations, which is so often found combined with roaming propensities in the adventurous Englishman. Another trait in the youthful Hatton's character was his strong leaning towards scientific research, and this had been developed by careful training under experts of repute, the results of which are noticeable in the work which he accomplished for the Company. An explorer without scientific acquirements is an artificer bereft of his best tools, and on this account alone it is to be regretted that so acute an observer and practical a worker in the hive of manhood should have been thus prematurely cut off. His discoveries and suggestions are nevertheless already bearing fruit. Mr. Pryer, the able Resident at Elopura, points out that Mr. Hatton was on the eve of a successful investigation when the sad accident happened that cost him his life; and the discovery of gold since made by Mr. Walker on the Segama River establishes the accuracy of Mr. Hatton's prognostications.[1]

Peace to the youthful explorer's ashes! As the broad banana leaves and the feathery palms of Sandakan wave over his untimely grave, they whisper anew the old truth, that high aims, a firm purpose, and honest work, ennoble the man, even when fate denies him the fruition of his reward.

WALTER H. MEDHURST.

*Formosa,* Torquay,
  *November,* 1885.

[1] Since the above lines were written a geographical chart of Mr. Walker's operations on the Segama River and its tributaries has reached London. On comparing his work with Mr. Frank Hatton's latest explorations, two remarkable coincidences are noticeable, namely, that when Mr. Hatton was thwarted, by an impassable swamp, in his efforts to reach the Segama overland, he had all but come upon the gold since discovered in the regions of the Upper Segama; and when the accident occurred that proved fatal to him he was close to the gold deposits subsequently met with on the Lower Segama.—W. H. M.

# CONTENTS.

## Part I.

### FRANK HATTON'S LIFE AND WORK AT HOME AND IN NORTH BORNEO.

#### I.

##### PERSONAL AND BIOGRAPHICAL.

PAGE

Introductory—The epilogue, sunshine—Childhood—School-life—At the College of Marcq, Lille—Master of French—Successes at King's College School in physical sciences—The School of Mines—Admiration for Darwin and Huxley—"Life is but a geological second"—Duty—A painless death—Favourite authors—A sad story—The prologue, shadow . . . . . . . . . . 1

#### II.

##### REMINISCENCES AND RELICS.

The lost diaries—A difficult task—Many-sidedness—"Man proposes"—First talks about Borneo—Choice of work—Borneo or Guy's Hospital?—"Too young! He will get over that"—Risks at home and abroad—Omens—Memories—Contributions to the press—A scientific controversy—The adventures of a drop of Thames water—At the Chemical Society—A visit to Rothschild's and the Mint—Packing up . . . . . 21

## III.

### A BUNDLE OF LETTERS AND THE MASSACRE OF WITTI.

PAGE

On the way—Sharks and divers—Ceylon and Singapore—Bungalow life at Labuan—Social amenities—Witti—In Borneo—Expeditions in the interior—Tropical floods—"Impossible to go on; impossible to go back"—Letters from home—An eventful day—Head-hunting—To Kinoram for a little rest—Food and dress—Missionary work—Romantic scenery—The perils of travel—Assassination of Witti and an exploring party—Sketch of Witti's career—Thoughts of home—Last letters . . . . . . 63

## IV.

### DISASTER AND DEATH.

Good news—Five days later—Sad letters—"A bright, fearless, brave life"—On the Segama River—Hunting in the jungle—The fatal accident—A devoted following—The silent passenger—Tropical scenery—Bornean highlands and the mountains of Pisgah—Inquest and verdict—A jungle cemetery—The pathetic story told by Governor Treacher . 95

# Part II.

## DIARIES AND REPORTS OF EXPEDITIONS, OFFICIAL PAPERS AND OTHER CHRONICLES.

### I.

#### LIFE AT LABUAN.

The smallest British colony—Four miles from the great island of Borneo—The North Bornean Malays—A native house—The Klings—The humming-birds of the East—The carpenter-bee and the mason-wasp—Coal Point—A deserted pit—Pig-shooting—The goat-sucker—A monkey comedy—Snakes—Native music—A brilliant sunset with a dark cloud over Borneo—Looking forward . . . . 119

## II.

### ON THE SEQUATI AND KURINA RIVERS.

First impressions of exploration—A novel experience—Making a Malay house—Working and watching—Digging for oil—"Orang Dusuns"—Astonishing the natives—Flying foxes—Exploring and sporting—Tropical vegetation—Lost in the jungle—Pangeran Brunei—A sick chief—Trading with the Dusuns—" Never seen a white man before "—Searching for coal—Christmas-day on the equator—The slave question—Protecting a fugitive—An anxious night—The New Year and a dark outlook—A Dusun house—" I was simply a nine days' wonder "—Keeping away evil spirits—" Well, well, sir ! "—Native women at work—Strange and picturesque scenes—Discoveries of coal and iron—Riding on buffaloes—Tropical floods—A perilous situation—Geology of the Binkoka district . . . . . 135

## III.

### UP THE LABUK RIVER AND OVERLAND TO KUDAT.

Tropical forests—A mysterious chief—Native ideas of gold——Discovery of a hill of pure talc—Leeches and rattans—Sin-Dyaks—A river accident—Head-hunters on the watch—" Like men with tails "—Omens—" Terrible news "—A strange ceremony luckily concluded—A lovely scene—" The giant hills of Borneo "—Collecting upas juice—Mineral prospects—Initiated into the brotherhood of the Bendowen Dusuns—" Oh, Kinarringan, hear us ! "—Talking to a dead man's ghost—Tattooed heroes, and marks denoting a coward—Rice harvests—"Only iron pyrites "—More brotherhood ceremonies—A model kampong—Hardships—Inhospitable Ghanaghana or Tunfoul men—A ghastly scene—Not head-hunting, but head-stealing—Pig-killing, and a dead man—Promise of minerals in the Sugut rivers—

Lost in the jungle—An angry native and a churlish tribe—The end of the journey—"In the Bornean bush from March 1 to June 15" . . . . . . . . 174

## IV.

#### FOUR MONTHS IN THE DISTRICTS OF KINORAM AND THE MARUDU.

Looking for antimony and copper—The Marudu valley—In the bed of the Kinoram River—Dangers and difficulties—Camping in a cave tenanted by bats and swallows—A romantic night—The horrors of leeches and ticks—Immense ravines—The natives "prayed me for rain"—Superstition obstructs the way—The "reported antimony" tracked to its "reported" hill—A treacherous guide—Sayup objects to white men—Discovery of copper—Descending a precipice—Limestone containing iron pyrites and a small percentage of copper . . . . . . . . . 222

## V.

#### EXTRACTS FROM DIARY OF THE LAST EXPEDITION.

Difficult operations—An ancient clearing—The fable of the Kinabatangan Cave—Dangers present and to come—Fever and leeches—The future coal-fields of Borneo—Durian—Fighting the torrent—Outcrops of coal—Lost—Expecting to prospect for gold—Relics of a murder believed to have been committed by the natives who killed Witti—Among the Muruts—A misunderstanding that nearly led to a fight—An offer to go out against Witti's murderers—Shooting rapids—Swamped—"Rain, rain, nothing but rain"—Narrow escapes—Dismal wastes—From the river to the sea—Thunder and rain—The last entry in the last diary—"River swift and deep" . . . . . . . 254

## VI.

#### HOW THE LAST EXPEDITION ENDED.

Letter from Governor Treacher—Mr. Resident Pryer's Report—Opening of the Inquest—The evidence—Adjourned for the arrival of the last expeditionary boats—Verdict of the jury 282

## VII.

### A POSTCRIPT IN LONDON.

A visitor—The European who last saw Frank alive—Mr. Herbert Ward who is mentioned in the last diary—In Frank's room at Kudat—About seven hundred miles up the Kinabatangan—Frank's call at Pinungah—Talks of home—Sport—Native superstitions—Among the Tungara men—Strange pipes—Poisoned arrows—" Good-bye "—Sadness and foreboding—" His men loved him "—The boy Oodeen—" Roughing it—Adventures and adventurers—Experiences at Kudat—Incidents related by Col. Harington. Count Mongelas lost in the jungle—Sports and Pastimes—Curious fishing excursion—Memorials in Borneo and London . . . . . . . . . 294

---

## LIST OF ILLUSTRATIONS.

| | |
|---|---|
| Frontispiece—Portrait of Frank Hatton. | |
| Tanjong Kubong, or Coal Point, Labuan [3]   *To face page* | 70 |
| Kina Balu from the Tampassuk River: the Steam Yacht *Borneo* at anchor . | 79 |
| On the Kinoram River   *To face page* | 80 |
| Frank Hatton's House [1] | 82 |
| Section of Stockade Surrounding Frank Hatton's House [1] | 84 |
| The Attack on Mr. F. Witti [1]   *To face page* | 86 |
| Portrait of F. Witti . | 88 |
| The Quay, Sandakan [1] | 94 |
| The last Journey [1] | 107 |
| Elopura, the chief Settlement in North Borneo [1] | 111 |
| Sketch of Frank Hatton's Grave at Sandakan   *To face page* | 112 |
| Principal Street in the native town of Sandakan, Elopura [2] | 115 |
| A Kling [2] | 123 |
| The Bungalow at Labuan—a quiet Corner   *To face page* | 124 |
| The Mason-Wasp [3] | 127 |
| Bornean Moths and Beetles   *To face page* | 128 |
| The deserted Colliery works at Labuan | 129 |
| Elk's-Horn Fern, and native Dusuns [3] | 147 |

## List of Illustrations.

| | | |
|---|---|---|
| Dusuns at a stream [3] | To face page | 162 |
| Dusun Women threshing rice | ,, ,, | 164 |
| The *Enterprise* in Abai Harbour | . | 167 |
| Through storm and flood in the jungle | To face page | 170 |
| At work on the Labuk River | ,, ,, | 180 |
| A deceitful and refractory Guide | ,, ,, | 181 |
| The Perils of an unknown river | ,, ,, | 188 |
| Frank Hatton is made a "Blood-Brother" of the Dusun chief Degadong | To face page | 196 |
| Talking to the dead man's ghost | . | 204 |
| Kina Balu, from Ghinambaur [3] | . | 221 |
| Portrait of Mr. Von Donop | . | 238 |
| The house at Pampang, Marudu River | . | 253 |
| "A friend in need;"—an incident of the last expedition | To face page | 272 |
| Mr. Resident Pryer and a group of native inhabitants of Sandakan | To face page | 287 |
| Mr. Herbert Ward | . | 296 |
| "Good-bye till we meet again in London!" | To face page | 305 |
| Overlooking Sandakan Bay [1] | ,, ,, | 307 |
| Colonel Arthur Harington | . | 312 |
| Borneo parang (in sheath) and Malay kris | . | 323 |
| Group of Bornean arms | . | 325 |
| Parang and reaper sheaths | . | 326 |
| Poisoned arrow-case and arrows | . | 327 |
| Pipes from the Tungara country | . | 328 |
| Bornean mouth-organ | . | 329 |
| Sirih-box, knife, and detail of decoration | . | 330 |
| Dyak women | To face page | 332 |

[The illustrations marked [1] are from an article entitled "Frank Hatton in Borneo" in *The Century Magazine*; those marked [2] are from a paper on Frank Hatton's diaries entitled "Adventures on the Equator," in *The English Illustrated Magazine*; and those marked [3] are from Burbidge's *Gardens of the Sun*, published by Mr. Murray. The biographer tenders his best thanks to the editors of the above magazines and to Mr. John Murray for the use of these interesting engravings.]

# Part I.

## FRANK HATTON'S LIFE AND WORK AT HOME AND IN NORTH BORNEO.

# NORTH BORNEO.

## EXPLORATIONS AND ADVENTURES ON THE EQUATOR.

### I.

#### PERSONAL AND BIOGRAPHICAL.

Introductory—The epilogue, sunshine—Childhood—School life—At the College of Marcq, Lille—Master of French—Enters at King's College School—Oxford and Cambridge Examinations—The Royal School of Mines—Admiration for Darwin and Huxley—"Life is but a geological second"—Duty—A painless death—Favourite authors—A sad story—The prologue, shadow.

I.

'NY more for the Continental express?'

"The electric lamps 'flashed into a sudden radiance' as the sun is said to do at daybreak in the tropics.

"For a few minutes previously to the simultaneous leap of light that transformed a dozen opaque globes into mimic suns, Charing Cross railway station had been in semi-darkness.

"There was much bustle of departing travellers. Parliament was up; for even the longest and most obstructed session comes to an end. Jaded legislators, men of fashion, ladies of society, were among the crowd bound for foreign shores. London was emptying itself from all its avenues of transit.

"'Any more for the Continental express?' shouted the platform inspector.

"A banging of doors, a shrill whistle, a last pressure of hands through carriage-windows, and the red lamps of the express for a moment challenged the white sentinels of Electra, only to leave the spectators gazing at the glistening track of steel along which the train vanished into the outer darkness.

"They were no mere holiday travellers, the two young men whose latest adieux were made to me. Their guns were not to be loaded for sport on Scotch moors. They were pioneers bound for the Eastern seas. Adventurers had gone before, and smoothed the rugged way for the allied aid of science, which London and Edinburgh now contributed to North Borneo, the one a chemist, metallurgical and otherwise, the other a doctor of medicine. Ahead of them were a respected Governor, a staff of officials and four years of diplomatic history, with a royal charter of her Gracious Majesty Queen Victoria to follow.

"It was, as I have already intimated, the autumn time of the year, when the aspect of empty houses falls with strange impressiveness upon the West-End streets. The dull windows shed no illumination upon the languid traffic of the finished season. There is nothing more cheerless than an empty house, more especially that which has been tenanted by your own family circle. Run up to town from your vacation retreat and note the pathetic dumbness of your 'household gods.' It is an experience in sensations. And how terribly empty is a familiar room when the familiar friend has left it, not to return for years!

"Such a room stands wide open, near the desk upon which I am writing. It contains a chest of empty pigeon-holes, each docketed with scientific titles; a nest of shelves crowded with the transactions of learned societies and technical works on mineralogy, metallurgy, and geology; a desk stained with many acids; a broken blowpipe; a pair of foils; a photograph of Professor Huxley; a kindly letter from Dr. Frankland; a cabinet of minerals in the rough; a barometer; and in one dark corner a package of miscellaneous books, papers, and manuscripts, relating to the sun-lands above which tower the sacred heights of Kina Balu. In that empty room (the relics of the former occupation of which are so eloquent to me, and may be to some of my readers) a student of the Royal School of Mines burnt the midnight oil. Recent investigations into the influence of bacteria on gases and kindred subjects gained for him considerable distinction at the Institute of Chemistry and the Chemical Society of London, and were recognized in the scientific organs of Germany and America. These labours may be said to have closed his student career. Endorsed by the best authorities, he was selected by the Governors of the new colony to explore its mineral resources.

"We had studied these books and papers together,

he and I, and had thus been enabled to see, through the eyes of many travellers, those almost unknown lands of tropical splendour to which the pioneers have gone. Since then a further collection of private letters and explorers' reports have been lent to me—official documents, and letters of interesting experiences. It is believed by certain friends of mine that, with this exceptional material at my disposal, I may compile and write a book of practical value (a pioneer volume, let me call it) upon the new colony and the newest British charter. The Directors have given me access to their correspondence upon the subject. In addition to this epistolary history, I shall avail myself of the best-written sources of information that bear upon the plan and object of the work in hand, the intention of which is to set forth the position and prospects of the new colony, and to tell the story of the East India Company's nineteenth-century successor.[1]

[1] Until thirty years ago the story of Borneo was that of an uncivilized country, the possession of which was a bone of contention between the Dutch and the English. Oliver Van Noort visited the island in 1598. A few years later his countrymen began to trade with it. In 1609 they concluded a commercial treaty with the rulers of the Sambas, and built a factory. After about twenty years of effort they abandoned the idea of establishing a settlement. In 1707 the English appeared on the Bornean coast. They built factories, but with no permanent success. In 1763 they take possession of Balambangan, and in 1774 the garrison is successfully assaulted by pirates. A year later the Dutch establish a factory at Pontianak, and in 1780 the reigning powers cede part of the west coast to the Dutch. In alliance with the Sultan of Pontianak, they destroy Succadana, and in 1787 are granted portions of the south coast. In 1812 an English expedition goes out against Sambar and fails ; to succeed, however, in 1813. In 1818 the Dutch, who during this war had been expelled by the English, return, and their Bornean colonies are now formed into a special government. Sir James Brooke visited Borneo in 1839, to

"While I sit before that pile of books and papers, from which the romantic story of the tropical island and its northern colony is to be extracted, the Continental express has transferred its travellers to foreign boat and train. Before I have analyzed half of my collection of letterpress and manuscript, the former occupant of the empty room will have stood face to face with Nature in her most lovely and yet most strange and startling forms. Sabah has been described as 'an earthly paradise.' The simile may hold good, from a British point of view, when the owners have built piers and roads and villages there on approved models; when the planter is on the spot and the new colonist is sowing his rice; when the cooling breezes of Kina Balu waft the punkahs of hill residences, and the wild 'gardens of the sun' are cultivated tracts of fruits and flowers.[2] This time may

succeed in carrying out, by his own personal energy, what the great East India Company had failed to accomplish. He founded Sarawak. With the aid of Admiral Keppell he annihilated the dangerous hordes of pirates that infested the western coasts. He successfully stamped out a rising of Chinese, in which operation the native tribes loyally came to his assistance; and he has demonstrated, financially and politically, the wisdom of those early Dutch and British adventurers who saw a splendid property in the island of Borneo. In 1848 the English Government, seeing the importance of a station in this latitude, purchased Labuan, an island off the coast of Borneo, and made it an English colony, with a governor and all the necessary officers and appliances of an efficient administration. Such is the brief history of Borneo, possession of which is now divided between the Dutch Government, the Sultan of Brunei, Rajah Brooke, and the British North Borneo Company, the latter endorsed in its undertaking by royal charter.

[2] This is only the suggestion of a possibility. The idea is conceived in a more rosy vein of imagination than the reality may have warranted. There are spots in North Borneo that might be described as "earthly paradises," rich in natural beauties, blessed with pure water,

come; and then the pioneers can rest, and we will talk no more of empty rooms."

\* \* \* \* \*

## II.

You have probably read these opening words before as a preface to "The New Ceylon."[3] You will forgive me for reprinting them here. They are the prologue to a tragedy. The young scientist was my son. I did not mention his name on that occasion, out of regard for his modesty, and as a check upon my own pride. Moreover, I thought his fame should herald him. He should write his own name upon his own book when he came home again. There is a belief among orthodox Christians that punish-

glorious in perpetual sunshine; but the pioneer cutting his way through the primeval forests, and sojourning with savages of the most degraded types, has many dangers and miseries to tell of that do not enter into the dreams of men who live on pleasant slopes by the sea, or in the more settled regions, where Rajah Brooke has brought a wilderness and its barbarians within the pale of civilization. The hopes of the founders of British North Borneo lie in a similar direction, and one's sympathies are with the pioneers; but I looked far ahead for that picture of rest in *The New Ceylon*, guarding myself with the reflection that the simile of paradise may hold good when the tropical colonist and the planter have taken and made the country their own. There are plenty of indications of treasure hidden away in Bornean forests and rivers; but the heart of Sabah is still tangled, wild, unexplored, without roads or even footpaths, populated by unknown tribes, "who neither eat rice nor salt, and who do not associate with each other, but who rove about the woods like wild beasts," with, on the other hand, here and there settled villages of quiet, peaceful natives, who are being gradually attracted towards the new government's stations and towns.

[3] *The New Ceylon.* Being a sketch of British North Borneo or Sabah, from official and other exclusive sources of information. By Joseph Hatton (1881).

ment follows anything like an idolatrous love which a father or mother may feel towards a child. The dear old Vicar of Wakefield in the play emphasizes this article of faith, or fear, in his solicitude for his daughter Olivia. It is considered neither British nor Christian to mourn, " over much," for anything or anybody, but " every one can master a grief but he that has it." If I am tempted, in these opening pages, to lay aside a mask of apparent contentment, to wear my heart upon my sleeve, and confess that for me the light of the world is evermore shadowed by his death, my readers will bear with me in remembrance of their own private sorrows; and if not for his sake, in honour of other pioneers who have yielded up their lives on the altars of science and civilization. Away in the jungle of an island slope in the Malay Archipelago, they have laid him beneath the palms. Pioneer in life, pioneer in death. The first English tenant of the little cemetery at Elopura, he rests from his labours.

III.

" One of the most remarkable young men of these days,"[*] Frank Hatton, though in no sense precocious as a child, developed a singular versatility of talent at an early age. Fond of music, he was a skilful pianist, and played several other instruments moderately well. He could ride, swim, skate, shoot, and had done long spins on the tricycle; he was clever at chess, was a good linguist, and wrote his native language with the polish of a gentleman and the finish of a scholar. A master of Malay, "the

[*] *Daily News*, May 8th, 1883.

Italian of the East," he was also conversant with Dusun, one of the local tongues of Borneo, and was as modest as he was accomplished. An authority on water filtration and other matters of scientific research, he died in his twenty-second year, a scientific explorer in the service of the Government of Sabah, leaving behind him a record that would have been honourable to a long and industrious life. His was the first white foot in many of the hitherto unknown villages of Borneo. In him many of the wild tribes saw the first white man. He was the pioneer of scientific investigation among the mountain ranges of Sabah, on its turbulent rivers, and in its almost impenetrable jungle. Speaking the languages of the natives, and possessing that special faculty of kindly firmness so necessary to the efficient control of uncivilized peoples, he journeyed through the strange land not only unmolested, but frequently carrying away tokens of native affection. Several powerful chiefs made him their "blood brother," and here and there the tribes prayed to him as if he were a god. When he fell in the unexplored regions of the Segama, his escort rowed his body by river and sea for fifty-three hours, without sleep, that it might be buried by white men in the new settlement of Elopura, an act of devotion which travellers in the equatorial seas will understand and appreciate.

I who write these lines am his father, but he was not only my son, he was my friend and companion. He lost his life while on his way home. The news of his safety and his good health preceded by a few days the telegraphic report of his death. When most happy, we have surely most cause for fear. His mother, who had never ceased to have forebodings of evil in regard to his safety, was at last, it seemed, about to enter upon a period of pleasant anticipations. We were entertaining several American guests at dinner, and talking of our plans in connection with his return, when the telegraphic lightning struck us down. For a time I believed that my career had ended with his. Such ambition as had hitherto guided me is certainly closed; from the first awakening of his genius, it had centred in him. It would have afforded me pleasure to have effaced myself in the contemplation of his rise and progress. I could have been content to lay aside my work and have for my epitaph, "He was the father and friend of Frank Hatton."

I had from his childhood estimated in his interest all the pitfalls that beset the path of youth and manhood. They were familiar to me. I had passed through the dangers and scrambled out of the pits. I warned him against them. He listened to my precepts and in most things accepted my guidance. My boyhood was stormy, his was peaceful. I went to school when I pleased, had tutors or no tutors, played truant, studied this or that, without system and without method. His career was the opposite of all this. He looked at the world of duty from a different standpoint. Guarding his young life from every adverse wind, I had my reward in a brave, upright, modest, scholarly son, to whom I hoped to have bequeathed my name, and the care of his mother and sisters. We had all come to regard him as the prop of our small house, and I knew that he was of "the stuff that great men are made." To-day, with the bright page of his young life before me, with letters concerning him still coming to me from all parts of the world, I feel that I owe a duty to his memory and to humanity to tell his story. Let the wisdom of my interpretation of this call be judged by the following consideration of the materials upon which it is founded.

### IV.

Frank Hatton was born at Horfield, Gloucestershire, a suburb of Bristol, England, on the 31st of August, 1861. I was at that time in my twenty-third year and editor of a famous west-country journal, the *Bristol Mirror*. Connected on my side with journalism and music, his mother brought him the health and common sense of the sturdy yeomanry of Lincolnshire. Frank was her second child, and she was his mother at the age of nineteen. Soon after his birth we went to live at Durham. Our home is described in the novel of "Clyte." Old Waller and his granddaughter are, to their author, very real persons; and there are quiet, sad hours in which he sees a radiant child gathering flowers in their garden. It will always be to him the house in which the old organist watched over the wayward belle of the cathedral city, but with a bright infantile face looking up at him while he is designing a fictitious story far less pitiful than that of which the boy at his knee is destined to be the hero.

From the north we went to Worcester. Here I became proprietor of *Berrow's Worcester Journal*, a town councillor, an officer of volunteers; and editor of the *Gentleman's Magazine*, dividing my days between London and the pleasant cathedral city. We lived at Lansdown, overlooking the pastoral valley of the Severn, which stretched away under our windows to the Malvern Hills. Frank had the full benefit of this pure Worcestershire air. The keeper of the toll-gate on the London road often opened the bar to him as he rode through on an obstreperous wooden horse, prancing along in mock solemnity towards the city of Dick Whittington. Having lived on the Wear and the Severn we migrated to the Thames, and finally settled down by the north gate of Regent's Park.

At the age of ten Frank went to his first public school, an establishment in St. John's Wood, conducted by Mr. Berridge. Soon afterwards he became a pupil at the better-known establishment of Mr. Barford, Upper Gloucester Place. His chief prizes during several years were for good conduct. He gave no indication at this time of the strong individuality which distinguished him a few years later. At home he cultivated a taste for music and war. Under the friendly tuition of a neighbour he became an expert on the drum. He had played the piano fairly well for years, his first teacher being the well-known organist of Worcester Cathedral, Mr. Done. His leisure hours were chiefly taken up with the construction of wooden fortifications, defended by a motley assemblage of toy troops and captured under the fire of real cannon. He was a collector of arms, pistols, swords, and knives, and his bedroom was quite an arsenal. A frequent visitor at the Zoological Gardens, he would bring home any stray dog or cat that would follow him.

Mr. John Leighton noting this fondness for animals in his youthful neighbour, taught him to ride, and gave him opportunities of proving himself both fearless and graceful on horseback. Occasional visits to the Upper Thames delighted him. He took a greater interest in out-door games than in academic studies. Popular with his companions, he was always their leader, not by any exhibition of physical prowess or mental superiority, but from a gentle yet firm habit of getting his own way. "For a youth to be distinguished by his companions," says Disraeli, "is perhaps a criterion of talent. At that moment of life, with no flattery on the one side and no artifice on the other, all emotion and no reflection, the boy who has obtained a predominance has acquired this merely by native powers."

V.

Towards the end of the year 1874 a gunpowder barge blew up in the Regent's Canal, wrecking the terrace in which Frank lived with his parents. Although he was hurled from his bed and deposited in the middle of the room amidst the *débris* of a shattered window, he accepted the situation with the greatest *sang-froid*. The necessity of changing our home for a time suggested the desirability of seizing the opportunity to send Frank abroad. It had already been decided that he should be entered as a student at the college of Marcq, near Lille, in France, and thither he went. He remained at this establishment, with occasional visits home, for upwards of two years. Reports concerning him were always satisfactory. He mastered the French language with singular rapidity. In his general studies he only made respectable progress. His prizes were for good conduct, natural history, and geography. When he left Lille he came home with the reputation of speaking French with the purest accent that an English student had ever obtained there, and with high testimonials to his manliness, his morality, and his honourable disposition. Trained previously in Protestant establishments, his beliefs and opinions had been stirred up by his Roman Catholic surroundings. For a short time he devoted himself to theological studies, comparing the faiths of the various sects, reading the Koran, and studying the Fathers. He came out of this personal investigation opposed to the formalities of creeds, with a determination to judge of the pretensions of the Churches for himself, strongly objecting to all kinds of clerical dictation, but with a generous toleration for all beliefs that were honestly held. He was only a boy, and he had not greatly distinguished himself in his studies; but he had a way of looking at things from a common-sense standpoint, and whatever views he formed, he held them with tenacity.

It was at this period of his career that he became a student of King's College School. His mother introduced him to the clerical head of the school, the Rev. Dr. Maclear. I was in America at the time. Dr. Maclear expressed a critical opinion unfavourable to parents who send their sons to be educated in France. Frank's mother ventured to say that I believed modern languages to be essential in the practical education of a boy who has his living to earn in these days, and that modern languages should be learnt in the countries where they are spoken. The head-master disagreed altogether with these views, and I suspect Frank's love for me would stand in the way of his respect for the wiser educationist. Clergymen having the command of English scholastic establishments are, as a rule, severe disciplinarians. Contrasted with the gentler methods of Lille, King's College School was, at best, a trifle uncongenial to Frank. He was never quite as happy there as at the College of Marcq. His King's College School reports show that he had a distaste for what is called "religious knowledge;" that he was proficient in French, made good progress in Euclid, his "general conduct" was "very satisfactory;" and his papers are marked for the Easter Term of 1877— " Physical Geography and Geology—fifth of fourteen who worked the advanced Oxford and Cambridge paper and has made good progress," while for the Easter Term of 1878, for the same studies he is set down as " highly satisfactory : obtained the third place of nineteen in the Oxford and Cambridge examinations."

## VI.

When he was a boy at Worcester Frank was asked what profession he would like to be when he grew to be a man. "An engine-driver," was his prompt reply. Asked in London at a later date a similar question, he said, " A capitalist, and live retired like So-and-So." Later still, when the proper time to discuss the subject came, and he had given evidence of a leaning towards scientific studies, he elected to be "a chemist and mining engineer." Natural history at Lille, physical geography and geology at King's College School, had prepared him for chemistry and mineralogy at the School of Mines. After a short interval of Continental travel, and some private readings with chemical experts, he entered upon the varied course of study then given at Jermyn Street and South Kensington, which he supplemented by geological tours around London, the Isle of Wight, Derbyshire, Cumberland, and other districts.[5] He passed in due course all the examinations in chemistry, mineralogy, magnetism, and electricity, acoustics, light and heat, and applied mechanics, "in the highest degree satisfactory." The time which he should have devoted to physics he gave up to investigations of more immediate importance, leaving this one link in his chain of honours to be picked up at a future day, and with it the Associateship of the School of Mines. He worked with unabated ardour at South Kensington for three years, from the age of seventeen to twenty. With his know-

---

[5] During a visit to Derbyshire he met Mr. S. H. Bradbury, who was then engaged in the literary preparation of his popular volume, *All about Derbyshire*. In the chapter on "Millers Dale," I find the following kindly reminiscence of Frank's holiday work:—"He taught me to look at the stone walls of the Derbyshire Peak, that rule off its roads and fields in hard lines of grey, with an interest that such prosaic things do not usually inspire. He found in them 'the fairy tales of science, and the long result of time.' He showed me the legacies which the prehistoric age had left in these limestone boulders; glacial action, volcanic disturbances, the shells of the sea-bed on the tops of the hills. He carried his geological hammer, his botanist's satchel, and his sketch-book wherever we tramped; to the caverns at Castleton, the quarries at Burbage, the lead-mines at Youlgrave, the dales, watered by the Wye, the moorland wilderness of Kinderscourt. I looked at Nature with new eyes when in his company."

ledge his character developed, and his political and theological opinions became firm. "He was," says Dr. Frankland, "one of the most genial, earnest, and talented students I ever had in my laboratory; he was a most indefatigable worker, and a skilful manipulator." Dr. Hodgkinson, speaking of him to me the other day, said "He was the only student of his time to whom I entrusted delicate and dangerous operations; he was implicitly reliable, and had a clean, firm grip of things; there was nothing that he could not do that he cared to do"

He had an intimate knowledge of the works of Darwin, Huxley, and Lyell. Professor Huxley travelled as Frank did for some months between Baker Street and South Kensington by underground railway. "If merit were properly recognized," said Frank, speaking of this one day, "instead of riding on that abominable line, Professor Huxley should travel in a coach and six." He was fully acquainted with Sir Joseph Hooker's Malayan and other adventures, and was always greatly interested in visiting Kew. During the latter part of his time at South Kensington he rode to and from Regent's Park on a tricycle, and had to answer a summons once for "furious riding" and upsetting a street porter. The officer who brought the charge asserted that he was riding at over eight miles an hour. The defendant produced the maker of the machine, who swore that nothing would make it travel at a greater speed than five. This, with a quietly humorous account of the affair from the tricyclist, brought the case to an end with a nominal fine.

In addition to his arduous work at South Kensington, he contributed a series of letters on chemical subjects to a provincial paper. He wrote several scientific articles for a technical newspaper published in New York. He contributed a score of biographical articles on modern scientists to a magazine, and he wrote a singularly entertaining essay on "A Drop of Thames Water," which was published in a London weekly paper; he translated a French drama by Sardou for the manager of the Princess's Theatre; and encouraged by Professor Becquet, of Lille, he began a translation of "The Valley of Poppies" into French. During his vacations he visited Holland, Belgium, Normandy, Germany, Italy, and France. A favourite remark of his was "a thousand years is but a geological second." Upon this declaration he argued that it is the duty of every one to see as much of the world, and to do as much in it as is possible in the short time allotted to us. "We know nothing for certain about the future; let us make the most of the present." This was his cue to exertion. "Time flies" was the motto that pushed him on. His portrait, and that of Mr. Ashton Wentworth Dilke, M.P., appeared in the *Graphic* on the same page—both young men, both travellers, both evidently stimulated by this acute sense of the brevity of man's existence. "Life must not be judged by years," said Dilke a few days before he died. There is nothing particularly original in these observations. It was Aristotle who said "it is by works and not by age that men should be estimated," and the lesson of "the geological second" is probably from Lyell, whom Frank had read continually. But it is interesting to know how such remarkable young men as Dilke and Frank Hatton have regarded life.

Horace Walpole's estimate of what was demanded from him was very much the view of the subject of these notes—"to act with common sense according to the moment is the best wisdom I know; and the best philosophy to do one's duties, take the world as it comes, submit respectfully to one's lot, bless the goodness that has given so much happiness with it, whatever it is, and despise affectation."

Frank Hatton always understood that although he had his own way to make, he might count upon the best education that money could buy and his own exertions procure.

### VII.

On these conditions he accepted his young life and made the best of it. If he worked hard, he played also. He entered into his recreations and amusements with the same energy that characterized him at work. Outdoor sports, the opera, the theatre, social gatherings; he enjoyed them all. There was a long, far-away look in his great eyes at times, and one thinks now of that absorbed expression with sad wondering. Except once in a way, when some scientific problem puzzled him, or he was "wool-gathering" (a charge occasionally brought against him, and the most serious charge he ever had to answer, Heaven bless him!), he was always cheerful and in good spirits. Once a somewhat melancholy visitor would talk of death, and Frank, invited to describe what he considered the least painful dissolution, replied, "To be shot dead in a charge on the field of battle." Asked would he select such a death if he had to choose—"I would not be a soldier," he answered, "unless Regent's Park had to be defended; but I do think that to be shot in a vital part is the nearest approach there is to a painless death." That friend has recalled this remark to my remembrance, and all the way from Borneo, in messages of condolence, has come the reminder that "in his death there was no suffering."

Frank Hatton, when he left England for the islands of the eastern seas, was in appearance the *beau-idéal* of a young English gentleman and student. Close upon six feet in height, he carried no surplus flesh. He had strong hands, with long fingers and almond-shaped nails. When he surprised us as an actor in a French piece at a King's College School speech-day I was not the only person who thought his hands were like Irving's. They were full of life, and his fingers suggested a special dexterity. This was one of the secrets of his manipulative skill in scientific experiments. He had a large foot, and he walked with a long, swinging stride. His eyes were big and brown and wide apart, his eyebrows black and perfectly arched. He had thick, brown, silky hair, a high but compact forehead, large ears, a generous mouth, a strong straight nose, and teeth of singular regularity and whiteness. In repose the expression of his face was thoughtful, almost sad; under the influence of conversation it was bright and full of animation. He enjoyed a joke keenly, often quoted Artemus Ward and Mark Twain, occasionally Dickens, but more frequently Shakespeare. It is not my desire to obtrude my feelings in regard to him upon the reader; but I find it difficult to get away from this picture of him as I recall the dearly loved figure and watch once again a hand waving to me its last farewell, from a

railway-carriage window, on that sad autumn night I
have already spoken of. With what tearful eyes I went
home to tell his mother (from whom he had already
taken leave) how cheerfully he went away; how they
were dried by-and-by when we began to have letters
from him, and how we rejoiced at his safe arrival;
how we waited for news of him when he had entered
upon his work; how when Witti, a fellow-explorer,
and his men were massacred, we resolved to send
for Frank home; how we received reassuring letters
from him and the Company; how he got on well with
the natives, and sent home despatches full of a strange
wisdom for one so young; how we, all of us, wrote
to him every week; how his letters thrilled us with
pleasure as they recorded his success; how we suffered when he was laid up with fever; how he was
better almost before we had had time to deplore his
illness; how at last he cheered us finally with the
news that he was starting on his last expedition prior
to returning home; how we got intelligence of his
safety and good health, and his nearing the end of his
journey; and how in the midst of our happiness came
tidings of his death; the joy and the misery and the
final heart-break of all this goes without saying. But
the story of the closing days of his brave young life is
full of a touching pathos that must have a fascination
for all tender souls. Considering the narrative as a
stranger might, who had never looked into his frank
brown eyes nor heard the music of his voice, I would
still, I think, be deeply touched by the brief record of
his industrious, heroic, and blameless career.

## II.

## REMINISCENCES AND RELICS.

*The lost diaries—A difficult task—Many-sidedness—" Man proposes "—First talks about Borneo—Choice of work—Borneo or Guy's Hospital?—"Too young! He will get over that"—Risks at home and abroad—Omens—Memories – Contributions to the press—A scientific controversy—The adventures of a drop of Thames water—At the Chemical Society—A visit to Rothschild's and the Mint—Packing up.*

### I.

I HAD hoped that if ever the brief story of my own career should be deemed worth the telling, he would have been my biographer. It had occurred to me, in this connection, that the famous people I had known and their influence on historic events would be for him interesting subjects of study. With these thoughts in my mind I had during his absence laid aside and collated many papers and letters for his perusal. When my time should come, I thought I would leave him the literary and journalistic notes of my labours and associations, that he might know me even from the time before he was born. It seemed to me as if I were putting my house in order for him. I likened myself to the old year that was going out; I thought of him as the new one that was coming in. I should rest from my labours. He would begin his work in the great world well equipped for his duties, and with a clearer knowledge of what they were than I ever had of mine. It is strange that I am left and he is gone. It is I who have to tell his story, not he mine. The world needed him far more than it needs me. He was a chemist learned in research, a metallurgist versed in geological mysteries; he had the gift of tongues, he was endowed with a faculty of government peculiarly valuable in the control of uncivilized peoples, he had the temperament and constitution, the intellectual grasp that are characteristic of great men. He was old enough to suggest all this in his habits and work, and young enough to give promise of a gracious manhood and a useful career. Yet he has gone, and I remain with my uneventful life, my commonplace story of journalistic and literary drudgery; and I have not even the poor consolation of printing for him a complete record of his work. He had no yearning for a fame that was not based upon a broad and deep foundation. His modesty was equal to his merit. But he intended to write a book on Borneo, a book of travel that should be many-sided, and for this purpose he kept careful diaries of his expeditions, and notes of his impressions. Only a portion of the first, and pencil memoranda of his last diary have been found. But extracts from the others which he furnished to the Governor and the Company, give warrant, on public grounds, for this labour of love upon which I am engaged. They are interesting contributions to the history of a comparatively unknown country. Their acknowledged value as mere extracts serves to emphasize the loss of the more elaborate manuscripts.

## II.

I am writing these chapters in the full belief that, sympathizing with my position, the reader will overlook the shortcomings of my work. It was my intention to set forth in minute detail all my joyous remembrances of him. The soul of modesty, he would have shrunk from such a record in print. I am trying to think what he might not have objected to have me say of him now. Desirous to honour his memory in this volume, I am trying to put myself outside the subject, and even to consider it editorially; I am trying not to be myself, but ending, I fear, in being very much myself; and so if any of my readers have lost a dear son or a much-loved friend, they will forgive me if I fall short of that high standard of biographic skill which a perfect critical taste in these matters has set up. I have before me the numerous certificates of learned examiners who endorsed the success of his studies in various branches of scientific knowledge. He was proud to bring them to me, because he knew they gave me pleasure, but he took no particular pains to preserve them on his own account. He valued the honour conferred upon him by the Institute of Chemistry, and was delighted to be a Fellow of the Chemical Society; but he did not use the letters that belong to these distinctions upon his address card, nor did he write them after his signature. "Some day," he said to me, "perhaps I may become a Fellow of the Royal Society, and that will include the rest." I think he could have become whatever he wished. He was a worker. Genius in his estimation meant labour. Whatever he thought it worth while to do, he did in earnest, and he took an interest in almost everything. He was on good terms with all kinds of toilers. Engine drivers on the Underground Railway, gasmen at work laying new mains, keepers at the Zoo, 'bus-drivers, tricyclists; he would talk to all of them about their work or play. "That boy of yours," said an American doctor, "gets to the bottom of things, he can't help it; if there is anything to find in Borneo, he will find it!" Thinking now of the hardships he endured out there, I try to remember the keen delight with which he made the arrangements for his journey, the vigour with which he studied up some special subjects it was desirable he should know, the happiness it was to him when he could show me, among his physical accomplishments, how well he could swim. And I was overjoyed to think that I had saved him from the drudgery of newspaper work, from the toil of writing stories when one would rather not; though I believe that had he been spared, he would have entered the world of letters with his full mind, his bright intellect and his travelled experience, and that humanity would have been the better for his sympathy and his labours.

### III.

His engagement by the British North Borneo Company was no work of mine. It was talked of in a general way for many months before any practical negotiations took place between Frank and the directors. In the meantime we read up together the history of the Eastern seas. We became authorities on the Dutch and Spanish and English claims to the island of Borneo. I did not think at that time that the business would go any further than this. But I recall that his mother would often look anxiously across the table at him when Borneo was the subject of our after-dinner chats. One day Frank came home and said he had accepted the position of mineral explorer and metallurgical chemist to the British North Borneo Company, "with your consent, of course." Then both his mother and myself began to argue against his choice of work. There had been an opening proposed for him as assistant chemist at Guy's Hospital. We hinted that perhaps he had better begin his career at home. "By analyzing poisoned stomachs?" he said quietly; "that is not a very interesting occupation, is it?" The position of chemist in a great dye works had been spoken of as likely to be vacant, and an American friend had offered him remunerative employment on the other side of the Atlantic in that same direction. "No," he replied, "I don't care for dye works. I would like to see America; and might I not come home from Borneo through Japan and by way of San Francisco and New York?"

"I fear you are too young for so serious and responsible a position as the Borneo Company offer you," I said.

"They don't think so," he answered, "and I have seen some of the directors several times. I am twenty. Life is so short, one cannot begin it too early. Besides, I must see the world; you have said so. You have proposed that I shall have six months of travel, that I shall go all through America. Here I am offered more than we ever dreamed of, a great Eastern journey, and everything that can make travel interesting, and with the prospect of a fortune at the end of it. I am to have a bonus on results, beyond my salary."

I went into the city, proud of the boy's courage, but with the traditional story of Borneo in my mind, and with ugly thoughts of fever and other tropical difficulties and dangers that beset the European path on the equator. Mr. Alfred Dent, the founder of the Company, and Mr. William M. Crocker, now its manager, spoke of my son in very kindly terms. They believed in young men, and in particular they believed in my son.

"Do you not think he is too young for the position?" I asked.

"Too young! He will get over that," said an elderly gentleman (looking up from a letter he was writing) to whom I was introduced.

This third gentleman in our conversation was Mr. William Henry Macleod Read, one of the first directors of the Company, and whose name is a tower of strength in that part of the East we were discussing.

"He is a fine young fellow," said Mr. Read, "and he will make his way."

"But the climate?" I said.

"Well, it is hot," he replied; "but I have lived out there most of my life, and I am over seventy."

Mr. Read was the picture of health, and I began to fear that I was playing the part of the over-anxious father. Nevertheless I carried home a bundle of papers, printed and in manuscript, relating to the Company, its work, its objects and affairs, resolved to study them and to master the modern story of Borneo. I was struck with the adventurous narratives of a Mr. F. Witti, who was in the Company's service; and I found that only a very small section of the Company's territory had been explored. Then I talked over with Mr. Dent the work which Frank would have to do. "It will be entirely different to that of Witti," he said, "who is a born explorer, one of those adventurous men who like danger for its own sake, and who prefer to wander up and down the earth in outlandish places rather than to settle in civilized quarters. When Frank travels, it will be under more favourable conditions."

The truth is, they did not quite know in London what would be Frank's real work in Borneo; but I made an express condition that if he had to undertake expeditions into the interior, he should at least have one efficient white officer (an Englishman) on his staff. In my ignorance of Eastern work, and especially of Bornean exploration, I tried to stipulate for English servants, but soon understood the impracticability of that idea.

Presently Frank was continually at the Borneo offices in the city. I think the most active of the directors took occasion to see him often. The Governor, Mr. Treacher, came to London. Frank met him and had a long conversation with him. A water-party on the Thames was given to the Governor. Frank was there. He became personally and well acquainted with the leading officials of the new government. He liked them. They liked him. The more they saw of him the more they approved their choice of the young officer who should form and establish their scientific department.

## IV.

I was in America while Frank was making his final preparations for leaving England. His letters to me during that period were full of his work. He was taking counsel, advice, and lessons in many things. Some of the learned and kindly men of the Geographical Society were helping him. He was deep in the mysteries of solar observations, navigation, surveying; in the intervals of these studies he was swimming, boating, shooting; these occupations and the collection of his outfit and scientific equipment found him at work early and late; so that at last, when all was prepared, the time for departure was welcomed as a period of rest. I never ceased to make inquiries as to the possible influence upon him physically and morally of his work. Crossing the Atlantic, I had a long conversation with Captain Murray, then of the *Arizona*, who had for a time commanded a trading steamer on the Amazon. He gave me many interesting accounts of his tropical experiences, and envied Frank the investigation of the unexplored rivers of Borneo. Colonel Knox, an American journalist and author, who had visited the Sabah coast, assured me I had nothing to fear, and much to be proud of, in the appointment of my son. " He will be well attended and well provisioned on his excursions, and his mind will be so full of his work that he will not have time to be sick." I received a shock on returning home. Consulting a medical friend, who knew Frank well, as to the influences of a hot climate upon a boy of his physique, I told him that the only illness Frank had ever had was an attack of bronchitis. " He could not go to a better climate, then," said my friend; "it will help him, and after being immured for so long in the laboratories at Kensington, his system will receive a fillip out there, and the trip will make a man of him. But of course you will insure his life?"

"No, indeed I will not," I said.

"Then the Company must," he said.

"Because he is going to a climate that will be good for him?"

"Oh, no," said my friend, "but for the same reason that you make an extra and special insurance on your life when you go to America—in case of accident. Not that, to my thinking, he will run any more risks out there than he runs every day in London, especially as a tricyclist."

"The cases have no point in common, let us not discuss them; do you think it is good for Frank to accept this appointment?"

"Good! It is a splendid chance for him—such a chance as falls to the lot of very few young fellows at the outset of a career."

He saw that his remark about insurance had troubled me for the moment. And yet I let Frank go. When I came home after saying good-bye to him, his mother said, "I shall never see him again;" and yet I did not say, "Come back."

Not long before we heard the first good news of his last expedition, a little shrine, which his sisters had set up to him, fell to the ground. I am not superstitious, but my heart seemed to stand still when they reported this to me; and I think we all looked at each other apprehensively. If afterwards, in our sorrow, we had calculated the date of that occurrence, I believe it would have proved to be on March 1st, 1882. When the despatch came which reported him well and in good spirits, and on his way down the Segama river, I remember our delight; but I awoke in the night from a troubled dream, with his voice in my ear. "But here am I, all alone, on an island of antimony," were the strange words he said. I mention these things without attaching any importance to them, but as curious matters, and as incidents that my memory persists in registering. His voice had been silenced for ever when I heard it in my dream. It could have had no spiritualistic association with his death. Though, as I said, I am not superstitious, my first "hoping against hope" arose in a fanciful reflection that so great was his love for me, and mine for him, that if anything serious had happened to him I should have felt it in some mysterious way; that I should have seen him perhaps, as the Corsican, in a play that had greatly delighted him, saw his brother on the field of death. In these days I find that I try to comfort myself with the reflection that his last moments were not embittered by a thought of us; that his death was too sudden for more than a fleeting knowledge of his hurt; that unconsciousness instantly followed his exclamation, "I am dead!"—that he died before he had time to think of the grief his death would cause at home; and, therefore, that he passed away happily.

The misery of such deaths falls to those who are left behind. We know that we had been in his mind. He had been in high spirits, with the knowledge that he was within a few days of the station where he would get letters from us. He was also on his way to Silam, Sandakan Kudat, to collect his things together, put up his diaries, pack his geological and botanical specimens, and then "homeward bound." He had met a young Englishman in the interior some days before the end, and had been talking of home, of Regent's Park, of London; and we knew that we had been in his thoughts, and possibly were so up to a few minutes before his death. It was characteristic of him to have dreamy reveries; there was often, as I have said, an inspiration of "far-away thoughts" in his brown eyes. His mind may have been busy with other scenes when he was struck down. The hint of thoughtlessness in the use of his weapon on this fatal day pictures him in my fancy marching to his boat heedless of his surroundings. "He met with an accident," writes one of his friends, "which might have occurred anywhere, and the kind of accident that is common in the history of sport and travel all over the world."

One night, in New York, a few months after his death, I sat and listened while Dr. Fordyce Barker explained to a little party after dinner the instant collapse that follows on a person being shot through the lungs.[1] One has often to bear blows of this kind,

---

[1] Dr. Fordyce Barker, who was intimate with Dickens, during that illustrious author's visits to America, was one of the guests. He started, among other subjects, a very interesting conversation.

"Have you ever made studies of deaths for stage purposes?" asked Dr. Barker.

"No."

"And yet your last moments of Mathias and of Louis XI. are perfectly consistent and correct psychologically."

"My idea is to make death in these cases a characteristic Nemesis; for example, Mathias dies of the fear of discovery; he is fatally haunted by the dread of being found out, and dies of it in a dream. Louis pulls himself together by a great effort of will in his weakest phy-

unconsciously given. I saw that pathetic scene in the jungle while the doctor was speaking, heard the last words, saw the boat with its dear freight gliding through the tropical night; and yet I was sharing in the talk over the wine, and I was thankful to the doctor for his emphatic opinion, that to be shot through the lungs means a sudden and painless death.

v.

In 1880-1 Frank contributed a long series of "Science Notes" to a country journal, under the *nom de plume* of "A Professor of Chemistry." They cover about forty newspaper columns. I find them in a scrap-book, annotated with a few memoranda here and there. The "Notes" are in themselves more or less instructive; they exhibit a general love of inquiry and a desire to thrash out controversial subjects. A cordial

---

sical moment, to fall dead—struck as if by a thunderbolt—while giving an arrogant command that is to control heaven itself; and it seems to me that he should collapse ignominiously, as I try to illustrate."

"You succeed perfectly," the doctor replied, "and from a physiological point of view, too."

"Hamlet's death, on the other hand, I would try to make sweet and gentle as the character, as if the 'flights of angels winged him to his rest.'"

"You seem to have a genius for fathoming the conceptions of your authors, Mr. Irving," said the doctor; "and it is, of course, very important to the illusion of a scene that the reality of it should be consistently maintained. Last night I went to see a play called 'Moths,' at Wallack's. There is a young man in it who acts very well; but he, probably by the fault of the author more than his own, commits a grave error in the manner of his death. We are told that he is shot through the lungs. This means almost immediate unconsciousness, and a quick, painless death; yet the actor in question came upon the stage after receiving this fatal wound, made a coherent speech, and died in a peaceful attitude."—*Henry Irving's Impressions of America.*

acknowledgment of the merits of great men, and an appreciation of their work, are manifest throughout the entire series. But it appears that Frank had an opponent with whom he occasionally crossed swords. One of his encounters is worth recording. It is sufficiently explained in the young professor's reply, and I think the subject is one that may not be uninteresting for its own sake.

In some notes of mine which appeared a few weeks ago in your columns, I made some statements concerning Mr. Joshua Prusol, which "a Reader of *Colburn's New Monthly* also" has taken very much to heart. In his very enthusiastic but somewhat indiscreet letter in your last week's issue, he makes some remarks which I feel obliged, in the interests of common sense and wholesome scientific thought, to contradict. In my refutation I will overlook the entire absurdity of the whole article, and shut my eyes, as far as possible, to the lamentable ignorance of scientific knowledge which it displays. I will treat the arguments, however, as those of a thinking man, and will now call in review the "theories" which your correspondent advances; theories, by-the-bye, which the merest tyro at science could easily refute.

The "Reader of *Colburn's New Monthly* also" begins by a dogmatic statement that "where there is no atmosphere there is no heat," and that "the heat we enjoy is not solar but atmospheric." As a proof of this he brings forward the cold of the Arctic regions, and states, entirely on his own authority, that "were the sun the source of heat, the intensity of the cold would increase, till in a short time there would be no heat, and thus the men would be congealed into statues." It is evident to me, from the above, that the gentleman in question does not know what heat is; it seems that he is bringing to life the old theory of caloric, a theory exploded at least a hundred years ago. For your correspondent's edification, and I hope instruction, I will give the following:—The heat of a body is caused by an extremely rapid oscillating or vibratory motion of its molecules, and the hottest bodies are those in which the vibrations have the greatest velocity and the greatest amplitude. Hence heat is *not a substance*, but a *condition* of matter, and a condition which can be transferred from one body to the other. There is also probably an elastic ether which pervades all matter and infinite space. A hot body sets this in rapid vibration, and the vibrations of this ether being communicated to material objects, gives them a more rapid vibration, that is, increases their temperature. If we stand in front of a fire, we experience a sensation of warmth which is not due to the temperature of the air, for if a screen be interposed, the sensation immediately disappears, which would not be the case if the surrounding air had a high temperature. Hence bodies can send out rays which excite heat, and which penetrate through the air *without heating it*, as rays of light through transparent bodies. Heat thus propagated is said to be radiated ; and the term, *ray of heat* or *calorific ray* is used in the same sense as ray of light is used. In a homogeneous medium, radiation takes place in a right line. The intensity is less the greater the obliquity of the rays, with respect to the radiating surface. Thermal rays falling upon a body are divided into two parts, one of which penetrates the body, while the other rebounds—that is, it is reflected from the surface. We live here at the bottom of an aerial ocean, which is to a remarkable degree permeable to the sun's rays of light and heat, and is but little if at all affected by the direct action of this heat. But the rays when they fall upon the earth heat its surface, and when upon the ocean evaporate the water. The air, in direct contact with the heated surface of the earth, which surface is reflecting back and radiating the solar heat, becomes warmed, and it is a principle of physics that hot air is lighter than cold air. This warm air then rises and flows northwards towards the poles, while the cold air from the Arctic regions flows southward to the equator. This is the principle of trade-winds, hot winds blowing from the equator to the poles, and cold winds from the poles to the equator. This is one of the causes which tends to modify the rigour of the Polar night. Another is that the heat stored up by the earth's surface during the summer months is radiated slowly, and thus the atmosphere is warmed by gradual radiation from the earth's surface of solar heat received during the summer. Absence of heat or " no heat," as the " Reader of *Colburn's New Monthly* also" puts it, has never been observed ; and as there is never an absence of motion in matter, insomuch as molecular motion always exists, there is probably no total absence of heat : for heat is motion. During the day, or Polar summer, the ground receives more heat than it radiates into space, and the temperature rises. The reverse is the case during the night ; the heat which the earth loses by radiation is no longer compensated for, and, consequently, a fall of temperature takes place. In tropical Bengal this nocturnal cooling is used for the manufacture of ice. . Large flat vessels containing water are placed on non-conducting substances, such as straw or dry leaves. In consequence of the radiation the water freezes, even when the temperature of the air is 60° Fahr. If the heat did not come from the sun, but were common to the atmosphere, there would be no evaporation, and therefore no clouds. It will now be seen how absurd a fallacy it is to talk of "heat dormant in the atmosphere." But as a convincing proof that heat comes from the sun, the following experiment is useful :—When a solar ray admitted through an aperture in a dark room is concentrated on a prism of rock salt, and then, after emerging from the prism, is received on a screen, it will be found to present a band of colours in the following order : red, orange, yellow, green, blue, and violet. This is the light and heat spectrum. (It demonstrates the fact that white light is composite.) If, now, a narrow and delicate thermo-pile or thermometer be placed successively on the space occupied by each of the colours, it will be scarcely affected on the violet; but in passing over the other colours it will indicate *a gradual rise of temperature*, which is greatest at the red. If the thermometer be now moved in the same direction *beyond the limits* of the luminous spectrum, the temperature will gradually rise for a considerable space beyond the light spectrum. This is the *heat spectrum*. It is therefore seen that the sun's light consists of rays of light and heat of different rates of vibration ; by their passage through the prism they are unequally broken or refracted ; those with shorter wave-lengths are the most refrangible. This experiment will also hold good for all sources of heat, as candles, the moon, electric light, &c.

The next point in the letter of the "Reader of *Colburn's New Monthly* also" is the vacuum, which he says I introduced into my notes, "to strengthen" my "ratiocination that heat comes from the sun." I am sure I did no such thing, as the observation has no connection with the matter. I merely stated a fact, that heat passes through a vacuum. Your correspondent tells me to "experiment with a vacuum, *enclosed both top and sides* with glass," and adds (somewhat after the fashion of the "March Hare" in "Alice in Wonderland," who, when the "Hatter" says that he knew butter would not suit the works of his watch, replies, "It was the best butter, you know,") that, "it must be plate glass to resist the pressure." How does one enclose a vacuum "top and sides," or which is the top of a vacuum and where are the sides ; and does your correspondent leave out the bottom altogether? However this may be, he concludes from this remarkable experiment performed with a vacuum, with "a top and sides," that "the atmosphere, the mother of heat, as far as possible is drawn out of it, and he will," referring to myself, "find that the heat is so wonderful within subject to all these favourable conditions that water is instantly congealed to ice!" Before going into the other "conclusions" drawn from these truly novel "top and side vacuum" experiments, I will briefly state the reason that water solidifies when the air is pumped out of a receiver in which water is contained. Whatever be the temperature at which a vapour is produced, an absorption of heat always takes place. If, therefore, a liquid evaporates and does not receive from without a quantity of heat equal to that which is expended in producing the vapour, its temperature sinks, and the cooling is greater in proportion as the evaporation is more rapid. Leslie succeeded in freezing water by means of rapid evaporation. Under the receiver of an air-pump is placed a vessel containing strong sulphuric acid, and above it a thin metal capsule, containing a small quantity of water. On exhausting the receiver the water begins to boil, and since the vapours are absorbed by the sulphuric acid as fast as they are generated, a rapid evaporation is produced, which quickly effects the freezing of the water.

By means of the rapid evaporation of bisulphide of carbon the formation of ice may be illustrated without the aid of an air-pump. A little water is dropped on a board, and a capsule of thin copper foil, containing bisulphide of carbon, is placed in the water. The evaporation of the bisulphide is accelerated by means of a pair of bellows, and, after a few minutes, the water freezes round the capsule, so that the latter adheres to the wood. In like manner, if water be placed in a test-tube, which is then dipped in a glass containing ether, and a current of air be blown through the ether, the cold produced by the rapid evaporation of the ether very soon freezes the water in the tube. Such experiments as these, which can, and shall, if necessary, be multiplied to infinity, show the entire absurdity of talking of "the atmosphere, which is the mother of heat, being drawn out," or of the "cold within the vacuum being the same which exists on the unapproachable mountain heights," or such kindred nonsense. (By the way, what is the "converging power" of a piece of plate glass? I am anxious to be informed.)

The next point to refute is your correspondent's assertion that heat does not pass through a vacuum. *Radiant heat is propagated in vacuo as well as in air.* This is demonstrated by the following experiment:— In the bottom of a glass flask (not a plate-glass one in this case) a thermometer is fixed in such a manner that its bulb occupies the *centre of the flask*. The neck of the flask is carefully narrowed by means of the blowpipe, and then the apparatus having been suitably attached, a vacuum is produced in the interior. This being done, the tube is sealed at the narrow part, and we have an exhausted flask containing a thermometer. On immersing this apparatus in hot water, or on bringing near it some red-hot charcoal, the thermometer is *at once* seen to rise. This could only arise from radiation through the vacuum in the interior, for glass is so bad a conductor of heat that the heat could not travel through the sides of the flask and down the stem of the thermometer in so short a time. (This may also be considered a proof that the hypothetical ether is present in a vacuum.)

The "Constant Reader of *Colburn's New Monthly* also" then goes on to deny my assertion that Tyndall, in common with many other observers, has recorded high temperature when at considerable elevations. The "C. R. of *C. N. M.* also" states that "the story of Tyndall is apparently a fiction, and is open and apparent nonsense, which I feel sure your Professor of Chemistry will be careful not to repeat." This is a very indiscreet remark, especially as the "Constant Reader of *Colburn's New Monthly*" does not seem to have read anything else but *Colburn's New Monthly*, which, admirable as it is, is not a scientific work, and is not sufficient to base one's scientific knowledge upon. I cannot do better than quote Tyndall himself in refutation of the accusation that I am an inventor of science facts which never existed.

In Tyndall's "Glaciers of the Alps," during the ascent of "Monte Rosa," over 15,000 feet high, when at an elevation of over 12,000 feet, Tyndall says:—"There was not a breath of air stirring, and though we stood ankle-deep in snow, the heat surpassed anything of the kind I had ever felt; it was the dead suffocating warmth of an oven which encompassed us on all sides, and from which there seemed no escape." The "Constant Reader of *Colburn's New Monthly*" also says that "Tyndall himself, although he is well known as an Alpine tourist in search of knowledge, to climb such a height would be quite beyond his physical endurance."

I am at a loss to understand why this statement is made, for every reader of even ordinary literature or of the London *Times* knows that Professor Tyndall has been up Mont Blanc (16,000 feet) several times, both alone and in company with Professor Huxley and Dr. Frankland. His ascent of the Matterhorn (14,000 feet) is a known fact, and Monte Rosa's summit has often been trodden by the Professor. In "Glaciers of the Alps," during an ascent of Mont Blanc, he says:—"At length success became certain, and at half-past three p.m. we joined hands on the top."

Tyndall, in "Heat as a Mode of Motion," quotes the following from

Sir Joseph Hooker's "Himalayan Journal," 1st edition, vol. ii. page 407 :—" From a multitude of desultory observations, I conclude that, at 7400 feet, 125·7°, or 67·0° (Fahrenheit's scale) above the temperature of the air, is the average effect of the sun's rays on a black bulb thermometer. The effect is much increased by elevation. At 10,000 feet, in December, at 9 a.m., I saw the mercury mount to 132° Fahr., while the temperature *of the shaded snow was* 22° *Fahr*. At 13,000 feet, in the following month, at 9 a.m., I saw it stand at 98°, with a difference of 68·2°; and at ten o'clock, at 114° (Fahr.), with a difference of 81·4°, while the thermometer placed on the snow had fallen, at sunrise, to 0·7 of a degree, or 31·3° below the freezing point, on Fahrenheit's scale." Tyndall's explanation of this phenomenon is as follows :— " These enormous differences between *the shaded* and the *unshaded air*, and between *the air* and *the snow*, are no doubt due," as I mentioned in my original note, " to the comparative absence of moisture at these elevations. The air is incompetent to check either the solar or the terrestrial radiation, and hence the maximum heat in the sun and the maximum cold in the shade must stand very wide apart." Quite dry air acts, in fact, towards solar heat as a vacuum and the heating of the atmosphere is all due to the presence of aqueous vapour in it ; as quite dry air transmits heat-rays without itself being warmed at all. This was proved by Tyndall at the last B.A. at Swansea. Such observations as these have been recorded by Sir J. Herschel, Dr. Livingstone, and numerous other eminent men, and I could quote page after page of similar observations in direct support of what I have stated.

The remainder of the letter in question needs no explanation or refutation from me, as its fallacy is so palpable that the most hasty of your readers will already have discovered the mass of errors of which it is composed. In conclusion, I may recommend the " Reader of *Colburn's New Monthly* " to invest a shilling in the purchase of an elementary primer of physics and astronomy, where he may learn the rudiments of a science about which neither himself nor, indeed, Mr. Joshua Prusol appear to have any real practical knowledge.

It was a little family joke against him, poor fellow, that he was "discharged" from this country paper. His "honorarium" was small, and he received it irregularly. Desiring to supplement some drafts of mine, on account of certain chemical apparatus which he had bought, he wrote for the salary due to him. No reply.

He wrote again. Then came his money and his dismissal. I noticed a flush of anger upon his face for a moment; it passed into a smile as he said, "I have got my cheque and my discharge! Well, *there is* work one can do for nothing, but not that sort of work." I told him that small troubles of this kind were often more irritating than great ones. "Little things will never bother me," he said, putting his cheque into his pocket and his letter into the fire. "One hasn't time, eh, pa?" And I don't think the little concerns of life ever did trouble him. As for time, he had none to waste; when he was not working, he was playing, and he did both with all his might.

VI.

At about this period he wrote a series of some twenty sketches of the careers and work of living men of science for the *Biograph*. Among his letters are pleasant epistles from several of the subjects of his papers, all pointing to the fact that he took pains with his work. He was not vague about dates, nor uncertain in his figures; he was very clear in his summaries of scientific facts, and he had an educated appreciation, and showed it unconsciously, of the labours he discussed and described. If he had done nothing else besides literary work at this time, he would have been entitled to respect; but these items of industry I am mentioning were accomplished in addition to his successful studies and examinations at South Kensington and the School of Mines. He contributed to *Bradstreets* (an American journal of high repute) several articles of an economic character, embracing such subjects as dye-works, aniline dyes, glass making, and gold and silver.

Prior to the brief sensation created by the so-called discovery of the manufacture of diamonds by Mr. Hannay, he had written for his country paper an interesting article on the chemical manufacture of gems. During the year 1880 he made some interesting experiments with Thames water, took samples of the river at the point where the *Princess Alice* was lost, and wrote an essay upon a drop of Thames water. He followed it, from its birth, down the river to London, and thence into the laboratory of the chemist, treating the subject "popularly," but with a fair balance of scientific information. I thought so well of his paper that I offered it to a publisher, believing it would make a useful handbook. The reply was that "we have a volume on the London water-supply in hand, otherwise we should have been very glad to undertake it." Frank then, on his own account, submitted the MS. to a London journal. "Cut it down and we will accept it." He cut it down. "More cutting" was the verdict. Then at last it was accepted, and a liberal cheque was his reward. But it was not published until he was in the midst of his work in Borneo. There are two examples of these youthful journalistic labours which I desire to reprint. They are, "The Adventures of a Drop of Thames Water," which appeared in the *Whitehall Review*, and "A Visit to Rothschild's and to the British Mint," which appeared in *Bradstreets*.

THE ADVENTURES OF A DROP OF THAMES WATER.

A SPARKLING aqueous crystal flashing in the sunlight, and reflecting all the colours of the rainbow. Down it came through the pure air, splashing at last into a pool among the roots of an oak in Gloucestershire. Here it made the acquaintance of innumerable other drops.

The short summer showers ceased, and then the sun burst through the clouds and shed a flood of golden radiance over the quiet landscape. Some drops rose at once into the air, and were borne away on the wings of the wind. Others, less fortunate, were swallowed up by mother earth; the one whose career I propose to follow was among the latter.

After soaking through the superficial soil it came upon a crevice in the rock, down which it bounded, dashing from side to side, dissolving and carrying away particles of rock, washing a fern, or starting a pebble from some projecting ledge. Presently it came upon an underground cavern, from the roof of which hung curiously formed stalactites, and along the bottom rushed a noisy stream. Our drop ran down the sides of one of the longest pendent masses, depositing in its course most of the foreign materials collected above, and thus contributing its little to the growth of the column. Soon falling off the stalactite it was carried on, with a host of companion drops, by the gurgling brook below. On a sudden there was a stoppage of the whole stream by the pressure of the oncoming water up a narrow channel. Our aqueous adventurer now ascended as fast as it had before descended. A minute later and it was running along the course of a noisy rivulet.

Away it went between green banks, washing the long grasses and the spreading burdock leaves. Dancing on in the sunlight, past dozing cottages and sleeping homesteads, the stream receives recruits from other rivulets and fountains, and soon fresh supplies pour in from either side. In due time our drop has helped to turn a mill. Near Kemble Meads it sails proudly under its first "bridge"—a few rough stepping-stones thrown into the streamlet. Now, as it approaches Lechlade, it encounters many fish. Still pure and limpid, it passes on, collecting but little organic matter from the banks, and that mainly of vegetable origin. Gradually the river widens: our little drop is almost lost in the immense volume of flowing water. But now its troubles begin. On the right of the river, about a foot above the water, a large pipe pours a blue liquid into the Thames. In the distance are tall chimneys, sending forth volumes of smoke into the atmosphere. The first pollution! Our drop dissolves some quantity of the factory filth, and continues its course less buoyantly. But soon it assists to wash sheep, and, loaded with some of their dirt, it becomes turbid from the entrance on either side of the water of drainage from manured land and the discharges of more fibre works. These latter are filthy liquids, sometimes blue from colouring dyes, sometimes brown from suspended rubbish. Sadly and slowly the tiny drop continues its course down the now polluted river, until it comes in sight of the spires and towers of Oxford, that city of classic renown, where they have still to learn the first principles of sanitary science. For here the noble river, that anon came splashing through flowery meads and pleasant pastures, is weighted with filth indescribable. By the time the city of domes and towers is passed the river contains 2450 parts of sewage contamination per 100,000 parts, and the colour is greenish-yellow. Our globule flows on, increasing in size and clogged with foreign matter.

Past Reading, Henley, Maidenhead, Staines, each place contributing to the pollution of the stream, our drop is used with its companions for bathing, for the washing of sheep and cattle. The river bears on its surface the putrid carcases of cats, dogs, and rats. It receives the foul discharges of hundreds of dye works, fibre works, paper-mills, and the sewage of numbers of considerable towns and villages. The entire flood is changed. It is here of a dark brown colour, and it flows along sluggishly. This once pure stream now conveys the germs of disease and death. By this time our drop has become the abode of myriads of animals. There are some with wheels, whirling about, twisting, turning, and rushing; some with long swords stabbing and thrusting. Others there are like balls, now contracting, now expanding; some with red eyes flaming and glaring, some with black, some with striped bodies, and some with no bodies at all, and each one filled with the desire of eating as many of its fellows up in as short a space of time as possible. There are hundreds crowded together in this one drop of water, which has to carry on not only all the dissolved and suspended filth collected above, but also these countless inhabitants. Presently our drop passes Windsor, catching a glimpse of the towers and turrets of the castle, and receiving the discharges from the sewers of the royal palace. The river is now wider and muddier. Steam launches dash along, tearing up the surface and boiling it into considerable waves. The fish have degenerated. They are now coarse and insipid. Pike have almost disappeared, and the water is tenanted by sluggish roach, coarse gudgeon, and flavourless perch, species which delight in polluted waters and feed on the filth. Angling has degenerated with the fish. The smart fisherman in knickerbockers, mackintosh, knapsack, and rod, is now unknown. He is replaced by the "professional angler." He is a middle-aged man, sitting by the river watching two or three rods lying near him, and holding another in his hand. Near him are a coloured handkerchief containing half a loaf of bread, a jar of bran, sundry onions, a knife, and a short pipe. From time to time barges interrupt his pleasures, and he and the drivers exchange a series of compliments, the fisherman calling the bargee's attention to the fact that he will knock his (the driver's) sanguinary eyes out, the bargee retorting by informing *piscator* that he will throw his blank carcase into the blank river. Here the argument generally ends, the driver contenting himself with shouting back polite remarks to the angler as long as he is in sight. The barges by no means improve the condition of the river, as the people on board cast all their refuse into the stream, thus contributing to the pollution of our sad and weary globule.

"Where is the sewage to go, if not in the river?" is a question which will be asked by many readers. The answer is that sewage water may be made drinkable. Croydon and Norwood are supplied with sewage water passed through a few feet of screened sand. As an example of the efficiency of this process it may be stated that a specimen of London sewage, before filtration through 15 feet of sand, contained organic carbon 4·386, organic nitrogen 2·484, and ammonia 5·557; after filtration these figures were reduced to organic carbon 0·734, organic nitrogen 0·108, and ammonia 0·012 per 100,000 parts of the water. It will be seen from this that the organic carbon and nitrogen, which include the germs of disease and other living organisms found in sewage, have been greatly reduced. If the stratum of sand had been thicker, the condition of the water would have been even better, and much of the organic and harmful impurities would have been converted into inorganic and innoxious matters. Chalk is a still better filtering medium. A specimen of the same sewage as above had its three important impurities still further reduced by filtration through fifteen feet of chalk. The figures were: organic carbon 0·582, organic nitrogen 0·092, ammonia 0·016.

Not only does this method of purification apply to sewage, but also to the refuse liquids from industrial processes, which could be thus materially improved before ejection into the river. It is true that, in the case of some towns on the Thames, processes for the purification of sewage are in use, but the standards of purity are too wide and are not enforced with sufficient vigour. We left our drop passing Windsor; it was in a sad plight, and progressing slowly. Now clouds gather. Rain-falls splash into the stream. The Thames rises gradually with the downpour. All day and all night it rains one unceasing torrent of drops. Miniature waterfalls run in from the meadows, bringing down all kinds of refuse—manure, soil, bits of straw, paper, and other *débris*. Soon the river overflows its banks; but still it rains without cessation. The stream becomes muckier than ever, owing to the stirring up of the mud at the bottom of the river. Our aqueous voyager passes Chertsey, Shepperton, Kingston. All is wrapped in silence here. The boathouses are closed. Not a soul to be seen. The smoke ascends slowly from the chimneys into the moisture-saturated atmosphere, and then hangs over the houses like a pall. All the windows are shut; there is no sign of life, for the people are sitting round their fires, trying to forget the weather outside. Slowly our drop approaches Teddington, and here it has a narrow escape of being pumped up into the tanks of the metropolitan companies. The river is in flood, and our drop sees millions of its dirty *confrères* gulped up by the suction pumps. They carry with them an enormous amount of the suspended and dissolved filth collected during the course of pollution which I have described.

Of the quality of the water delivered to London by the various companies, that of the West Middlesex is the best of those drawing from the Thames. The Grand Junction comes next. This latter water contains on an average ·231 organic carbon, ·032 organic nitrogen, and ·001 ammonia. The other companies' waters vary in purity, but even the efficient filtration to which all the companies submit their waters cannot remove all the noxious constituents, and no one ought to be asked to drink water which has been contaminated, no matter how slightly, with animal matter or excreta.

The drop of Thames water whose adventures I am chronicling, having escaped the pumping-stations of the great companies, is now quickly approaching London. It is in a very bad state, and is swollen very much. Who could say what it did not contain? Animalculæ in abundance still peopled it; organic matter in quantity, both dissolved and suspended, was in it. It contained nitrates of potash, ammonia, soda, and other salts. It had nitrates of the same bases, also free ammonia and common salt in comparative plenty, besides salts of lime, magnesia, and so on.

Past stately Richmond and Kew, and now on to Hammersmith, the number of dead animals floating on the stream had increased tremendously. Our drop was caught for a time in a quiet pool, and it watched its companions sailing past with their numerous passengers. Now a bit of straw floated by, curling and twisting in the eddies. Then a fragment of an old play-bill, recording some performance long forgotten and erased. Anon a scrap of wood, a bit of stick, or a piece of coloured rag passed our drop, and now the putrid body of a cat in a revoltingly decayed condition. Then a dog in a similar state floated past, the remnant of a filthy rope dangling from its decomposed and skeleton neck. Weighted with new and still more terrible matter, both alive and dead, the crystal drop that fell from the clouds to refresh the thirsty earth and minister to the health and happiness of man struggles, a messenger of disease and death. It is in sight of London.

The progress of the drop of Thames water to Westminster was slow and monotonous. Now it wended its way with the sluggish current and the ebb tide; now it was left high up on the bank at low water, when the river bared itself, showing the masses of accumulated filth which composed its bed. To the right and left, in front and behind, as far as the eye could see, stretched thousands of houses, streets, buildings, museums, schools, offices, churches, shops, and gin palaces, with the Houses of Parliament and Westminster Abbey in the foreground. What a beautiful city! A city of embankments, promenades, and fine buildings, a city of noble bridges and splendid architecture! One by one the lights glimmered from myriads of windows, shops, and lamps, as night lowered her mantle over the vast metropolis. On a sudden there is a blaze of light from the Embankments. It seemed as if day had changed its mind and come back again. A stately Needle stood up in relief against the bright background, giving to the scene an almost Oriental appearance. The waves on the river were tinted with silver, and the eddies about the bridges looked like pools of molten metal. Our idealized globule admired the people who could thus create an artificial sun at will—admired them, in spite of their ignorance of sanitary laws and their waste of that great fertilizing power which they fling into their noble river.

Daylight found our traveller past the Tower. Ships and hay-boats lay moored at the city wharves' walls. The sailors were getting ready to begin their course down with the tide. The sun got up and blazed out, parching the lips of the boatmen and festering every noisome carcase which floated on the river. It burnt the heads and eyes of the dockhands toiling at their arduous tasks, and it sent Mayfair home to its ice and its sunshades. Many of the companions of our aqueous voyager soared aloft, reclaimed by the sun, each one leaving its *débris* behind to its fellow globules. Our drop wished to be taken up also, but it sailed along in the shade of the buildings, which prevented its evaporation. Soon the tide ran out, and our drop was caught in the mud-bank and was left by the stream. It watched the river uncovering itself, and it surveyed the stuff accumulated on the banks. Here was an old coal-pan half-covered with mud, there a kettle of ancient date. Now a boy throws a basket of rubbish on the bank, such rubbish as vegetable leaves, cabbage stalks, a dead rat, cinders, an old tin pot, an empty sardine box, potted-lobster tins, dirty paper, and such like odds and ends, which slowly sank into the mud, there to await the returning tide. Presently a cart of filth is discharged upon the bank; it contains a miscellaneous assortment of rubbish collected from all sorts of sewers, gutters, and corners. As the sun shone down upon it, gases of all descriptions rose from the awful heap. Sulphuretted hydrogen was the least offensive. There lay our drop, in company with a dead dog and a sardine tin. It watched the flies deposit their eggs on the body of the putrid animal, and the larvæ come to life under the favourable beams of the sun. Soon the skin and the flesh were swarming with white grubs, crawling about and devouring the animal in question, an operation the further contemplation of which our drop was spared by the new tide. Gradually the dead dog was covered with water, and then it rose to the surface, surrounded by bubbles of gas and floating larvæ.[2]

London is now left behind, and Rotherhithe, Greenwich, and Erith passed. Great ships, majestic ocean steamers, sail up to the docks, bearing the wondering foreigner to the greatest city in the world. The scene from Erith to Woolwich and Gravesend was, to our drop, terrible. To the right and left the enormous filth-ducts of the metropolis were pouring forth day and night their torrents of liquid into the Thames. The previous pollutions of the river were as nothing compared to this vast contamination; Oxford, Reading, Windsor, nothing in comparison to the pollution of London. The river was fast becoming an open sewer, and our heaven-born traveller asked itself whether it was water at all, or only a patch of moist mud and filth. Even animalculæ had been getting scarce, and fish had long since disappeared. The shore's mud, the bed of the river

---

[2] Among Frank's memoranda of work done in the laboratories at Kensington I find the following:—*Analysis of Thames Water where the "Princess Alice" went down.* Results of analysis expressed in parts per 100,000. Sample taken from just below Beckton Gas Works. Total solid matter, 105·56; organic carbon, 6·08; ammonia, 1·0; nitrogen as nitrates and nitrites, 0; total combined nitrogen, 2·016; previous sewage or animal contamination, 0; chlorine, 27·20; hardness, temporary, 17·14, permanent, 18·58—total, 35·72. *Remarks.—* Fœtid odour; very turbid; fearfully polluted; little better than sewage; the sewage contamination is present, and not previous; no poisonous metals. Then there is a note for "Results of Microscopic Examination," but without any entries.

filth, all was foul and horrible. Now our drop passed the spot where
the *Princess Alice* went down. This was the worst place on the
river—one might say the most polluted. The accumulated filth of
four millions of people had been shot into the stream, that stream
which already carried the refuse of considerable townships, villages,
works, and factories. The scene was pleasant enough, in spite of the
river, and the people on board the ill-fated vessel were most likely
enjoying the bright prospect of the country. There is a peculiarly
horrible feature in this catastrophe, which was not sufficiently dwelt
upon. It was not alone the water that drowned the victims of the
collision; they were choked by the filth. One mouthful of the
Thames at that spot is enough to poison any one. It killed the strong
swimmer. A little of the water bubbled into his mouth, and then,
sick and fainting from the nauseous matter he has swallowed, he
sank. This was the fate of many victims of the *Princess Alice*
catastrophe. The newspapers called attention to the horrible fact.
There was an inquiry instituted, which ended, as most of these com-
missions do end—in nothing. There is much ado and writing of Blue
Books, much money is spent and orders are given, and when the
report is bound and put on the shelf, the work of her Majesty's
Government is too often considered at an end. For an example of
this I may say that some seven years ago a Rivers' Pollution Com-
mission summed up the Thames in the following words:—"We, therefore, recommend that the Thames be, as early as possible, abandoned
as a source of water for domestic use, and that the sanction of her
Majesty's Government be in future withheld from all schemes in-
volving the expenditure of more capital for the supply of Thames
water to London." This was written seven years ago, and yet nothing
has been done. The Thames has not been abandoned as a source
of potable water, nor is there any likelihood of its being given up.
Fever and cholera have already more than once been brought to
London by the Thames. Moreover, it is terrible to think that in
these days of "light and leading," one cannot drink a glass of water
without the fear of being poisoned by sewage. Cannot something be
done meanwhile to help those scientists who are anxious to rescue
the foreign matter now poured into the Thames for the fertilization
of the land? The late Government were on the right tack when they
decided to buy up the water companies. The public will consent to
be poisoned by a private company, but when it becomes a Government
question, they will not be so complaisant. The local parliaments of
the chief provincial cities have bought up their water companies;

why should London lag behind the enterprise of country boards of health?

We left our heavily-weighted voyager off Picklow's Point. It had now become so crowded with loathsome matters as to make one turn sick to think of it. The once pure globule was floating sadly along, when a boat rowed out from the shore. In it were two persons, a gentleman and a Thames boatman—a calm, self-possessed man. The scientist threw into the water a Winchester quart bottle, attached to a cord. Our little limpid traveller floated into the vessel, with a crowd of its dirty companions. The scientist pulled forth the bottle, when it had filled, and labelled it thus:—"Specimen collected from the spot where the *Princess Alice* went down." The much-tried globule was carried in its prison-house to the laboratory of the chemist, where in due course it was evaporated, released from the parasites and *débris* that had clogged it, and permitted to return to the clouds from which it had originally fallen, as pure and bright as nature made our great river, the Thames, and as pure and bright as science can maintain it, if science be permitted to do so. When will London arouse herself to the awful significance of this true narrative of the adventures of a drop of Thames water? Is the subject to degenerate into a party question among politicians? Or shall we wait until some new and terrible form of epidemic falls upon the great multitudes who populate the banks of the river? We can solve foreign problems; we can regulate the Turk; we can preside over the watery fortunes of the Nile and the Ganges; let not our posterity have the right to curse us that, though we illuminated its banks with electric lamps, we were content to have our great and glorious river converted into nothing better than a common sewer.

The second article is selected from among several which appeared in *Bradstreets*. It is dated January 15th, 1882:—

## A VISIT TO ROTHSCHILD'S AND TO THE BRITISH MINT.

*London, January 5th.*—From outside, neither the Royal Mint nor Rothschild's refinery present an imposing appearance. A street, reminding one of the back slums of Calais, with quaint French signs, French shops, and French people, leads up to a pair of large and decayed wooden doors, the entrance to the works of Baron Rothschild. An old man, with sabots on his feet, opens the door and ushers the visitor into the presence of the director, a stout, genial-looking Frenchman, who bows a great deal, and talks a great deal more. Rothschild's employés belong to "the gay nation" on the other side of the English Channel. I had the privilege of being shown over the large and interesting establishment of the world's greatest financiers a few days ago, and the following is a *résumé* of the processes in use at Rothschild's for purifying gold and silver:—

The gold as delivered is very impure. It contains large quantities of silver, copper, iron, and other metals. The first operation consists in melting the crude metal in a large clay crucible. By this means a partial separation of copper is effected. The copper is oxidized, and, rising to the surface of the molten metal, is skimmed by means of a ladle. When as much copper as possible has been thus removed, the molten alloy of silver and gold, still containing a little copper, is ladled out and granulated by being poured into cold water. The granulation is to give an increased surface for the action of the acid in the subsequent operation. This granulated metal is then treated with nitric or sulphuric acid, according to the method adopted in the parting. Messrs. Rothschild use the latter process, which is generally adopted in France, Germany, and Austria, because it is much more economical than the nitric acid method. The sulphuric acid process can be applied with success to the refining of silver containing only $0.0005$ per cent. of gold; but the metal for treatment requires to be alloyed with a somewhat larger proportion of silver than is required in the treatment of nitric acid. When the metal has been granulated as described above, it is introduced into large leaden digesters, with about two and one-half times its weight of concentrated sulphuric acid, and it is very necessary to maintain the acid in excess in order to retain the argentic sulphate, formed during the action, in solution. The temperature is then raised to boiling, during which operation volumes of sulphurous anhydride are evolved with the conversion of the silver and copper into argentic and cupric sulphates respectively. The chemical action continues from three to four hours, and the mass is kept constantly stirred with a wooden pole in order to expose fresh surfaces of metal to the action of the acid. The acid liquid is then run off, and a small quantity of stronger acid added to the residue of finely divided gold which is left in the bottom of the digester. The gold is thereupon boiled up again, so as to insure the complete separation of the sulphate of silver. In Messrs. Rothschild's works two products are thus obtained; namely, finely divided, but almost pure gold, and a solution containing argentic and cupric sulphates. The gold, after most careful washing, is boiled in a platinum vessel for a short time, with a further proportion of concentrated sulphuric acid, after which the washing is repeated, and the gold is dried, melted, and cast into bars. The melting was performed in " Piccardie pots," and my friend, Professor Roberts, of the Royal Mint and Royal School of Mines, pointed this out as remarkable, as the fusion of gold is now, as a rule, performed in the best and strongest plumbago crucibles, it being very risky to fuse gold in a clay pot.

The acid liquors containing argentic and cupric sulphates are next treated for the recovery of the silver. The liquid contained in a vessel lined with lead is diluted, and then heated by the passage of steam from a boiler through perforated leaden pipes into the solution. The sulphate of silver dissolves in the boiling water, and is precipitated therefrom by the introduction of scrap copper, the reduction being continued until the solution ceases to give a white, "curdy" precipitate upon the addition of a solution of salt. The solution of cupric sulphate is run off by a syphon to the crystallizing tanks, and the finely divided precipitated silver is washed and afterwards compressed into cakes with a hydraulic press, which is also used for the expulsion of water. The cakes, after drying, are melted in " Piccardie pots" and cast into bars. All these operations, except the fusions, are conducted in one large room, and during the whole of the boilings with sulphuric acid large quantities of sulphurous and sulphuric anhydrides, together with volatilized sulphuric acid, are given off. No attempt whatever is made to condense the fumes, and the workmen engaged are exposed all day to the deleterious gases and vapours. There is not even a good draught to carry away the fumes into the air, in spite of a very tall chimney which is constantly pouring forth clouds of black smoke and contributing an important quota to the fogs of the metropolis. When Messrs. Rotuschild's neighbours complain, the millionaire proprietors silence them with the present of a bar of silver or gold, according to the importance of the complainant.

From this scene of precious metal and bad vapours, I passed on to the crystallizing tanks, situated in large vaults underground. Here the crystallization of the sulphate of copper goes on. Gas jets threw light on great walls of blue, tanks of blue; and innumerable facets of blue crystals flashed back the illumination with singularly beautiful effect. Monte Cristo's cavern could hardly have appeared at first blush more strangely impressive. Some of the crystals were eight, and even ten, inches long, and of a most perfect form. There were several tons of sulphate of copper stored in the drying-room, and I asked the director what market he had for such vast quantities of an article which, to me, seemed of so little use. "*Pour les marchands de 'pickles,'*" he said, smiling.

Messrs. Rothschild's works, it is said, only just pay their expenses as a refinery. I am told they are only carried on as a purely financial matter, in order to enable the owners to flood the markets of Hamburg, Paris, Berlin, or other of the important commercial centres of Europe, with a million of money at almost a moment's notice. A large quantity of the pure gold and silver produced is, however, sent into the Royal Mint, which is situated almost next door to Rothschilds. Having taken leave of the courteous director of Rothschilds, I proceeded, under the guardianship of the well-known Professor Roberts, F.R.S., to her Majesty's Mint. Here I saw the chlorine system of parting gold and silver. This process obviates the expensive necessity for alloying the gold with two or three times its weight of silver, for no other purpose than to insure success in the process of parting. The gold containing silver is melted in a plumbago crucible, fitted with a lid with an aperture to receive a clay pipe connected by tubing with an apparatus for generating chlorine gas. The clay pipe is passed to the bottom of the melted mass of gold, the surface of the latter being covered with a layer of borax, which thus acts as a condenser and prevents the loss of metal by volatilization. The chlorine, as it passes through the molten metal, is at first quickly absorbed, attended by the conversion of the traces of arsenic, antimony, bismuth, lead, &c., into their respective chlorides. The silver present is also converted into chloride, and, rising to the surface, forms a layer of fused argentic chloride. The first stage of the operation is marked by the escape of white vapours, consisting of chlorides of the baser metals, and after a while orange-coloured vapours begin to appear, indicating that the process is complete. The crucible is then withdrawn, and the gold allowed to set, when the still fluid argentic chloride is poured out into a flat mould (a slab of suitable form) for its subsequent reduction by iron and diluted acid—sometimes by carbonate of soda. The gold is cast into ingots suitable for rolling for sovereigns.

The day I visited the Mint they were making nothing but shillings; this, however, is a typical process, and a description of it will be practically a description of the coining of all the other pieces. The alloy of silver and copper and a trace of unremoved gold is melted in a plumbago crucible capable of holding 200 ounces. By a suitable mechanism of cranes and levers, the pot is lifted bodily from the furnace and its contents poured into a row of ingot moulds fixed on a truck running under the crucible. The bars of silver are then cut to suitable lengths and rolled to the required thickness of the coin in rollers worked by machinery. The rough ends are again cut off, and two portions of the size of a shilling are taken from each strip of metal and sent forward for assay. Until these results are finished, the strip cannot be sent on, and if the assay is not satisfactory, the metal is remelted. The strips of metal, about a yard and a half long, if containing the proper percentage, are conveyed on wooden trucks to the cutting-room. Here discs of metal of the size of a shilling are cut out of each strip at the rate of 500 a minute, and two machines were at this work when I was there. The waste from the cutting of the circular discs is sent back to the melting-pot, and the discs are transferred to a machine to give them the edge. Any discs which have sustained injury while passing through the various machines are picked out and sent back to the melting-pot. The machines which give the edge to the coin turn out at the rate of 800 a minute. On emerging from these machines, the metal is very brittle and requires annealing. The discs are therefore placed in pots and heated in an annealing furnace for about an hour. They are then taken out and thrown into sawdust, from which they are separated by sieves. Here they are afterwards packed on trucks and sent to the stamping-room, where they are stamped and milled in eight machines, which turn out thirty shillings a minute. Again packed on trucks, the coins are transferred to the weighing-rooms. Balances worked by steam and fed by a long hopper weigh the shillings at thirty per minute. After weighing, they drop down a glass tube and into a box provided with three compartments—one for coins that are too heavy, the centre one for medium, or proper weight, coins, and one for those which are too light in weight. According to their weight they fall into one or other of these three compartments, and are thus separated. The heavy and light coins are returned to the melting pot, and the medium ones are sent to the Bank of England.

The assaying of the samples of metal is performed in a small laboratory in another portion of the building. Gas muffles are used for the cupolations, and seventy-four cupels are put in one furnace at once. The methods of cleaning the buttons and hammering before weighing are both peculiar to the Mint, and Professor Roberts, in drawing my attention to these details, said, "It is upon such matters as these that success and failure depend."

It will be especially interesting to my readers to be reminded, in connection with this semi-technical sketch of refining and coining in

England, that in some parts of the United States the method of parting gold by nitric acid is still in use, notably at the San Francisco mint. There, the properties of gold being first determined by assay, one part of gold is made up, and two parts of granulated silver are added. The metal is then transferred to earthen receptacles capable of holding 130 pounds in each jar. Nitric acid of thirty degrees' strength is added, and the jars are placed in hot water to facilitate the action. When the action of the acid is at an end, the jars are filled up with water, and the weak solution of argentic nitrate formed is run off from the subsided gold. The finely divided gold is washed in a filter several times. It still contains silver, in order to remove which it is boiled with concentrated sulphuric acid, two pounds of acid being added for every pound of gold. The sulphate of silver is removed, and the gold, after repeated washing, is dried. The solutions of nitrate of silver are precipitated with common salt, and the argentic chloride formed is reduced with zinc. The purity of the resulting metal is about 991 per 1000 for the gold, and 998 per 1000 for the silver. In England the nitric acid parting method has almost entirely been superseded by the chlorine process, which, there is no doubt, is more economical and more effective than any other acid methods, whether sulphuric or nitric acids. Parting by acids is never complete; the gold always contains traces of silver, and the silver always traces of gold; more complete separation is undoubtedly obtained by the chlorine process. Only one firm in England still uses the nitric acid process. In America the process is used by a few firms which have a ready market for the gold in the finely divided state furnished by the nitric acid method, and it is for this reason, of course, that it is employed.

## VII.

On a Thursday night (March 3rd, 1881), two years to the day prior to receiving the telegraphic news of his death, I sat in the midst of a great throng of scientific men in the theatre of the Chemical Society at Burlington House, to hear Frank read two papers before the Society, under the presidency of Professor H. E. Roscoe. The subjects were: (1) "On the Action of Bacteria on Various Gases," and (2) "On the Influence of Intermittent Filtration through Sand and Spongy

Iron on Animal and Vegetable Matters dissolved in Water, and the Reduction of Nitrates by Sewage and other Agents." The papers were the result of investigations which the author had conducted over a period of several months in competition for a prize of 50*l*., offered by Professor Frankland, and the Associateship of the Institute of Chemistry. Professor Roscoe introduced the young lecturer in a few pleasant words, noticing the elaborate diagrams which Mr. Hatton had prepared for the complete illustration of his subjects. The platform was decorated with many, to me, mysterious charts, to which the lecturer drew attention with a wand as he proceeded to explain his experiments. Commencing a little nervously, he speedily regained his customary self-possession. He spoke clearly and well, and was complimented by all who took part in the discussion that followed. The papers, which are printed in the transactions of the Chemical Society, are so technical that it will be sufficient, I think, to give a summary of them and some remarks thereon from the report of the meeting which I find in the *Chemical News*.

The President called on Mr. F. Hatton to read a paper " On the Action of Bacteria on Various Gases." The experiments were made to ascertain the nature of the action exerted by various germs on the life and increase of bacteria, and to observe what influence the bacteria had on the percentage composition of the gases. The bacteria were obtained by shaking fresh meat with distilled water. The aqueous extract was filtered and exposed to the air for twenty-four to thirty-six hours; it was always found to be full of bacteria. A small flask was half filled with mercury, filled up with the bacteria solution, and inverted in a mercury trough.

The gas under examination was then passed up, a small glass vessel was introduced under the mouth of the flask, and the whole removed from the trough. The liquid was examined daily as to the condition of the bacteria, the sample being removed by a piece of bent glass tubing having an india-rubber joint. After about a week the gas was pumped out by means of a Sprengel, and analyzed. Atmospheric air was first tried. The bacteria lived well during the fifteen days of the experiment (T. 15° to 22°). A large absorption of oxygen took place, but it was not replaced by carbonic anhydride; in a second experiment (T. 25° to 26·5°), 20 per cent. of oxygen disappeared, and only 17 per cent. of $CO_2$ were formed. Pure hydrogen after fourteen days had no action on the bacteria; the gas contained 0·34 per cent. $CO_2$, 98·94 per cent. H. Pure oxygen after ten days was converted into $CO_2$ 29·98 per cent., O 70·02 per cent. A mixture of CO 46·94 per cent., $CO_2$ 1·27, O 1·27, N 50·51, was next tried after fourteen days; the gas contained $CO_2$ 17·77, CO 0·55, H 7·58, $CH_4$ 2·50, N 71·57. In all of the above cases the bacteria flourished well. Cyanogen was next tried. The solution of meat turned gradually to a thick black fluid. On the fifth day very few bacteria could be seen. From this time, however, they increased, and on the twelfth day were comparatively numerous. On the fifteenth day the gas was analyzed; it contained CN 5·35, $CO_2$ 57·59, O 2·24, N 34·79; a second experiment gave similar results. It appears, therefore, that cyanogen is fatal to bacteria as long as it exists as such, but that it soon decomposes into ammonic oxalate, &c., and that the bacteria then revive, especially in sunlight. Sulphurous anhydride was next tried; the bacteria lived during the fifteen days; the gas contained $CO_2$ 7·87, O 0·00, N 2·13, $SO_2$ 90·10. Similar results were obtained with nitrogen, nitrous oxide, nitric oxide, carbonic anhydride, a mixture of H and O obtained by the electrolysis of water, and coal gas; in all cases the bacteria lived well during the experiment. The author next experimented with a solution of urea (0·98 per cent.) and phosphate of potash (0·4 per cent.), sowing it with bacteria. The bacteria lived well during the fourteen days of the experiment; small quantities of gas were evolved containing 0·53 per cent. $CO_2$, 2·64 per cent. O, and 96·82 per cent. N. An experiment was made with spongy iron, air, and bacteria. On the fourth day, all the bacteria had vanished; the air was analyzed on the fifth day, and consisted of $CO_2$ 0·26, O 0·00, and N 99·74 per cent. Experiments were also made with acetylene, salicylic acid, strychnine (10 per cent.), morphine, narcotine, and brucine; none of these substances had any effect on the bacteria. On the other hand, phenol, spongy iron, alcohol, and potassium permanganate were very destructive to these microscopic growths.

Dr. Frankland expressed his satisfaction with the results obtained by the lecturer in his laborious research. He confessed that they had surprised him not a little. The fact that bacteria, which were real organisms and could not be shielded under the term putrefaction, lived and flourished in $SO_2$, CO, CN, &c., seemed to him very extraordinary, and the question arose whether the germs to which infectious diseases were probably due were not similarly endowed with a power of great resistance to ordinary influences. Mr.

F. J. M. Page said that Dr. Baxter had proved that with some fever-producing liquids, their virulence was destroyed by chlorine and sulphurous acid, and that he had seen some experiments at the Brown Institution which led to the same conclusion; so it seemed that at all events in some cases, the virulence of infective liquids was due to organic matter, essentially different from the bacteria observed by Mr. Hatton.

Mr. Hatton then read a second communication "On the Influence of Intermittent Filtration through Sand and Spongy Iron on Animal and Vegetable Matters dissolved in Water, and the Reduction of Nitrates by Sewage, &c." Filtration through sand :—A 14-feet verticle glass tube, three and a half inches in diameter, was filled with sand. The water was passed through at the rate of four litres per day. Experiments were first made with peaty water diluted with its own volume of distilled water. The organic carbon decreased 1·527 parts per 100,000, whereas the organic nitrogen was but little affected. The addition of a nitrifying material, in the shape of 5 c.c. of stale urine added to four litres of water, did not promote the oxidation of the organic nitrogen of the peat during filtration. A filtered infusion of rape cake was substituted for the peaty water, and similar results were obtained. Some experiments were then given as to the effect of sewage in promoting the reduction of nitrates. A 5 per cent. solution of clear fresh sewage containing no nitrates was added to a solution containing 0·0853 grm. of nitre. The mixture was shaken in a large stoppered bottle, and estimations of the nitric nitrogen made from time to time. For a time the nitric nitrogen steadily diminished, until, in fact, the sewage itself began to nitrify, and then the amount increased. At low temperatures the sewage does not seem to nitrify. It was found that when a solution containing nitrates and sewage was allowed to stand in contact with air, the oxygen in the dissolved air increased 4·5 per cent., while that in the air above the liquid decreased 5 per cent. In sixteen days the N as nitrates and nitrites decreased from 0·406 part per 100,000 to 0·075. Thick sewage was much more active than clear sewage. Spongy iron, when shaken up with a solution of nitre, converts the nitrogen into ammonia and free nitrogen. Filtration through spongy iron rapidly reduces the nitric nitrogen, converting it for the most part into ammonia. Filtration of peat solution and solution of egg albumen through spongy iron rapidly removed both the organic nitrogen and organic carbon, no nitric nitrogen being formed, all the nitrogen being reduced to ammonia. In some cases the carbon seemed to give rise to some marsh-gas.

Other papers were read on "River Water" by Professor Tidy, and in the discussion which followed, Dr. Gilbert, Mr. Bischoff, Mr. Hawksley, C.E., Mr. Kingzett, Dr. F. J. M. Page, Mr. W. M. Hamlet, and others took part. The President commended highly the patient and useful research of Mr. Hatton, and Professor Frankland, replying to some points of Professor Tidy's paper contending for purification by flow, said he hoped that Professor Tidy would, having heard Mr. Hatton's paper, no longer believe in the destruction of bacteria by a cold bath in the Thames; "when they withstood the action of cyanogen and sulphurous acid, it was difficult to see why they should commit suicide by bursting their envelopes by endosmosis." Dr. Gilbert followed in the same direction, protesting against the tendency of Professor Tidy's paper, which underestimated the danger of water contaminated with sewage. The President emphasized the lasting importance of Mr. Hatton's investigations; and, in reply, Professor Tidy modified the impression the meeting had received from his remarks, and confessed in strong terms that he was a water purist, and " had not the least doubt that sewage ought not to be discharged into the Thames."

I remember that when Frank came home he gave us an amusing illustration of Dr. Tidy's oratorical manner—not ill-naturedly, as he had great respect for the Professor. When making an emphatic point Dr. Tidy has a peculiar action of his right arm, and seems as if he thumped his back with his fist. Poor Frank imitated this oddity of manner, to the great amusement of the family and a couple of scientific friends, adding, however, " I think Dr. Tidy knew he was wrong, and only argued for the sake of arguing. Of course he knows that no amount of flow in our rivers will get rid of bacteria; peaty matter will disappear, but the oxidation of germs is a different thing. He knows that well enough; but he wanted to have a controversy with Dr. Frankland, and, considering what a bad case he had, he conducted it splendidly."

Among the letters upon this subject I find one from Dr. Henry E. Armstrong, the Secretary of the Chemical Society, which I venture to quote :—" The first part of your paper, which is obviously the main portion of your research, will, I imagine, not give rise to discussion. You have established a large number of facts, and your descriptions of them will doubtless be received with great interest." After the papers had been read,

Mr. H. Watts, editor of the *Chemical Society's Journal*, writes: "I am instructed by the Publication Committee of the Chemical Society to inform you that they regard your papers on the action of bacteria on gases and the oxidation of organic matter by filtration, &c., as very important contributions to our knowledge of these matters, and well worthy of publication in the Society's journal."

## VIII.

I returned from America in July, to find Frank nearly at the close of his arrangements for leaving England. It seemed only the day before that he was playing with toy-guns, exploding "drawing-room" fireworks, illuminating the garden with magnesium wire, manufacturing miniature lightning, and building wooden forts to be taken by tin soldiers. And now he was experimenting with electric exploders for mining, taking observations of the sun, testing sextants, discussing chronometers, trying rifles, and making occasional excursions into iron and coal mines in the midland counties. It was a constant surprise to me to contemplate the business-like way in which he conducted his affairs, the calmness with which he made his arrangements. If he had been an experienced pioneer, or an established scientific expert, he could not have tackled his work more methodically. "And I shall soon be back," he would say to his mother in the midst of it all. "Two years—what is it? Of course it will seem long to you, but to me, you know, my dear, it will be nothing at all. When you went to America with father it seemed an eternity. The time drags when you are waiting and in one spot; but when one is travelling, and amidst new scenes, and has absorbing work, the days are not long enough."

It was settled that Dr. Walker, a clever young Scotch surgeon, who had been appointed to the chief medical post under the new government, should be his travelling companion. This reconciled us all very much to the situation. If he were ill he would have a friendly adviser at his elbow. Dr. Walker came and dined with us at a little farewell dinner. Dr. Hodgkinson, (Frank's principal tutor and friend in the chemical laboratories at South Kensington) and Mr. William M. Crocker, assistant managing director of the British North Borneo Company, were of the party. We all tried to be very merry. . . . It became Dr. Walker's duty in his new occupation to receive and examine the dead body of his friend; while poor Mr. Crocker had to bring us the bitter news of our loss. Is it the instinct of fear or love that makes women feel the approach of misfortune? It was ten o'clock one never-to-be-forgotten night in the spring of 1883 that Mr. Crocker came to us on his terrible mission. We had been talking over Frank's return, and the way in which we would celebrate it. "We will keep our silver wedding," I said. "And you shall have on that day," said an American guest, "a silver brick from the Berkshire mine!" We did not "keep our silver wedding;" we never shall. The moment my wife saw Mr. Crocker's face she said, "Something is the matter with Frank!" "Calm yourself," he said gently. . . . I find my pen continually drifting in this direction. . . . I fear there is no other method of telling his story except in this fragmentary way. There is no other for me; and I am inclined to think the friendly reader may not object to it. If one adopted the strictest literary method, there is no discipline of mind or pen strict enough to shut out the continual intrusion of the supreme motive of the record itself. The *dénouement* is continually before me. How shall I prevent the shadow of it falling right across my work?

## III.

# A BUNDLE OF LETTERS AND THE MASSACRE OF WITTI.

On the way—Sharks and divers—Ceylon and Singapore—Bungalow life at Labuan—Social amenities—Witti—In Borneo—Expeditions in the interior—Tropical floods—" Impossible to go on; impossible to go back "—Letters from home—An eventful day—Head hunting—To Kinaram for a little rest—Food and dress—Missionary work—Romantic scenery—The perils of travel—Assassination of Witti and an exploring party—Sketch of Witti's career—Thoughts of home—Last letters.

### I.

LETTERS came to us from Paris, Marseilles, and other cities *en route*. But they began to be most interesting from the time that Frank arrived at Singapore. From Marseilles, on the 20th of August, 1881, he wrote: " I had a splendid day in Paris. We got in at about six in the morning. At twelve o'clock I was going for a walk, and the first people I met were all the Farwells, of Chicago. I took them to the Louvre. Then we went up the column in the Place Vendome; and after that, shopping, of course. . . I have been down to the vessel. She is rather fine. The steward seems inclined to be a beast, and I wish we had gone out by the P. and O. I don't care to be sailing under the French flag. Dr. W—— is a very agreeable fellow. Beautiful fruit and flowers at Marseilles. . . . You are quite mistaken in thinking that going away will make me no longer care for home. It is a good thing to go away, so as to learn the value of such a home as I have."

"Off Naples," he wrote, "steaming along the blue waters of the Mediterranean is very pleasant. As regards eating, this French vessel is a floating palace-hotel. The passengers are, however, rather slow. Please send me by first post, care of Johnston, Singapore, the portrait of Miss ——, which I don't know how I came to leave behind. My stateroom is a fine one, and I have the port-hole continually open. We have lots of meals! First, a table-d'hôte breakfast at nine; then a fruit luncheon at twelve; a table-d'hôte dinner at six; a tea at eight, and a 'snack' at ten. Send me the cartridges I ordered. The sea is lovely, the weather not too hot. Mamma must never be anxious about me. I am perfectly well, and if I am ever ill I shall let you know."

"When we left the Red Sea," he writes off Ceylon, "the weather became much cooler. I went on shore at Aden, and drove over to the tanks. The natives say the tanks were constructed about A.D. 1100. Only three that I saw contained water. Aden is not a nice place. There is no sign of vegetation, and it is very hot and bare. There were a lot of African boys in their native 'dug-outs' round the steamer, diving for money all day, in spite of sharks. I did not see the sharks myself—and, in fact, the only 'wonder of the deep' that I have seen at present is the flying fish. I think the stories of travellers are often very much coloured.

"We left Aden on Saturday, and it takes nine days from there to Ceylon. The worst of the journey is now over. The second day from Aden was very rough. I was sick one day, and seedy the next, but on the third I was all right. I have at last got my 'sea legs on,' and now I don't mind how much the ship pitches. There are one or two good fellows on board, whom I have made friends with. I would not go by Messageries Maritimes again. One gets so tired of table-d'hôte living day after day. Table-d'hôte breakfast, table-d'hôte dinner, and so on. Rupees are now the coins we always use. I won six rupees to-day on the run of the steamer. The highest run we have made as yet was 338 miles; but the usual run is 280 to 305. When about five days from Aden the engine had to be repaired, so we stopped fifteen hours for that, and only went one mile an hour under sail.

"Life on board an ocean steamer is very monotonous, and there is but little news to send you. The ship is pitching a good deal just now, which makes it rather a difficult thing to write.

"I feel sure I shall come back safe and well to you, as I mean to take great care of myself, run no risks, and do nothing but work. The more I see of the world, the less I feel inclined to indulge in any of its so-called pleasures; for the greatest pleasure possible for me will be to come back to you. Fine sunsets, but the weather is as a rule very cloudy, and a good deal like the weather at home. It has rained once since I started, for about five minutes.

"I went down to the luggage-room about a week ago and got out your portraits. I now have half an hour's talk to you all every day, and it is such a pleasure to look at you."

II.

"Arrived here safe and well at nine o'clock yesterday," he wrote from Singapore, the 17th of September, 1881. "Do you think a chapter on my voyage out, with short sketches of Naples, Port Said, Aden, Galles, and Singapore would be any use? It would do to begin my book with, at any rate.[1]

"I went on shore at Ceylon and had a drive about the country. Cocoanut palms were growing every-

---

[1] In a memorandum-book that eventually came home in his boxes I find some rough memoranda for his book, in diary form. The following are a few of these notes intended for use in a chapter on the voyage out :—*Port Said*, August 28: Intense heat; engage boats; fellow spoke English; landed; Seyd Ali offered his services. Seyd was dressed in a purple robe reaching to his feet. Rather handsome. He wore a Turkish fez and first-rate English boating boots. His charge was one shilling an hour. Seyd : "Will de gentlemen go post office?" "No, take us to the Arab town." A walk of about fifteen minutes along the sandy streets of Port Said. The Rue de Commerce, quite destitute of vehicles, brought us to the Arab town. Visit the Mosque, which smells terribly. Then walk up the back streets of the Arab town. People lying at their doors, too lazy to brush away a fly from their faces. Arrive at the market-place. Feast day. Swings with three Arab girls ; very picturesque in yellow head-dresses. Men selling melons. Carrying water in pig-skins. Walk back. Turkish soldiers. Visit the Café Chantant. Palpable force of assumed gaiety. Female band of scowling women. The gambling, *rouge et noir*. *Mem.*—Enlarge on the assumed air of gaiety, the selling of indecent photos, &c. —*Suez Canal*, August 28 : 104° in the shade. Old Egyptian reeds. Immense banks of sand. Blue jelly-fish. Ismalia—green desert city. Beautiful flowers—asters. Scrub on the banks. Water, yellow to bright green. Temperature while going on second day—cabin, 103°; under the awnings, 110°; and 50° C. in sun. The ship. The commissaire, a curious burlesque Frenchman. "Ah! I do not know; you must ask the Agent des Postes ; it is not in my department." *The*

where, each tree being loaded with fruit. Bananas, nutmegs, and pine-apples grow by the roadside. The country is very charming and very damp, as the rainy season is now at its worst. In Singapore, however, the weather is very good. It rained yesterday a little and cooled the air. The temperature is about 80° to 82° in the shade during the day, sinking to 75° in early morning and midnight. Mr. Read lives about two miles out of Singapore, and his house is surrounded by tropical gardens full of tree-ferns, palms, bamboos, travellers' trees, as under :—

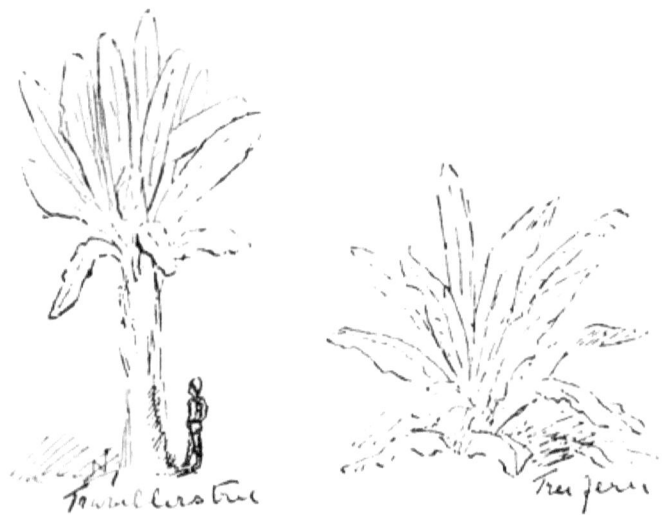

Travellers tree.   Tree fern.

"It is not a first-rate garden, either. The great drawback is the grass, which is very coarse. Singapore is the nicest town I have seen yet.

"All the people have gone to Borneo—the engineer,

*Captain:* "Ah, ze piano (P. and O.) is very bad." *General:* "But surely there cannot be two pianos?" *Captain:* "Ah, no, ze

the Governor, &c. Our ship is due on the 20th, and we shall start about the 21st or 22nd."

On the 27th of September he tells us he has engaged his native servant and starts for Borneo on the morrow. "Yesterday the fort fired minute guns (fifty) for poor President Garfield, and all the flags in the harbour and at the consulates were half-mast. I was very sorry to hear of his death. My best love to all our American friends.

"The affectation and petty snobism of certain 'swells' here is ridiculous. A friend of mine, whom I met on the steamer, a barrister, Mr. ———, when making his calls, passed the house of a lady whom he had to call upon, but he dared not go in because he was on his way to Lady ———, who would take it as a deadly insult, if any one was called upon before her. Mr. Alabaster, a pleasant fellow whom I met on the steamer (private legal adviser to the King of Siam), invited me to Bangkok, in Siam, when I am on my way home, to spend a week with him." [2]

---

PIANO. Ah, yes; not ze P. and Oh!" Cannot land at Suez. Two Frenchmen kissing. Frenchman—" Ah, mon cher cousin!" in a fearful state of perspiration. *A remarkable sunset*—a few clouds collect in the evening, tinted with gold as sun goes down behind a distant range of rugged purple hills—foreground in green scrub; the banks are lined with old Egyptian reeds—curious after-glow—wonderful water tints of purple and red, with purple-tinted sky above. Ten minutes later the moon appears—after the sunset very bright. . . . French officials very bumptious. Pass nothing but British ships, except one Prussian corvette. *French sailor:* " Ah, la, la, il y a tant de vraies Anglais! " English sheep!"—The other pages of the little book contain memoranda on methods of skinning squirrels and preserving birds' skins, notes of experiments in tropical photography, &c.

[2] "We last week announced the death of Mr. Henry Alabaster, private secretary to the King of Siam. Some of our readers will be interested

III.

*Labuan, Borneo, viâ Singapore, Oct. 17th, 1881.*

MY DEAR FATHER,—I have got your two letters of Aug. 28th and Sept. 8th. I get a chance of writing once a fortnight here.

Our passage from Singapore to Labuan was not at all pleasant. The *Royalist* is an abominable ship, and I was ill, but the journey was soon over. I made friends with the owner, Mr. Cowie, who lent me his pony at Labuan. When we arrived here, Lemprière, the secretary, and Cook, the treasurer, who stay at Labuan, were out wild boar shooting. But we went up to the Company's bungalow, where I am now staying. I had orders to remain in Labuan until the arrival of the Governor, who is away at Sandakan. Walker was to go on to Sandakan, so I left him on board the *Royalist*. I landed all my things, including my chemicals, camping outfit, and everything I have got. Cook and Lemprière were very kind. I called on the Governor of Labuan, who invited Walker, Cook, and myself to dine with him at Government House. A very good dinner, and we played billiards till two o'clock in the morning, which out here is very late. I played nearly everything I know on the piano, and made great friends with the Governor. I have dined there once since then, to meet Mr. de Crespigny (who called on me the next day), from Sarawak (in his ship), and also Father Jackson, and Mr. Everett, of Sarawak, who is very nice, and is staying up with me at the Company's bungalow.

The other day Lemprière, Everett (of Sarawak), and I went up to Coal Point—a famous place in Labuan—to shoot. There is a deserted coal-mine there, upon which thousands of pounds have been spent; and jungle is now growing all over most valuable machines, railways, and other gear; it is a very melancholy thing to see. I will send you some photographs of it in my next letter. I am writing a sketch

---

to learn that he was a friend of the late Frank Hatton, the young scientist who lost his life in Borneo. Mr. Hatton had arranged to visit Siam, on Mr. Alabaster's invitation, and had obtained special letters of recommendation to the King for that purpose. It is a pathetic coincidence that a box of floral wreaths sent out to be laid upon Hatton's grave in the little jungle cemetery at Elopura, Borneo, was delivered by mistake at Bangkok, Siam, where his young friend Mr. Alabaster had died."—*Court Circular*, November 29, 1884.

which I will post by next mail, entitled "Bungalow Life in Labuan." This life is very pleasant as regards sea-bathing, shooting, riding, and eating. But the mosquitoes *are awful*, especially just now; they are biting very badly. There are few bad creatures on the island, except pythons, some wild boars, some green and other harmless snakes, and centipedes, but one somehow thinks nothing of these things out here. The temperature is usually 80°, but sometimes sinks to 71° or 72° after rain.

When we were at Coal Point, we met the Papar boat, just come from the Company's station on the Bornean coast at Papar, with the Resident, Mr. Everett, brother to the Everett of Sarawak, on board. There was an affectionate meeting, and the Resident came to stay with us at the bungalow. He is a good fellow, and a fair geologist and mineralogist.

I stay here till Mr. Treacher comes; he is expected about the 19th. I shall ask him to let me, as you say, put my laboratory up here, and make my headquarters here for the present, and I expect this will be done. I shall probably go first to Abai, the nearest point to Kina Balu. You may be quite sure I shall be prudent about expeditions, &c., and that I shall run no *unnecessary risks*.

Ever your loving son,

FRANK.

IV.

On the 17th of October, writing from Labuan, he tells us he is enjoying his life at Labuan—bathing, shooting, photographing, and overhauling his chemicals and apparatus. A fortnight later he speaks of a pleasant little gathering at Governor Leys' bungalow, and sends his kind regards to a young American. "Tell him the rifle-shot gun and revolvers have all been in play." He adds, "I generally go about here in a pair of white trousers, a flannel shirt, a waist-belt, a coloured handkerchief, and a white helmet and shoes—quite a toff, eh?" Further on he says, "My two cockney phrases from that farce at the Princess's, 'Ain't she a lady?' 'Oh, she are, she are!' are getting acclimatized here. The insects are awful. One could make quite an

TANJONG KUBONG, OR COAL POINT, LABUAN.

To face page 70.

extensive entomological collection sitting in a room with a lamp at night."

*Victoria, Labuan, Borneo, Nov.* 2nd, 1881.

MY DEAR FATHER,—It is decided that I am, for the present at least, to have my laboratory here in Labuan. I wrote a letter to Mr. Treacher, when he landed, on the subject, and he said yes, so that is arranged. I shall go up the coast by the next *Royalist* from Singapore; that will be about the 14th of November. I shall go up to Tampassuk to Witti. I am getting on slowly with the language.

Yesterday there was a grand dinner party of all Labuan at Government House, to meet Mr. and Mrs. Treacher on their return from Sandakan. Here is a plan of the table and where we sat:—

Governor Leys.

| | |
|---|---|
| Mrs. Treacher. | Hon. Treacher. |
| Mr. A. Hart Everett. | Hon. Hamilton. |
| Mr. Frank Hatton. | Mr. Davies. |
| Mr. Gueritz. | Mr. Lemprière. |
| Mr. Cook. | Father Jackson. |

Captain Harington.

Mr. Gueritz is Captain Ross's agent for our only regular steamer, the *Cleator*. Mr. Cook is the Company's treasurer. The Hon. A. Hamilton is executive council, executive committee, police general-in-chief, harbour-master, &c., of Labuan. Mr. Davies is our new Resident, going to Papar in place of Mr. A. Hart Everett, who goes to Abai. Mr. Lemprière, the Governor's secretary. Father Jackson, a Catholic priest, come from Afghanistan to convert the natives, which he will never do.

I recited "The Private of the Buffs" at Government House after dinner, and afterwards played upon the piano.

I will send home very shortly a sketch of " Malay Types," which I hope will be of some good. I got soaking wet to-day—caught in the jungle "on *my pony*" in the most awful thunder and rain storm I ever heard or saw. The rain came down in sheets, and being blown in my face from the sea by a frightful wind—a tornado, in fact—I thought I should have been blown away; and the thunder was simply fearful, the lightning blinding.

Your ever loving son,<br>
FRANK.

## V.

On the 1st of November he writes in admiring terms of Governor Leys, of Labuan, and sends a photograph of him, "taken by myself, and a very bad one; but when I get my laboratory put up, I shall be able to take much better ones." Then he refers to a short article he has written on Labuan, which he fears is not good enough for the *Century*. "Governor Treacher," he says, "is very kind, and Mrs. Treacher charming. I enclose some other photographs. Witti is not popular here, or with anybody, but I shall judge for myself. I am going to Tampassuk some time to see him. Could you send me out some more water-colours, note-books, insect-collecting boxes, sticking-plaster, some tubes of chloride of gold, porcelain ebonite trays, eau de Cologne, &c.?"

On the 14th of November he announces that he is to "go to Witti and Everett at Abai. Witti, after our consultation, then goes to Papar to explore. There is a new Resident at Papar. Everett and I go up the coast to the *oil* at *Marudu Bay*. The boring machine has arrived in the *Royalist* from Singapore, and, I think, my cartridges. Your two letters, Oct. 6th and Sept. 27th, have also arrived. Never think all the advice you can give me is ever a bore. I am so glad to get letters. My two months' expedition is organized. I have six men, and more if necessary, and a practical English workman, from Bath, who was in the employ of the Labuan Coal

Company for some time. He is my *aide-de-camp*. His name is Smith." .... At a later date he sends the following sketch:—

Kudat, North Borneo, January 17th, 1882.

MY DEAR FATHER,—My answers to your last letters you will get after this, as they have gone to Sandakan by mistake. I have just returned, or rather been driven back, from an expedition up the Bongon River, Marudu Bay. The rain was too much, and as the whole country was flooded, further progress was impossible. My aide-de-camp is still searching for coal at Siquati, and I go on a long expedition up into the interior next month. Don't be afraid about me, my pistols carry considerable weight. The story of my expedition up to Timbong Batu is rather interesting, especially the way I got back. My party consisted of F. H. Abdul (my boy), whom I shall perhaps bring home; Fareich, Houssa, two Arab policemen; Bilal, a Suluman; and Bablogan, a Bajow. After great difficulties we made our way through the sopping wet jungle, sinking often above our knees in mud and slush. When we got to the Dusuns, at Timbong Batu, the Bongon River was about thirty feet wide; but here it began to rain in torrents, and soon the stream was as many yards wide and twenty or thirty feet deep, rushing along at ten to thirteen miles an hour. Here I remained shut up four days; rain all the time without a moment's stop. I only got one hour to investigate the river bed, and then all it yielded was quartz with pyrites, which may be auriferous. Higher up the stream, at Kaparkan, perhaps I shall find metals. As things were looking serious at Timbong Batu, I determined to make a rush for Bongon. We had three water buffaloes with us, so, packing the things on these animals, we struggled through the pouring rain to Datu Omers, a place one-fourth the distance to Bongon. Here I got a prahu, so I left Omers at ten o'clock in this dug-out—myself, Abdul, Bablogan, and my guide Datu Mahomet, leaving the other men to bring the buffaloes overland. The prahu we got was small and leaky, and the wicked stream was rushing along with tremendous force. We went down at nine or ten miles an hour. One man was on the look-out all the time for floating wood and overhanging trees, which we encountered every moment. Evidences of the great floods were apparent all down the stream, and by-and-by we came to a stop before the immense trees which had fallen across the river. Bamboos and driftwood had stuck there and formed an effectual bar to our passage. The water was here, perhaps, thirty or forty feet deep, and roaring along one vast rapid for miles. At one place the river had overflowed its banks and rushed into the jungle, thus getting rid of half the water which otherwise would have gone on to Bongon. We first tried to cut our way through the barrier, and while standing with precarious foothold on fallen trees, with the water roaring underneath and the fear of crocodiles, the rain came on again. Down it poured in torrents, and really matters looked serious. Impossible to go on, equally impossible to go back, as we could not have made a mile in a day against such a stream. What to do was the question. We had no axe to cut our way through, and it was *Friday*, and the 13*th*, and do what I could, I could not help feeling a little superstitious. Matters were now at their worst. Wet through, and with thirty feet of roaring stream below the prahu, which itself was leaky. On the right, dense jungle; and on the left, tall, cutting grass swamp. The right was the only chance—to drag the boat through the tall grass, mud, and water, risking snakes and crocodiles. But four of us, we found, were unable to pull the prahu. Now an unlooked-for help came in the shape of three Sarawak men in a little boat, who, more daring than their fellows, were coming down trading to Bongon. With their help, after half an hour's stiff tugging, we got the prahu past the obstacles; the grass was tall, rank, and cutting like a knife. We were now past the worst, but not out of danger—a sharp look-out had to be kept, as the stream often threatened to hurl us under some overhanging tree and sweep us into the torrent. However, we arrived safe at Bongon at five o'clock, and there I learned that such floods had not been experienced for ten years.

Give my dearest love to mamma, Nellie, Bessie, and my kind wishes to all my friends. *I am afraid travel will make me a wanderer.*

Your ever loving son,<br>
Frank.

VI.

Next came several letters descriptive of his earlier expeditions, consisting chiefly of notes from his first diary and extracts from his reports, which will be found printed at length in Part II. of the present work. These letters contained the previous and accompanying rough pen-and-ink sketch.

On February 5th, 1882, he writes from Singapore. We knew later that he had gone there to recruit after a two months' expedition " up the coast " and an attack of fever. He does not refer to this latter fact; but speaks of the expedition he is organizing "from Labuk to Marudu," touching which he says he hopes shortly " to report something which will make me worthy the title they give me here of ' scientific explorer.'" On the 16th he has returned to Labuan, and refers to the sketch of that tiny colony which he had written for a magazine. "It is only a bit of first impressions, and nothing like the report of my second expedition which I have sent home to the Company. Don't be too sure about *great* mineral wealth in North Borneo. It ought to be there. Two or three months, I hope, will show; but, as you know, I am not over sanguine. I am rather disappointed with Kurching, the capital of Sarawak. . . . . Yes, Borneo is 100,000 times better for me than Guy's Hospital, to which I never could have gone, and never will go now.

*Kinaram, April 20th*, 1882.

DEAREST FATHER,—I have just got nearly through one of the most arduous and difficult enterprises which I hope it will be ever my lot to undertake. I went to the Labuk River in search of antimony on March 3rd, having left Sandakan on March 1st. With the greatest difficulties we got up the rivers, and our long journey overland was an experience I shall never forget. I have got your nice letters in reply to my first report on Sequati, and they cheered me more than you can think; I got them in Central Borneo from Smith, who had gone back to the coast to fetch food. A description of one of our most eventful days may interest you, so I will give it as written in my diary. The result of my expedition is that from Labuk to Kinaram, all through the following countries—Lomantic, Tandar Batu, Kagibangan, Tampias, Tonaonona, Tampoular, Sogohtan, Daralai, Bendonin, Senemlan, Byag, Niaasane, Ghanaghana, Tuntone, Danao, Koligan, Lasas, Virtno, Bundo, Moroli, Munnus, to Kinaram—there is no trace of any mineral of commercial value. At Kinaram I am on the track of the copper, which I shall, I hope, shortly discover.

We arrived at my men's camp from our short trip at 10.30. The place was well posted below a bend in the river, at the foot of a hill 1000 feet high. Potatoes, kaladi, melons, cucumbers were now plentiful, and my famished men got a feed of something more than rice, for which they were very thankful. The country here is very mountainous, and as the river is restricted by high banks, the current is tremendous; and all the Dyaks, Sulus, &c., said I was very brave to go up at all. .... The Dyaks here are true head-hunters; and only a few days ago a head was taken at a bridge over a torrent. The man was walking over the felled tree, which in this country always constitutes a bridge, when four men rushed on him, pushed him down the steep bank, and, jumping down after him, took his head off in a twinkling. I saw the victim's head and hand in a house not far from the scene of the murder. The headman said himself that three weeks ago seven heads had been taken from slaughtered men of Tingara, with which country he, Sogolitan, was fighting. The bodies of these men were thrown into the wood near us, and all the men said that at night, when the wind blew from a certain quarter, there was a fearful smell of dead animal matter. ....

We nearly had a fight with these people next day.

I stand the climate in a most wonderful way; poor Smith is knocked down with fever when I am perfectly well. I think it is because it is not my fate to have any ill-luck in Borneo. In five villages where by certain rites I have been made a brother of the natives, at my call 300 spears would come out.

Your dear letters, and mamma's, and Nellie's, are the only things that I look forward to. Bessie writes to me now and then. I can only write this one long letter now, as I have my hands full of work. In about two months I go back to Labuan, and I shall take a rest of a month or so.

Dearest love to mamma, Nellie, Bessie, and all my dear friends, English and American.

Ever your most loving son,

FRANK.

*Kudat, May 18th, 1882.*

MY DEAREST FATHER,—I have come down from Kinoram for a little rest. I have a little station there now, consisting of my house, the men's house, and the guard-house, with a stockade all round them and a flagstaff in the middle. I have had some very wonderful and interesting experiences, some very happy and some very wretched days. I have now two white men under me in my department—Smith, whom I have sent back to Siquati, and Beveridge, who is coming from Sandakan looking for me. I hope to find him near Kinaram when I go up this time. I can speak Malay, and I am quite at home with the people. On our last journey, however, we nearly had several rows with Dyaks, who knew absolutely nothing of the Company, and had never seen a white man.

Your letters, with all their kind advice, are a great pleasure and comfort to me, and many times I have received them when wet, tired, and hungry in the jungle.

My best love to you, my own dear father.

From your loving<br>FRANK.

## VII.

In a letter to his mother, June 26th, written at Labuan, he says, "although I have been in the Bornean jungle for three months, I don't smoke—only once in a way a cigarette. When in the bush, my dinner generally consists of American meat (when there is any), a biscuit (cabin H. & P.), sweet potatoes, and a pickle, the whole followed by a bottle of beer. Sometimes we get a fowl; but to the Dusun fowl Mark Twain's remark on carving, 'use a club, and avoid the joints,' would very much apply." In another letter he speaks of "brandy merely as a medicine," and of the "treat" afforded by some Swiss milk and cocoatina which we had sent him. "My dress when travelling," he says, "as a rule, is a thick brown canvas jacket and strong blue trousers, the ends turned into my socks, tied round tightly with string, to prevent leaches getting at me; but they attack one, in spite of all one can do. I wear strong canvas shoes and a helmet, a waistbelt, and sometimes sword as well as pistol. Behind me come my two followers, one carrying my rifle and the other my shot-gun; then six natives with rifles and bayonets; next two men with picks, and in the rear the camp things and carriers. But the camp things which I brought out are all broken up. Nothing in heaven or earth can stand the Bornean bush."

On the same date he writes to his sister Helen (a student in the Royal Academy schools), "You had

KINA BULU, FROM THE LAMPASSUK RIVER: THE STEAM YACHT, "BORNEO," AT ANCHOR.

better come out here and do some sketches for the *Graphic* or *Illustrated*. There are hundreds of things to do, and nobody to do them. All is new and everything picturesque. Kina Bulu would make a splendid subject for a big picture, while near my house in Kinoram there are some wonderful bits of hill and river. There is one view from the outside of my stockade which is simply lovely. The river is a rushing torrent, and one can see up its course for miles right away to the mountains, which tower up one above the other away to Kina Bulu. The peaked one, like the Matterhorn, which is 7000 feet, I ascended lately with

M. le Comte de Montgelas, who had come to the Kinoram to see me. We climbed within 100 feet of the top and could get no further; the thing was simply a precipice. The getting up was 'horful.' The slope was what you see in the diagrams. (See below!) Then there were countless (very much countless) leeches and other abominations, and nothing to eat, as it had been forgotten (!!) by the horrid native policeman whom I felt inclined to kick down the hill. When we got down the Dusuns wanted to collect a poll-tax—a water jar—for being allowed to go up their hill. They nearly collected something else."

On October 27th, 1882, he writes to his youngest sister, who at that time was at a convent school in the Ardennes. She is troubled, it seems, in regard to the religion she is to adopt, whether she should be a Protestant or a Catholic. "I am sorry," he writes, "to hear you are so much struck with the beauties of 'Dominus vobiscum,' &c.; but you will soon get over that. Experience, experience—that is the only thing; but when obtained in Borneo, it is hardly obtained. There is one fact which may interest you which came under my notice a short time ago. There is a Catholic missionary

ON THE KINORAM RIVER.
From a sketch by Frank Hatton.

out here in Sabah. He converted two Dyaks; one became a thief, the other a murderer. That missionary has not yet been eaten by savages; but poor Witti has been slaughtered by Muruts, and when it comes to a question of practical value, *of real use* in a savage country, all the priests of France and Belgium, with all the bishops and cardinals of Italy and Spain, and the Pope thrown in, with all their gear, and their books, and their candles, and their relics, could not equal the worth of poor Witti. 'But no mattaire!' We will talk of this anon. There is very little longer for me out here, and one night a cab will drive up to the dear old gate at home, and out will get a sallow, long, Oriental wreck, and the cabman will say, 'Here's a hobjec'!' and you will say, 'Who is this person?'

"Now, good-bye, dearest Bessie; you know *my letter is only chaff*."

*Kudat, October 27th*, 1882.

MY DEAREST NELLIE,—I have not written to you for no end of a time, but I have not written to any one for an equally long time. I have been away up in the mountains for nearly four months; such an awful country—so pretty from the coast; but when you are there, but for the trees, travel would be impossible—the slopes are so steep. The scenes of torrents tearing over boulders with cliffs 500 or 600 feet high, rising in sheer precipices from the river-bed, are, however, very grand; and if they were in England, the whole place would be dotted about with "Gibbs and Gibbesses." The rainy season is just coming on, and when it rains here, it does rain simply in torrents. Borneo is not a place to build one's country house in, or a place to live in for pleasure. One "great philosopher" said, "The best thing to do with it, would be to sink it under the sea;" another said, "Borneo? Borneo? Borneo, sir, is a sandbank!" These persons held extreme views—but I will refrain from inflicting my adventures and opinions upon you, as I shall have such a long time for that when I get home, and now I do so wish the months would fly a little quicker. I can speak Malay and Dusun; I am (now poor Witti has been murdered by the savages) the only white man who can speak the latter language, and therefore a very desirable person for an inland Resident, "though *Hi* says it as shouldn't." I shall be quite content to carry your water-colours—the oils are too heavy—about, and be an Oriental wreck for six months after I come, for really I have had some very hard times here, roughing it in a manner which I would defy even an African explorer to put into the shade. But it is all experience. You see, my writing has even become Oriental, i.e. shaky.

Ever your affectionate brother,<br>FRANK.

*Kudat, October 28th,* 1882.

MY DEAREST FATHER,—I have just returned from "the mountain fastnesses" of Borneo, where copper exploring has occupied me for more than three months. I will not give you a detailed account of all my adventures and experiences, as it all appears in my Kinoram report, No. 1, which will arrive at the same time as this letter, or should do. I am quite well now, although I have had a very bad leg. You need not tell mamma so. Your letters and papers have all reached me, and give me more pleasure than I can tell you. The ring I shall always wear for your sakes.[3] My thoughts of coming home to you all, are thoughts of unalloyed pleasure, although you will find me much altered, I expect; and I shall feel so

FRANK HATTON'S HOUSE. (*From a Water-colour Drawing by Himself.*)

strange at first, and yet so happy. Do you think of coming to Marseilles? I am not sure that I shall come home in a French ship: a P. and O. is a good ship as well. I am so glad to hear you say that the Governor and the Company appreciate my services, although hitherto so unsuccessful. The district being explored now, comprises

---

[3] A ring sent to him in commemoration of his twenty-first birthday.

all the mountains contained in the spur from Kina Balu to Tumbo-yonkon, including both these peaks. It will take us some time, and it is an awful country. It may give us copper; it has done so already in small quantities. Enclosed is a picture of my house in Kinoram. I can't draw, you know, or paint either—so much the worse,—but I will do both when I get home.  Ever your loving son,

FRANK.

*Kudat, October 28th, 1882.*

MY DEAREST MOTHER,—I have received all your nice letters, and they give me, I cannot tell you how much pleasure. I have hardly ten months more, and then hurrah for merry England! Now, I am going to tell you something which I did not tell papa, and I tell you now because you will surely learn it from the papers, and I know you are too strong-minded to get anxious about me; I can take care of myself. Poor Witti! He was travelling in a Murut country, and having slept in a native's house, left the place next morning with his eleven men. They had a small native-made boat, in which they were going down stream. They came to a shallow place, where every one had to get out into the water and drag the boat. The rifles and weapons were put in the prahu. Witti waded ashore to make some notes. In the middle of all this they were attacked by some hundreds of savages, who fell upon Witti and his unfortunate men with spears, sumpitans, swords, &c. Witti, *it is said*, had a spear thrust right through his body; and even after receiving this awful wound, he turned and fired his revolver six times. Four cartridges were damp and did not explode, with the other two he killed two men. Of the rest of his followers, three escaped to tell the sad tale, the others were killed or died in the bush.

Now, please don't get frightened at this, as I am in a different district. I suppose papa has heard of it already; if not, it is news, but it is only my account. I am saving a little money, but it takes such a long time to mount up. Just think, only a few months more, and I shall be with you all again. I may go back again to the East, if there is nothing for me to do at home; but I would rather stay with you, dearest mamma, even if I had to put my bit of money into a newspaper, and become a J—l—t; but no matter, a time will come, as the walrus said, to talk of many things—of Borneo, and bees'-wax, and of many other things.

My dearest love to you.  Your ever loving son,

FRANK.

## VIII.

It had fallen to my lot to tell the story of Witti's death in the London and New York press. The cheerful accounts I had received from my son at about the same period, if they relieved my anxiety on his account, did not discount the sorrow I felt at the calamity which had befallen Witti, for he was a familiar and friendly person to me. I had read all his reports

SECTION OF STOCKADE SURROUNDING FRANK HATTON'S HOUSE.
(*From Drawing by Himself.*)

and letters to the Company; I had studied his character from many sides and much information; I had had reason to fear that he might be seriously hostile to my son, and had in later days reason to feel confidence in his friendly admiration of his young colleague; and the report of his death arrived just as I had mailed a letter to Borneo, thanking him for his courteous treatment of Frank, and inviting him to London whenever he should take his next vacation. Poor Witti! he had few friends, it seems; but the few were staunch and true, and even his enemies did not doubt his courage. The story of his connection with Borneo, and his life and death in the service of the new Government of Sabah, are romantic. He was the only foreigner connected with the Company. He wrote and spoke English almost perfectly, was an excellent French and German scholar; had mastered Malay and the local dialects of Borneo; and was essentially a clever and dauntless explorer.

A few explanatory words are necessary to introduce even the brief sketch which I am enabled to give of the life and death of Mr. F. Witti, who appears to have had neither friends nor home, that any one in England or the East knew of, outside Borneo.

The grant of a royal charter to the British North Borneo Company practically enabled that association to annex the territories north of the Dutch under treaties from the Sultans of Brunei and Sooloo. The first idea of making this country a commercial enterprise was American, which, apart from the intrinsic interest attaching to so novel an undertaking, gives to British North Borneo, or Sabah, a special interest for the United States as well as England. Mr. F. Witti was originally an officer in the Austrian navy. He was, I believe, induced to go out to Borneo by Baron Overbeck, who assisted in the transfer of certain American rights to the English Company. Mr. Witti, an adventurous and enterprising traveller, after visiting the country, came to London to seek official employment in connection with the new powers. His services not being welcomed as promptly as he expected, he disappeared from London, and it was thought by the Managing Director of the Company that he had sought other occupation. It seems, however, that, fearing on account of his nationality he might not be endorsed by this English Company, he went out to Borneo on his own account. His appearance there was under somewhat romantic circumstances. Having had much experience of the sea, he had " worked his passage," and landed in Borneo as the mate of a coasting vessel. He made his way to one of the principal residences, and his services were at once secured. He was appointed by the Resident to undertake certain geographical and other explorations, and his surveys and reports were so well done that in course of time the authorities in London gave him a settled and definite appointment as an officer of the Company authorized to conduct a series of expeditions of general exploration. He penetrated into many districts of the country never before visited, and one of the latest maps of the new territory is chiefly the result of his travels. During four or five years he had been engaged in this special and interesting work. At length he intimated to the Governor his intention of investigating the country lying between Kimanis and the Sibuco river, and it was on this journey that he lost his life. During the progress of the expedition Governor Treacher intercepted him by messengers with a special despatch of recall, requesting him to postpone his visit to the locality about the Sibuco and at once to return to Kimanis, the nearest residency. I have seen Mr. Witti's reply to the Governor; the last letter which was ever received from the unfortunate explorer. He acknowledges the recall, and with all the courtesy that he can command excuses himself for disobeying it; he refers to the importance of the work he has

THE ATTACK ON MR. F. WITH.
Drawn by W. H. Margetson.

To face page 86.

undertaken, and hopes that its success may lead to condonement of his breach of discipline. His idea was to complete the preliminary survey of British North Borneo, or Sabah, which he would almost have accomplished by an investigation of the line of country approaching the confines of the cession.

In the course of this letter he quotes from "The New Ceylon" a passage in regard to the junction of a river called the Kinabatangan with the Quamote, in respect to which Mr. Pryer (the Resident at Sandakan) says, "This is quite an unexplored river, owing to its interior being in the hands of a fierce tribe, the Tinggalums, who sometimes make a raid upon the Kinabatangan."[1] Poor Witti quotes these words in his last letter, and expresses his intention of entering this country. Mr. Pryer suggested that a fort at the junction of the rivers to keep the Tinggalums in check, would, with a firm but friendly administration, soon lead to the establishment of a thriving station, the district being prolific of valuable tropical produce. Witti in his letter dwells upon these points, and says he has no reason to doubt that he will go through the country safely, several of his men having been there before. He pleads the importance of his trip and his own earnestness as an excuse for going on, and thenceforth, of course, is outside the Company's authority.

Six or eight weeks after the receipt of this letter three natives, who had been of Witti's party, returned to Kimanis and reported his death under treacherous and terrible circumstances, whether at the hands of Tinggalums, Muruts, or head-hunting Dyaks seemed to be a matter of doubt. These native attendants

[1] This locality is in the region of Frank Hatton's latest exploration.

(mostly Malays) described the assassins as Muruts. I am inclined to think they were the very Tinggalums to whom Mr. Witti had referred in the letter just quoted. Frank Hatton passed through several tribes of Muruts much further to the north, and received from them considerate and hospitable treatment. The Muruts are nevertheless head-hunters.

F. WITTI.
(*From a Photograph by Lambert and Co., Singapore.*)

Witti had made a successful trip, and was evidently on his way back to Kimanis. He had bought several boats from the natives, and had paid them liberally with cloth and the other articles of exchange; and he had evidently every confidence in the friendship of the people. It is too common a habit of explorers in savage countries to divide their parties for the conveniences of travel. Throughout the history of martyrdom in the cause of geographical and scientific knowledge, it will invariably be found that explorers have often come to grief when they have committed the mistake of weakening their advance. Mr. Witti had with him seventeen men. He delegated half of them to go on with his boats to a certain point of the river, he arranging to follow them later with the other men. In the meantime he allowed his body-servant to carry his Winchester rifle and the others to stray about, while he sat down near the river with his despatch-box and papers for the purpose of making some notes in his diary. While thus engaged, several armed natives suddenly appeared from the jungle and an ambush formed of rocks near the stream. Without warning they sent a volley from their sumpitans at Witti and the men nearest to him. The sumpitan is a kind of blow-pipe through which a poisoned arrow is deftly discharged, and I remember that in Witti's first report to the Company he described this weapon and thanked his stars that on his first expedition he had been called upon to use no antidote against it. One of the arrows, it seems, pierced him in the breast, and three or four of his men close by fell mortally wounded. Witti seized his revolver, but the humidity of the atmosphere or damp occasioned by fording rivers appears to have interfered with its efficiency. Only two barrels were discharged, and these killed two of the assailants; the remainder rushed upon him, one of them spearing him to death, the others despatching his men. Three of his party ran away at the first attack and secreted themselves. They say that the whole action was very quick, and that within a few minutes the assassins cut off Witti's head and the legs and arms of the others, which they threw into a prahu and then made off, some of them into the jungle, others down stream. The three natives who

had escaped then tried to find their way to Kimanis.
They wandered about in the jungle for several days
and nights, living chiefly on leaves, and finally found
their way to the residency, where their evidence was
taken. The account is very circumstantial, and though
natives do not always tell the truth, the Governor has
had no reason to modify these details. Before Witti
left Kimanis he made a will and arranged for the
proper settlement of all his worldly affairs, evidently
impressed with the serious character of the work he
was voluntarily undertaking.

## IX.

On December 3rd Frank writes from Singapore, " I
am down here until the 30th, when I return to Borneo.
I have had a touch of fever, which luckily I have now
quite got rid of: I think I stayed too long in Kinoram. See my last report; I think it is the best I have
done; it will tell you everything about my work. At
the Governor's request I am sending home a box of
specimens. On my return to Borneo I start on my
last exploration—up the Segama and all round Silam
and Sibokon—a country that is quite unexplored. And
the next time I am down here, I shall be *en route* for
England. 'Hurrah for merry England!' But a
thousand times hurrah for merry home. I don't
think, after all, I shall be very rich when I arrive. My
salary was not much. . . I speak Dusun now as well
as Malay, and am going to write down all the dialect
words in the language of N. Borneo, as many of each
as I can remember and collect for some printed forms
of the Asiatic Society which I am to have from the
Bishop of Singapore. . . I shall leave Borneo on

the 1st of August, take the first French mail, and arrive at Marseilles by the 15th of September; on the 18th, in the evening at 8 p.m., I shall be with you, my dear—so expect me and order anything for dinner except fowl!" On the 9th he writes to me his last letter but one. He says,—

*Singapore, December 9th,* 1882.

MY DEAR FATHER,—I leave here on the 19th for Silam. Is it not a nuisance? I cannot get your letters out of the Labuan bag; about six mails now will be waiting me in Borneo. I have just returned from Johore, and I think of going to Malacca next week. I am quite well and happy again. I am afraid I wrote a miserable letter some time ago, but please remember I had the fever badly and the "blues" worse.[1] I would so like to feel sure, or not sure, that the directors

---

[1] This refers to the only sad letter he wrote to us. It was dated Kudat, November 10. I had, in response to a letter in which he said he was very happy, expressed a hope that he would not forget that we at home could never be very happy without him. This reached him when he was ill, and drew from him a bitter cry. He was down with fever, and was badly hipped. "I am not very old," he wrote, "but during the last fifteen days I have been experiencing the feelings of an octogenarian on the brink of the grave." He thought we had misunderstood one of his most genial letters, and he for once did not spare me nor himself. "I have had twenty days of wretchedness and agony —so homesick that I have thought of throwing the whole business up and coming home." If he only had! If I had only received his letter in time to act upon it. Accompanying it, and in the same envelope, was another letter of the same date, on the eve of his starting to Singapore on a few weeks' leave for the benefit of his health. The other letter he wrote is "only to show you what I can do when I am down with fever—take no notice of it, and don't show it to mamma. Kudat is a wretched hole, and I was very ill and miserable. The copper in Kinoram exists—I hunted it down, but only found it in pockets, and in no workable quantity. I shall come home by French mail on the 12th or 13th of August next. I often think of getting into the train at Dover, then away to London, then clatter and rattle in a cab to Titchfield Terrace. . . . Now, good-bye, dear papa, my only friend—and don't think anything of that fever letter—and don't show

are satisfied with me and my work. If I am to get samples of wood, gums, &c., for research, the Royal Society had better give me a grant. Dr. Hodgkinson might perhaps see to this. I am now a member of the Straits Royal Asiatic Society, and one of their agents in Borneo. I am going to write them a paper on Sabah, but I think I had better consult Mr. Treacher first. I went to an essential oil factory yesterday, and procured samples of citronella oil, lemon oil, nutmeg, patchoulli oils, &c. Rather an interesting place. Please tell me in full what you think of my last report. I think it is my best. I have yet Siquati to finish, Kinoram Geological Report, with maps, &c. But, most of all, I want to know if my work is approved of. Cowie is a good fellow. Did you see Barclay Read?

I think I look a little "too utter" in my photo. *Que pensez-vous?* I am collecting data, though slowly, for my book. Witti did not take many arms, or pay much attention to the weapons which he did take; I do. In my book I shall write some things which do not appear in my diary and reports.

Your most loving son,<br>
FRANK.

His last two letters are from Sandakan. He discusses the question of his position and the future. The Company want him to take a holiday in the east, but not to return home. They wish to extend his engage-

it to mamma, it will make her sad." I suppose there is nothing more depressing than jungle fever. Attending this depression which afflicted Frank at Kudat was the keen disappointment of the failure of a great copper find. He had tracked the indications of the metal over miles of country under serious difficulties, and had literally hunted it down to its source. It was at the time the one great hope of the Company. Examples of copper, antimony, and gold had previously in more than one instance been palmed upon their explorers by natives and others; but here was a genuine find. Frank had followed it step by step from the place where it was found (far away from its source) to its origin, to its first outcrop—and the result, while it was in its way a scientific triumph, was not a financial success. These two letters did not reach me until he had left Singapore on his last expedition, and on the day I received them satisfactory and cheerful reports of him by telegraph and letter had been received at the Company's offices in London.

ment, and the managing director suggests a residentship, combined with scientific investigation.[6] I feel complimented by this expression of confidence in their young official, but will listen to nothing so far as I am concerned that does not first contemplate his return to London for a personal and family consultation. The photograph (referred to above) sent from Singapore, taken just after his recovery from fever, emphasized this resolve, to say nothing of his hardships, his dangers, and the utter void his absence had made in our little family circle. More than once I had gone to the Company's offices in Old Broad Street, with the intention of telegraphing to him, "Come home!" But fate would have it that I was always met there with some cheering account of him, a compliment from the Governor touching his work, or a pleasant record of him from some traveller or official who had seen him. When the news of poor Witti's death came, I went up to the city with that old familiar message, —"Come home!"—in my mind; but on that very day despatches were received from the Governor, with satisfactory accounts of Mr. Frank Hatton, and it would have seemed cowardly, I thought, in his sight

---

[6] "He might," said the managing director to me, "take six months' leave and visit Java; the country would interest him in many ways, its system of government, as you know, is unique. You referred to it in 'The New Ceylon.'" A few months later, and at about the time Frank would, under this arrangement, have visited Java, came news of the terrible earthquake there, the atomic dust of which is said to have accounted for the wonderful sunsets—the blood-red after-glows—which followed, and were noted throughout Europe and even in America. I saw the snowy prairies beyond Chicago bathed in their ruddy light, and in London I was told they literally seemed to set the Thames on fire.

to have requested his return at such a time. "Moreover," says one who knew him well, "your telegram might not have reached him for months; and if it had, he would not have come. His engagement was for two years, and nothing would have induced him to break it; besides, he liked his work, hard and dangerous as it was, and he would have gone through with it, whatever might have been the end of it."

THE QUAY, SANDAKAN (EVENING).
(*Drawn by Helen A. Hatton. From a Photograph by Mr. Robson.*)

In his last letter he said, "coal has been found in Marudu, small quantities of copper in Tumboyonkon, my laboratory goes up at Kudat I don't think the Company can spare me. But I am coming home. I want to see all your dear faces again, and have a talk with my old friends in London... This is a unique experience and position; but is life worth living so long away from you all? No... I am just starting on an expedition up the Segama—my last trip, and when I have done this, I shall go inland no more."

## IV.

## DISASTER AND DEATH.

*Good news—Five days later—Sad letters—" A bright, fearless, brave life "—On the Segama River—Hunting in the jungle—The fatal accident—A devoted following—The silent passenger—Tropical scenery—Bornean highlands and the mountains of Pisgah—Inquest and verdict—A jungle cemetery—The pathetic story told by Governor Treacher.*

### I.

AND it was so. He went inland no more. They carried him to the coast, where he rests from his labours. He had passed safely through perils innumerable, and was on his way home. But it was his English home that was in his thoughts and ours; not that other home to which we all are marching. This is how the news came to us, while we were counting the months that stood between us and him. He went away in the autumn. With the fall of the leaf we should see him back again. What a pleasant time it would be! His mother had in view a surprise for him in Paris; his sisters dreamed of trips with him on his favourite river. I thought of the dear fellow busy with his first book. We drank his health and wished him joy, and all the time he was asleep and knew it not; nor did we, for we heard good news of him even after they had set up a wooden cross over his grave, and carvéd upon it, " F. H., 1883."

On Monday evening, March 19, I received from the British North Borneo Company the following welcome letter:—

11, *Old Broad Street, E.C.*,
*March* 19*th*, 1883.

MY DEAR HATTON,—The following extract from one of our despatches will interest you in case you have no letters by this mail:—

"Mr. Pryer has received a note from Mr. Hatton, dated 25th January, from near Penangah. He was in good health, and about to descend the Segama River."

After this, I believe he is going into Silam, where there are four Europeans, and from which place he can return to civilization by Cowies' steamer.

Yours truly,
WM. M. CROCKER.

Five days later, on Thursday the 22nd, Mr. Crocker brought me (and I have often felt sorry for him when thinking of the painful character of his mission) the following telegram from Sir Walter Medhurst, at Shanghai, to the British North Borneo Company in London:—

Bad news from Borneo—Baquette shot himself—accident—Von Donop and Callaghan ill at Elopura.

There was one hope for us—the selfish hope that the code-word was a mistake. Our kindly messenger of sorrow gave us this hope to break our fall upon. "Baquette" was the code-word for Frank Hatton; but there was the code-word "Banquette," which stood for another officer of the Company. It was hard to wish that death had taken some other, and not our dear one. We tried to cherish that forlorn hope, nevertheless. But in his mother's heart all hope died out with the very first suggestion of trouble. The next day was Good Friday. The Company had telegraphed to Shanghai for details. But we could get no reply until Saturday. From Thursday night until Saturday morning we lived through the suspense. Thank God he knew nothing of our anguish. We beguiled some of the time on Friday sending a special messenger into the country to ask some unnecessary question about the telegram. The local churches tolled their sad bells for a death that occurred eighteen hundred years ago. The next morning London awoke as usual to its daily miseries and joys; and in a sort of dull dream I travelled to the city, over the ground which he and I had often traversed together, and entered the offices where I had often had news of him. Sympathetic hands laid before me the second telegram from Sir Walter Medhurst:—

It was Hatton—he was elephant shooting—his rifle caught in the bushes and exploded—he was shot through the lungs and died instantly—an inquest was held at Elopura. There are no written advices.

II.

And we drew down the blinds, for now we knew that he was dead. How we accepted the inevitable needs no telling. During the day a minstrel played under my window "Home, sweet Home," and I tasted all the bitterness of it. Then came the necessity of occupation. But it had to be in his service. So we made arrangements to bring him home.[1] We visited

[1] "*British North Borneo Company*, 11, *Old Broad Street, London,*
"28*th March*, 1883.

"DEAR SIR,—The Court of Directors have learned with extreme regret of the fatal accident that has befallen your son, Mr. Frank Hatton, as reported by the telegraphic advices of Sir W. Medhurst; and I am desired on their behalf to convey to you and to the other members of your family the deep sympathy of the Court at the loss

cemeteries and churchyards to find him an English resting-place. Telegrams went out to the East, a coffin was provided and sent to Borneo from Singapore, and the date was fixed for the dear remains of him to be embarked for home. Tennyson's sublime poem "In Memoriam" had once been my chamber-book, and I took it up again now and found a melancholy kind of comfort in it. I followed the imaginary track of an imaginary ship, with its "dark freight of a vanished life;" for by the time we should have met the vessel, information came that he might not be removed for two years. And then came letters from abroad, supplementing the many tender messages which the mails had already brought us from all parts of the United Kingdom. They were more eloquent I think than is customary on the occasions which elicit "letters of condolence." I turned to "In Memoriam" to find that the poet had resented the proverbial remark that death is the common lot. None of my correspondents, however, wrote to me in that conventional strain; yet the poet's exclamation against the phrase that "loss is common" touched me keenly, for I was an actor in the tragedy he had put into four throbbing lines of verse:—

> "O father, wheresoe'er thou be,
> Who pledgest now thy gallant son;
> A shot, ere half thy draught be done,
> Hath still'd the life that beat from thee."

you have sustained by this sad occurrence, which has also deprived them of the services of a most energetic, valuable, and painstaking officer. Instructions will be sent by this next mail to the Governor as to the disposal of your son's remains, and the collection of his papers and property in accordance with your wishes.

"Yours faithfully, ELPHINSTONE, *Vice-Chairman*.
"*Joseph Hotton, Esq.*, 14, *Titchfield Terrace, N.W.*"

Those sadly welcomed letters from over the sea; I cannot close this chapter without printing a few of their eloquent and tender tributes to him. They are from his friends, from those who had seen him since I had, who had touched hands with him in that interval between our good-bye and his silence. One is from Mrs. Treacher. It is addressed to my wife, and comes to us "with one or two pieces of music in my care which belonged to your dear one, and I am sending them to you by this mail, for I know how precious they, with everything else that belonged to him, must be to you." And then she adds, "words are such empty things, and it is so hard to try and say what one feels for trouble like yours. I only heard the sad, sad news yesterday, and I cannot keep the tears from my eyes. I feel for you very, very deeply; it seems a trouble almost too hard for you to bear, knowing how we all feel it here. *He leaves a very bright recollection of himself in all our hearts—the recollection of a bright, fearless, brave life, through which we could always catch a glimpse of his strong love for home.*" Opening this packet of the dear fellow's music, it was quite in keeping with the rest of the story that the first piece should be Chopin's "Funeral March." The other two were Wagner's march from "Tannhäuser," and De Groot's "Le Réveil des Faucettes."

From Sandakan Andrew Beveridge, the Australian gold-miner who was with him on his last expedition, wrote, "If I consulted my feelings I should not write to you. As the comrade of your son, and being with him at the last moment of his life, my duty impels me to give you the few plain facts which have caused so dreadful a bereavement to yourself and family. . . . I found your son breathing his last, supported by his native attendants. I am certain he came by his sad end through accidentally shooting himself with his rifle. I need not go into particulars, as no doubt you will receive the evidence as given at the inquest; believe me, I knew the worth of your son's brave spirit and comradeship." [2]

Mr. Alfred Dent wrote from Shanghai, "So sudden an end to such a promising career will cast a deep gloom over our service in Borneo for a long time to come. I had been looking forward with great pleasure to meeting him after his long and tedious exploration on the eastern coast. We shall have only his writings instead of his face to look into now. I promise you that they and all his belongings shall be held in the respect they deserve. No one has worked so laboriously and pluckily for us as Frank during his travels in unknown districts, and few people have interested themselves more than he has done in the early history of our enterprise."

I forbear from making any further extracts from these letters. They are more or less private, and they are all very sad. Now that I can read them again with something like calmness, I note how far they are above that common idea of consolation—that "it is all for the best." Another thing also strikes me, that many persons whom we meet in society and elsewhere, and regard as happy, nurse at home sorrows we have never heard of. I could relate some touching stories of men and women who in the shadow of my sorrow have told

[2] "Mr. Beveridge," writes the Governor (June 20th, 1883), "has just left us, his health having entirely given way under the strain of the hardships which your lamented son's spirit enabled him to bear so well."

me of theirs.³ Through our own misfortunes we become acquainted with a multitude of fellow-sufferers.

### III.

The details of his death came by-and-by, mixed up in the mails with fresh letters of condolence,¹ inquiry, and

[3] In an American journal to which I have contributed some journalistic notes and literary reminiscences I recently had occasion to refer to this sentiment of "a fellow-feeling," and I illustrated it with the following most melancholy incident. This note is dated August 21, 1884:—"Two or three weeks ago Mr. Gilbert a'Beckett, one of the *Punch* staff and a well-known dramatic author, called upon me. 'I have just dropped my son to see the cricket match at Lords' (which is close to my house), he said. Then I thought he suddenly avoided the subject, remembering that I had now no son. A few days ago this fine, handsome boy, a college lad of about fourteen, on a holiday visit at Thorndon Hall, shot a bird; it fell into a pond; he swam in after it, was seized with cramp, and was drowned. Life is a tragedy. Chronicling and reviewing its current history, in the course of one's journalistic business, one is obliged more or less to deal with its comedy side, but how frequently we are all pulled up by the discharge of a gun, a sudden cry, a collision at sea, the breaking of a locomotive crank, the flooding of a distant valley, a proclamation of war, to go back to the admission that life is a tragedy. A'Beckett, I hear, is inconsolable; yet by-and-by he will have to 'make merry,' and go on writing for *Punch*.

[1] Among these were two from namesakes, one an army officer in India, another from Mrs. Bradshaw, wife of the editor of the *Nottingham Journal*, who wrote that her father married a Miss Hatton, and that Hatton had always been one of their family names. The point of this lies in the heroic and tragic story which my correspondent relates. The details of my son's death impressed her forcibly by "their strange similarity" with those which led to her brother's death in a foreign and distant land. "It seems," she writes, "more than passing strange that after the lapse of more than thirty-three years this other sad fatality should occur, and that two brave lads bearing the same name should be the victims of a like catastrophe." My sympathetic correspondent encloses me the following remarkable and impressive narrative, which was found among her brother's effects, which were forwarded to England by a brave Cuban doctor, together

tributes to his memory; but it was not until the first week in May that the written despatches and records with a letter from the young fellow himself. This is the young adventurer's letter:—

"Some years ago I grew tired of home and the monotonous humdrum of my daily toil, and resolved to visit different lands. I had already been over a great part of Europe, but was not satisfied, so I determined to go to Australia. After much hesitation, my father gave me a good outfit, bought me both farming and mining implements, tents, and everything which we considered might be necessary, gave me a tidy sum of money, paid my passage on board an A 1 clipper, had a cabin built for me and my companions on deck (for there were five or six of us in company), and said, 'Good-bye!' to us a few miles down the Mersey. I see him now standing on that little steam tug which separated us. He had lost a worse son than I had a father. We had a cheerful and merry voyage of ninety-seven days. We landed at Melbourne. After a few days of sight-seeing, when we managed to get rid of a good deal of our money, we went up country to look for gold. Ah me! what a life we led! It chills my blood to think about it. Toil, toil, toil, so wearily from morning till night, sometimes up to the waist in water, sometimes up to the knees in mud, sometimes in quartz so hard it was like chiselling at steel, and finding no gold, getting poorer and weaker and thinner every day, ready to sink at night as we lay out in the open air, covered with a rug, and thinking of the comfortable homes we had been such fools to leave. Sometimes we would wake up half frozen, while our feet, which were towards the fire, were scorched. Well, I went on digging and had better luck, turned shopkeeper, and lost all my money again; then turned cattle driver, was first one thing and then another, till I scraped enough money together to take me home. But I would not go to England. I was determined, when I did go, it should be as a rich man, not as a pauper. So I *stayed on*, and moved about from place to place, seeing strange sights and doing various things, till I worked my way down to the coast, a healthy man with a well-lined purse. Then I fell in with a Yankee skipper who was engaged in the coasting trade aboard a schooner of about 200 tons burden, with a crew of six men. I took a passage on board the schooner, and calculated on landing in North America in about twelve months. We set sail for Peru, got on the Brazilian coast, landed at various stations to barter our cargo; had all sorts of sport—at one place a bit of lion hunting,

of the inquest were complete. The facts may be briefly
condensed in this place. The official record is printed
at another chamois hunting, then a bit of shark fishing, and first one
thing and then another, until at last we found ourselves on the coast
of Chili. Here we were becalmed, so we landed. The British Consul,
hearing of our arrival, sent me an invitation to stay with him, and
here I am, comfortably lodged in his house, smoking a pipe and writing
this. To-morrow we are going inland to see if we can rouse a few
lion-cubs or other small fry for sport. To-morrow night I shall
finish this, and give an account of our excursion."

\* \* \* \* \* \*

Seven days later the letter was continued as follows :—" Here I am
in bed, in the British Consul's house, scribbling a few lines as best I
am able with a pencil. I was to have finished my letter the night of
our hunting party, but I have been obliged to postpone it. We went
into the mountains cub hunting, but we made a terribly long march
before we found anything. About two o'clock I was getting through
some tangled brushwood, and my gun went off, shooting my arm
through above the elbow. My word, how it bled! All the shot went
clean through, making a hole as big as an apple, and splintering the
bone. I very soon fainted from loss of blood, and when I came round
I was lying on the back of a mule, being taken gently down the
mountains towards the coast. My newly-found friends were very
kind and attentive, especially the Consul—he is a downright good
fellow, a regular Englishman. He came alongside and told me all
about it. He said he had been travelling in this style for three hours,
and he was taking us to the nearest station where we could find a
doctor. There is only one doctor about every three hundred miles in
these parts, and we were fortunately near one. They had tied my
handkerchief tightly round my arm to stop the bleeding, but it began
to feel very bad with the jolting of the mule and the tight bandage.
When we got down to the coast we hired a small boat, and I was
lifted on board. We were then sixteen hours on the open sea, and all
this while you can imagine my shattered arm was not very comfortable. At last we got *home*, and the doctor was quickly on the spot.
He soon saw what was amiss, and told me he should have to take off
my arm, as it had been too long without attention to render recovery
possible. I didn't much like parting with so valuable a limb, for we
had been together many years, and it had done me good service at one
time or another. It had given many a man a hearty welcome in
civilized countries, and knocked many an one on the head in the jungles

in the second part of this volume. Frank Hatton was conducting an expedition in the north-eastern part of Borneo. It consisted of four boats. He was in the first

so I was loth to lose it. But there was no help for it, so I asked the doctor to give me a cigar and a cup of coffee, and to get on with his work. He asked me "if I should like my eyes bandaged," but I declined with thanks. He got out his knife and saw, and in about half an hour had performed as nice an amputation as ever I beheld, for that was not the first I had witnessed by many an one. He told me to keep up my spirits, which I am now doing to the best of my ability. I expect in a few more days to go aboard the schooner, for that Yankee is still here, and vows he will wait for me, if he stops twelve months."

\* \* \* \* \* \* \*

The following is an extract from the Cuban doctor's letter:—
"Poor fellow! he suffered and died like a hero. At the time he was writing so cheerily, the cold hand of death was on his throat. When he was brought under my care, I saw in an instant that mortification had set in—they had tied his arm so tightly—and no power could save him. What courage!—to smoke while I operated! When my saw was in the middle of one of the ligaments of his arm, he exclaimed in good French, 'Doctor, excuse me a moment, you take my breath; give me that cup of coffee!' I gave it to him, and he recovered his strength. I asked him 'if I should bandage his eyes,' and he said, 'Ah, doctor, you forget that I am an Englishman.' Ah, these English, they are like iron men; they are calm and brave and cold. He appeared to recover in a short time, and I began to hope, but the mortification suddenly revived, and he sank like a meteor. He asked for his pipe, which I gave him. He smoked calmly, and remarked he did not feel so well! Poor fellow, he was within an hour of death. He grew feebler each minute, till he could not smoke, and he sank into a slumbering condition. I endeavoured to arouse him, and asked his name and birthplace, but he could not reply. I gave him a spoonful of brandy, after which he said, 'God bless—' and fell back upon his pillow. I held the cross over his eyes, but they saw no more of earth. He was interred in the little churchyard in Chili, where British subjects are buried, and there is to be found there a simple wooden cross, erected at the head of his grave, and on it is this inscription:—

"'To an Unknown Hero,'
"March 21, 1857."

one, and Mr. Beveridge, an Australian mining expert, in the last. Frank fired from his boat at an elephant and wounded it severely. Leaping ashore, accompanied only by his mandore, a Malay, named Drahman, he gave chase. They came up to the elephant, which had stopped, and was roaring. Thinking possibly that his Winchester rifle was too light for a final attack on the elephant, he went back to the boats for a party of his native attendants. Arming them with Sniders, he led them into the jungle. The elephant, however, had moved off, and it being now nearly dark, he was persuaded by Drahman to return. On the way back he was walking with his Winchester at the shoulder. When penetrating the forests he had always been in the habit of carrying a stick for the purpose of pushing aside the overhanging vines. On this occasion, as he stooped to pass under a creeper, he raised his rifle to lift up the obstruction. The weapon became entangled in an unusually strong growth of vines, whereby the muzzle was suddenly twisted towards him, slid down his shoulder, and went off, the trigger being pulled by some twigs of the creeper.[5] The ball entered at the

[5] *Truth*, in mentioning the accident, points out the fact that many persons lose their lives in the work at which they are proficient, and instances Speke being shot by his own gun while partridge shooting in Somersetshire, and Whyte Melville dying by an accident in the hunting-field. Recently conversing with Mr. H. H. Johnston, the young African explorer (whose volume on the Congo is one of the most interesting of recent books of travel), he confessed that he had had more than one very narrow escape from serious wounds or death while carrying a rifle in the jungle. Mr. Governor Treacher considers the Winchester unsafe for jungle work. It is, nevertheless, a favourite weapon with travellers. Mr. Stanley carries a Winchester; so also do Mr. Joseph Thomson, Mr. H. H. Johnston, and other African explorers. I have lately examined many Winchesters. The trigger,

collar-bone and came out at the back lower down, severing two main arteries. His men were round him in a moment, and seized him before he fell. "*Oodeen, Oodeen, mati sahya!*" ("Oodeen, Oodeen, I am dead") he said in Malay, as he laid his head on the shoulder of his Tutong boy, whose name is Oodeen, and who was devoted to his service. It was at this moment that Mr. Beveridge arrived on the scene. He heard the shot and the cry of the men, and leaping from his boat, (only some 150 yards away), within four or five minutes at the most was by his young chief's side; but Frank Hatton was breathing his last. So surprising was it to Mr. Beveridge that "Tuan Hatton," noted for his coolness and his care in the management of his weapons, should have shot himself, that he exclaimed, "Who has done this?" The men, most of them shedding bitter tears and crying, "Better we had died," explained the incident, and after satisfying himself that their story was only too true, he had the body carried to the boats. One of the most affectionate acts of devotion followed. Eleven of the explorer's men, under the direction of Mr. Beveridge, paddled the body to Sandakan by river and sea, a distance of nearly 170 miles. They never slept, night or day. They only rested three times, to cook and eat a little rice. For fifty-three hours

it seems to me, might be better protected than it is. A distinguished member of the Sabah Government said to me recently, "I am only surprised that more accidents do not happen. I was shooting in the jungle not long since, when my rifle was caught in the creepers. They are as strong as steel, and spring back upon you in the most extraordinary way. 'That is how poor Frank was killed,' I said, as my rifle was suddenly twisted out of my hand. The density of the Bornean jungle is beyond all description."

## Disaster and Death.

they paddled their native boat down the hitherto unexplored river to the sea, and then along the wild coast to Sandakan. Here is a subject for poet and painter, the silent passenger and the dusky rowers, who only pause under sun and moon to lament the dead and to eat rice enough to give them strength to reach the distant Residency. In the daytime the boat glides silently along by the unpeopled banks of the unknown river. A white bird, a stray deer, a wild bull, or a company of chattering monkeys pause to look at the unfamiliar sight. The burning sun shines straight down upon them. Now and then they shoot

THE LAST JOURNEY. (*From a Drawing by E. J. Meeker.*)

along under the shade of the nipa-palm. At night still onwards, the only sounds the cries of wild animals in the forests, until at last the murmur of the sea greets them. Then, by-and by, they are among the breakers. They push on outside the headlands. At length they reach the bay where a week or two hence their silent passenger was to have landed to meet friends and prepare for his well-earned holiday in England. It is night when they anchor off the Residency, midnight, and the mournful news goes round the little town, among the handful of Europeans, and the crowd of natives and Chinese. Says a correspondent recording the incident in the *Straits Times*, "The European population were sadly dismayed when it became known that one of their bravest and most genial friends was no more, and that his body was lying at Sandakan. With tearful eyes one asked the other if it could be true that Frank Hatton was dead!"[6]

There are many curiously striking coincidences in connection with the young explorer's death which may possibly be hereafter related. One of them may be noted here. Rarely in his letters or reports, or in such extracts from his diaries as I have yet seen, has he taken up much space in anything like eloquent descriptions of the natural scenery of Borneo. But I have before me some notes of one of his most remarkable journeys, from the Labuk River to Kudat, nearly four months of river and jungle travel. Once he pauses to describe a "splendid view" which he obtained from the summit of a ridge of land 3000 feet above the sea level,

---

[6] "The *Melbourne Argus* contains the report of a paper read by Mr. De Lissa at a meeting of the Geographical Society of Australia, containing an eloquent tribute to the young London scientist whose accidental death in the interior of North Borneo will be remembered. 'Among the intrepid explorers and scientific men who have done so much for Sabah,' said the speaker, 'can never be forgotten the brave, young, and clever Frank Hatton, who, at the early age of twenty-two, had already made a name in Europe for his scientific abilities, and who, with his chosen Malay followers, intrepidly explored the unknown regions of Borneo. Never shall I forget my intense sorrow, shared as it was by a sobbing community, when his death was announced at Elopura. He will be always remembered among the pioneers of Borneo as the gentle and heroic Frank Hatton.' The Singapore branch of the Asiatic Society recently recorded in their minutes a note of the society's high appreciation of Frank Hatton's work, and during an official survey of the Segnama country a range of hills were named after the young explorer and 'blood brother' of many native tribes."—*Daily News*, October 11th, 1884.

and in his graphic sketch he indicates the very country in which just a year later it was to be his fate to bring his worldly travel to an end :—

"To the north," he writes, "lay the Kinabatangan Valley, with the Silam Hills in the distance; eastwards stretched the Labuk, girded by hills rising one above the other up to the noble crags of Mentapok. In the distance, again, was the Singat Vale, with range upon range of tree-capped mountains rising right away to Kina Balu, which, seemingly near, towered like a fairy castle up into the blue sky. I shall never forget this lovely scene, but more especially shall I remember the wonderful tints and shades presented by the distant 'giant hills of Borneo!' A blue sky showed up every crag of the principal mountain, which stood out purple and black. The setting sun shed its rays on rock and tree, and the water streaming down the time-worn sides glinted and flashed, while the nearer hills were clothed in every shade of green. A few white clouds appeared in the distance, and as I neared the Dusun kampong of Toadilah night-clouds were closing in the glorious landscape. It was a most exceptional view, and one which this season of the tropical year can alone afford."

When he died in the following March, he was on his way to those very "Silam Hills" he writes of. If the mountains of Pisgah are as real as these Bornean highlands, he has ascended the sunny heights and entered "the better land."

An inquest was held at Elopura in the Bay of Sandakan, and adjourned from time to time during two or three days, until all the boats came in and each man could give his evidence. Dr. Walker said the wound was perfectly consistent with the statements of the mandore and the boy Oodeen. It was inconsistent with the theory that one of the other rifles might have accidentally exploded, as Frank Hatton was taller than any of the natives, and the bullet had entered from above. Further, it seems that the men acted on a general order from Mr. Hatton never to carry their weapons loaded, and only to load when there was something to shoot at. Questioned as to Mr. Hatton's relations with his men, Mr. Beveridge said, "Mr. Hatton was on the very best of terms with his men; they would do anything for him. Half of them were crying." A native said, "Mr. Hatton always cleaned his own gun; we were afraid to touch it." Ungong, another native, said he arrived on the scene with Mr. Beveridge, four or five minutes after they heard the shot. "Mr. Hatton was dead. We all cried. I had been with Mr. Hatton a year. We all said, 'Better we had died than this.'" The jury, which consisted of twelve Europeans, recorded the following verdict :—

The jury are of opinion that Frank Hatton came by his death from the accidental discharge of his rifle on the evening of the 1st of March while returning from elephant shooting at Sugoon Tukol, which is situated about sixty miles up the Segama River, and about 160 miles by water from Sandakan, and whilst he was pushing aside a vine with the aid of said loaded rifle carried in his hand.

The jury much deplore the sudden death of Mr. Hatton, who, as an explorer and mineralogist, had proved himself of much value to the British North Borneo Company and to the world generally, and on account of his many social qualities.

Governor Treacher in his despatch pays a high tribute to the deceased, "whose reports of journeys in the interior, and of metalliferous researches," he says, "amidst circumstances of much difficulty and oftentimes of personal danger, will remain as reliable records in the annals of the North Borneo Company. He was devoted to the work he had in hand, and his scientific attainments made him enthusiastic in his interesting pursuits. Personally his amiability endeared him to all who came in contact with him—he was as popular among his brother officers as he was trusted among the natives (who followed him so faithfully to his death) in his inland journeys." Mr.

ELOPURA, THE CHIEF SETTLEMENT IN NORTH BORNEO.
*Drawn by E. J. Meeker. (From a Photograph by Mr. Robson.)*

Resident Pryer bears equally high testimony to the "brilliant beginning and promising future" of the deceased, in concluding which he says, "Mr. Hatton's geographical notes will be of great value, and his name will be attached to the first correct chart of the Kinabatangan River."

The remains of the young scientist were interred at Elopura on the 4th of March, followed to the grave by the Resident, all the Europeans, and many inhabitants, Chinese and natives, of the district. From the lowest native to the highest European functionary a general grief was manifest among the strangely picturesque crowd. The funeral took place at eight o'clock in the morning. The procession formed opposite the public offices, and followed the coffin to the grave (a distance of about a mile), where the service of the Church of England was read by Mr. Pryer. The burial-place was a jungle clearing of about an acre, on a gentle slope half a mile from the sea. It has since been consecrated, and by this time other silent neighbours keep sorrowful company with the first European tenant, upon whose primitive headstone might be duplicated Pope's lines on Harcourt, which touchingly interpret my own experience of one of the kindest, most manly, most amiable fellows that ever lived :—

> "To this sad shrine, whoe'er thou art! draw near.
> Here lies the friend most lov'd, the son most dear;
> Who ne'er knew joy, but friendship might divide,
> Or gave his father grief but when he died!"

### IV.

As it is from the pen of Mr. Governor Treacher himself (who has acknowledged it with supplementary notes of praise and regret), I am constrained to print the following eloquent tribute and pathetic narrative which appeared, surrounded with a black border, in the official gazette of the Government, the *North Borneo Herald* :—

### MR. FRANK HATTON.

IT is our sad duty to chronicle in this, only our second issue, the occurrence of a most melancholy accident resulting in the death of a

Sketch of Frank Hatton's Grave
at Sandacan, British North Borneo
from a drawing by G Templer Pickers

promising young officer of the Company's service. Mr. Frank Hatton, after an arduous exploring journey up the River Kinabatangan, and a very plucky though unsuccessful attempt to reach the Segama overland from the former river during the prevalence of the rainy season, was compelled to make the journey by sea, and reached the Segama with his party in open boats on the 27th of February, after what he has described in his diary as "a terrible voyage." His duty was to prospect the Segama district for gold, to the existence of which the testimony of all the natives of the east coast unanimously point. With this object, accompanied by Mr. Beveridge, the companion of all his journeys in Borneo, and by a party of Malays, he ascended the river. His diary is continued to the 1st of March, on which day he enters the note, "Just one year ago left Sandakan for the Labuk," the first inland journey he had made in the territory, and this was the day that was to terminate for ever all his work in this world. The last entry in the diary is to the effect that at 3.40 p.m. on the date named above he had reached a certain point up the river. Soon after this it appears he came across an elephant on the bank, and firing at it with his Winchester repeating rifle, he wounded it. The animal made for the jungle, and the deceased immediately started in pursuit. He was unable to get up to the quarry, and darkness coming on with the rapidity usual in tropical climes, he and his native followers determined to give up the chase for the day and return to their boats. On the way back Mr. Hatton, leading the way, came across a creeper growing across the track. He, somewhat wearied, probably, by the fatigues of the day, attempted to remove it with the butt end of his rifle. The weapon is known to have had an exceptionally sensitive lock. Some sudden jerk occasioned by the elasticity of the creeper caused the loaded weapon to explode, and the bullet passed right through his breast. He fell into the arms of his "boy" (a native servant), who was walking behind him, and was only able to utter, "*Udin, sayia mati*"—"Udin, I die!" And in three or four minutes all was over. Mr. Beveridge had been following up the river close behind in another boat. He heard the shot fired, and hurrying up to the spot whence the sound proceeded, was informed by the followers of the terrible event which had just transpired, and arrived only in time to see poor Hatton breathe his last. This sad event is, if possible, rendered still more sad by the fact that the lamented officer had been, according to the evidence of Mr. Beveridge, in the highest spirits for several weeks previously, rejoicing in the fact that he was shortly to terminate his labours in Borneo and rejoin his family, to which it was patent to all who had experienced the pleasure of his acquaintance, he, as an only son, was attached by ties of more than ordinary depth and devotion.

Mr. Hatton arrived in the country in October, 1881. He was of somewhat slender build, and apparently not possessed of a robust constitution, and it was consequently thought by many of his brother officers that he was scarcely fitted to stand the hardships of inland journeys in a jungle-covered country such as this, without roads or house accommodation for the traveller. But what he may have wanted in physical strength the deceased made up in strength of mind and in that pluck and determination to carry out his mission, however arduous and dangerous, which we find in the Englishman in all quarters of the globe. This pluck and determination had carried him safely and triumphantly through difficulties which could never have entered into his thoughts when he accepted in London the appointment of Commissioner of Mineral Explorations to the Company.

During the short time he was with us Mr. Hatton had examined and furnished an exhaustive report upon the valuable resources locked up in the Sekuati petroleum oil shale. He made an adventurous journey from Sandakan to the Labuk River, up that river and across country to Kudat. He subsequently spent some months in a patient exploration of the country at the head of Marudu Bay, where he met with and discovered samples of native copper and copper pyrites, coal, and other minerals which will in time doubtless be developed in the interests of the Company's Government. He then paid a short visit to Singapore to recruit himself after his prolonged sojourn in the jungle, and on his return to Borneo proceeded to Sandakan, where he entered upon the expedition which has so disastrously terminated in the death of a gallant and enterprising young officer. By his modesty, his ingenuousness, and by his attainments, he had won the sincere regard, and, in many cases, the affection of his brother officers. Before leaving England he had made the commencement of a reputation by his chemical researches. His native followers were strongly attached to him, and he had shown an exceptional facility in acquiring influence over and inspiring confidence in the untutored inland tribes. He has, we believe, left behind him a very complete vocabulary of one dialect of the Dusun language, which we trust the Government will take steps to have published in the interest of the junior members of the service. Mr. Hatton's age we gather to have been not more than twenty-one or twenty-two years. All who knew him prophesied for him a distinguished career. To the great Disposer of all things it has seemed good to ordain otherwise. Whom the Gods love die young.

PRINCIPAL STREET IN THE NATIVE TOWN OF SANDAKAN [1] (ELOPURA).
(*Drawn by Helen H. Hatton. From a Photograph by Mr. Robson.*)

The second part of these notes and reminiscences is devoted chiefly to the publication of such por-

[1] "The native town is very picturesque, as will be gathered from our illustrations of the wharf and the principal street. The buildings along the quay are made of bamboo with Nipa-palm "attaps." The principal street is little more than a palm-stem gangway, elevated on piles above the water. It is a curious sight when crowded, as it is now and then, and it is none the less strange in the early morning, when the earliest risers are abroad. The new town which is being built by the Company is on the slope of the hill that rises above the native village. It was from Elopura that Frank Hatton set forth on his latest expedition; it was to Elopura that his body was brought by his native followers in that fatal month of March, 1883."—*English Illustrated Magazine.*

tions of the diaries of the late Frank Hatton as have reached England, together with his reports to the Company. It will represent, as far as is now possible, the material upon which he would have founded his book on "North Borneo," and his manuscript is given intact. A postscript supplies, from two of his comrades, information which adds to the interest of the record, and gives point to some of its revelations.

END OF PART I.

## Part II.

DIARIES AND REPORTS OF EXPEDITIONS, OFFICIAL PAPERS, AND OTHER CHRONICLES.

## I.

### LIFE AT LABUAN.[1]

The smallest British colony—Four miles from the great island of Borneo—The North Bornean Malays—A native house—The Klings—The humming-birds of the East—The carpenter bee and the mason wasp—Coal Point—A deserted pit—Pig shooting—The goat-sucker—A monkey comedy—Snakes—Native music—A brilliant sunset with a dark cloud over Borneo—Looking forward.

#### I.

MIDST the diplomatic correspondence of Holland, Spain, and England in reference to the cession of North Borneo or Sabah to a British company chartered by her Majesty the Queen, a few notes on the civilized bit of country off the coast may have a special interest both to the Old World and the New. Should they not

[1] This is a mere holiday sketch. It was written with a view to

prove attractive in themselves, they may be so regarded from the standpoint of an introductory sketch to unexplored Borneo itself, all the more so as the island upon which they are written is, in American phraseology, "the jumping-off place" in the China seas *en route* for the wonderful regions that surround the sacred mountain of Kina Balu.

Labuan is an island lying a few miles north-west of Borneo. It is one of the smallest and least known of the British colonies. Ceded to her Majesty in 1847, it possesses the privilege of English government, and at one time promised to be an important coaling-station for the fleet. Approaching it from the European route, you make the little harbour in a steamer plying thither from Singapore. Landing at the only town in the island, Victoria, a row of houses, dignified by the name of the "Bazaar," is the first thing one sees. All the trade and commerce of Labuan is transacted in this combination of stores.

publication in a magazine and before the writer had visited the island of Borneo. His work had yet to begin. He was at this time experiencing his pleasantest days in Bornean waters, looking out wonderingly at the distant coast-line of Sabah, and making arrangements for his first expedition. Colonel Harington, who was his comrade during these days at Labuan, has read the proof of this first chapter, and I append some of his notes, which form an interesting supplement to the article. Later on, in the postscript to the extracts from Frank's diaries and reports, which follow this holiday essay, Colonel Harington has something to say of the author and his work. Now that one looks back, the story of the young traveller seems full of warning omens. Had he returned home in safety they would not have been remembered. But his death gives pathetic point to his description of the sunset that impressed him one evening at Labuan —"on the distant coast of Borneo a dark cloud hung heavily; lightning was visible at intervals, and the far-off thunder rumblings gave signal of an approaching storm."

Most of the establishments are in the hands of the Chinese. The locality is redolent of their food and their tobacco. The celestial shop-keepers describe themselves as "general dealers," which means that bad tinned milk, biscuits of ancient date, curious wines, fossilized potted meats, gunpowder, shot, and old muskets are to be had from them at various prices. They also deal in Manchester and German cotton goods, and an endless variety of cheap "sarongs," the universal dress of the country. Over each shop-door are pasted Chinese characters in black, on a red ground. One of these I found stood for "good luck" and another for "salve."

Walking on past these odoriferous stores, the only two imposing structures in Labuan come in sight. These are the Government offices. Two large low buildings, roofed with red tiles, and built, as nearly all buildings are in the islands of the Malay Archipelago, on piles. Two brass field-pieces are stationed in front of the Government offices. These guns, by-the-bye, were taken from the Dutch in 1850 at Cossipore. The Union Jack flies on a large flag-staff close at hand,[2] and in the distance is a stockade mounting four small pieces. These six guns, together with fifty native police, armed with Snider rifles, constitute the Labuan army. There are at present half a dozen European residents and officers on the island, and a population of between 5000 and 6000 mixed natives, made up of Kadyans, Malays, and a few Borneans, Klings, and Bengalees. The Malays about the coasts of Borneo are a miserable and degraded race, well described by Mr. St. John as

---

[2] Every rope taut and ship-shape—the pride of the Honourable A. Hamilton.

the most indolent and contemptible on earth. Their average height is about 4½ to 5 feet. There are no tall Malays in these regions. A square head, with long, lank, black hair, a sullen hang-dog look, a short stumpy figure, high cheek-bones, and a retreating forehead,—an old Malay is as near an approach to the " missing link " as can be found. In character the North Bornean Malays are cowardly and servile. Devoid of all spirit or enterprise, they are content to live in their old way until their " pile dwellings " fall down upon them. The women do all the house-work and most of the field-work also. The curse of the Malays is their confirmed idleness. The Labuan coroner told me that he recently held an inquest on the body of a little child who fell into a ditch and was drowned, while a Malay sat on the bank chewing betel, too lazy to get up and help the little one out of the water.

A country Malay's house is better kept, perhaps, than his town home. It stands as a rule in a small cocoanut plantation, built on high piles, the rooms being fourteen or fifteen feet from the ground. The whole of the exterior is made of dried leaves of the nipa-palm, sown together with split rattans, and supported on a framework of wood. The interior is lined with roughly-cut planks.[3] The entrance to the house is up a flight of creaky steps, which leads to the verandah, a favourite seat of the family. Here the grandmother sits all day chewing her betel or smoking her long roko. The mother is out in the fields, digging or pruning the fruit and vegetables. One Malay " lady," who lived close to my lodging in Labuan, was in the habit of

[3] The roof is made of attaps, which form an excellent protection against the constant heavy seas.

spending her days "pig hunting" (i.e. wild boar hunting) with a clumsy old musket. She recently got into trouble for shooting a neighbour's cow instead of the boar she was after. Since then her friends evidently doubt her capacity as "a sport." The musket has disappeared.

A KLING.
(*Drawn by Helen H. Hatton. From a Photograph by Frank Hatton.*)

The Klings are by far the finest type of natives in Labuan. They are rather darker in complexion than the Malays, and are on the whole a sturdier and finer-looking race of people. The accompanying illustration is a portrait of my Kling *syce* or stableman. It is from a photograph. I had much difficulty in persuading the subject to let me take a picture of him, as he said it was wicked. But "*backsheech*" induced him to overlook the sin. When, some days afterwards, I showed him a print of himself, he merely asked if it was intended for him, and did not express any surprise or astonishment at all, although it must have been the first time he had ever seen his own face.

The Chinese do the greater portion of the trade in Labuan, and nine out of ten of them are not too honest, especially the boys, who come to be engaged as servants. They have a kind of "trades' union" or secret society, whose orders they must obey. If the society forbids a boy to accept a certain sum per month, he cannot choose but obey, as any boy who fights against the society is very soon worried into submission.

II.

Bungalow life in Labuan is pleasant for a while, but soon becomes monotonous. The bungalow in which I lived was built on piles, and stood about four feet from the ground. A large verandah ran round three sides of the house, which was almost surrounded with tall cocoanut-trees. In front the verandah "expanded" into a kind of open room—that is, a room without walls—and this is the pleasantest place to sit in in all eastern houses. One large room served the purpose of dining, drawing, and writing room. This was about sixty feet long, and thirty feet wide, and had no less than eight doors in it. The following is a plan of it, and may be taken as a general idea of the familiar bungalows of Singapore and the Straits Settlements.

THE BUNGALOW AT LABUAN: A QUIET CORNER.

Drawn by Helen H. Hatton, from a photograph by Frank Hatton.

To face page 124.

PLAN OF HOUSE IN LABUAN.

During the monsoon season a splendid breeze could be got by opening the numerous doors. All cooking is done out of the bungalow in the cook's offices, built forty or fifty yards away, and the food is carried in by servants. The rooms marked "bath-room" in the plan are merely little cellars, with a tub of water in each, and a small tin can with which to pour the water over the "tubber."

During my stay at Labuan I get up as a rule at

six o'clock, and have a first breakfast, quite à la française; then go for a walk or bathe along the beach, and get back at eight to half-past eight o'clock. The thermometer, which is about 78° to 79° at six o'clock, rises to 83°, and as a rule touches 85° to 87°, or sometimes 90°, from eight o'clock to twelve o'clock. Nothing much is done between eight to ten (the most trying part of the day), except sitting down in the verandah and enjoying the cooling breeze, if in the monsoon season, or watching the sun-birds hovering over the large pink and yellow flowers that cluster round the verandah. These sun-birds are the humming-birds of the East. They are tiny creatures, richly coloured with lines of gold and yellow, brown, blue, and red. They rifle the large spreading flowers with their long beaks, and are as tame and as impudent as London sparrows.

Here, in the East, lunch or *tiffin* is taken at one o'clock, and dinner at six or seven. The most agreeable time of the day is from four until six o'clock. It is quite dark at half-past six, and the sun rises about five to half-past five in the morning.[4]

There are, as might be expected in the tropics, quantities of insects, especially in old bungalows and in the vicinity of felled wood. The carpenter bees had made their homes in my verandah and all the wooden framework was hollowed out by these remark-

---

[4] Colonel Harington tells me that Singapore merchants have breakfast at 8.30 to 9, a most substantial meal with, generally, claret, hock, &c. They lunch at 1—another substantial meal, at which the "sparkling wine of France" very often appears; and after office-hours they drive back to their houses in the environs of the town, and a regular dinner is served at about 7.30.

able insects. Some of them measured at least three inches from wing to wing. The wings are beautifully coloured with iridescent tints, and the noise one of the creatures makes during its flight is like that of twenty humming-bees rolled into one. The mason wasp, an extraordinary creature (which looked as if it was carrying a valise by its tail), had been equally industrious in building its house upon the verandah roof. Occasionally this ponderous insect will make

THE MASON WASP.

its nest in one's bedroom; and bats have a habit of hanging by their legs all day from the ceilings, and disporting themselves at night. Little green, insect-eating lizards run like flies on the ceiling in pursuit of that worst and most troublesome of pests, the *mosquito*. These insects are sometimes so numerous in the bungalow, and cluster in such quantities, that the white wood is black with them. Hunting mosquitoes at night under one's mosquito curtains, with a candle and a damp cloth, is one of the exciting preludes to sleep in Bornean waters. Many an hour I have spent in this manner, slaughtering the buzzing little demons, and wondering for what special purpose such insects are created. I have mentioned the most common of the insects which infest houses in Labuan; among the rarer ones are large spiders, five or six inches across their extended legs; an occasional centipede, large moths,[5] various kinds of beetles, which fly in the room at night and put out the candles in an objectionable, if not alarming, manner.

One of the pleasantest and coolest places in Labuan is Tanjong Kubong, or Coal Point, on the north-east side of the island. Here coal-mining operations on an extensive scale were formerly conducted; here are four seams of coal, and a most expensive plant is on the ground; but the apparatus, machinery, buildings, and engines are now all going to ruin. At one time the mines were leased to the Oriental Coal Company of London and Leith at a yearly rental of 1000*l.* In 1876 as much as 5800 tons were turned out; and in 1877 a larger output than this was made. In 1878 the colliery was given up, the miners were sent away, the Europeans left the place, and now, in 1881, jungle covers a large portion of the houses and plant. The great drawback to successful mining was water;

---

[5] Colonel Harington writes, "The moths are marvellous. I wonder if Frank kept any of the specimens we got at Labuan: one, a beautiful fawn-coloured moth, had a wonderful luminous eye, the colour of a fine ruby." A specimen of this moth and a number of remarkable beetles came home among some other curious things, but more or less damaged by the damp of the tropical atmosphere, which had penetrated even into tin-lined cases and trunks. The accompanying illustration shows the moth referred to. Its two wings measure six inches across. The beetle in front of the box is about the size of a canary.

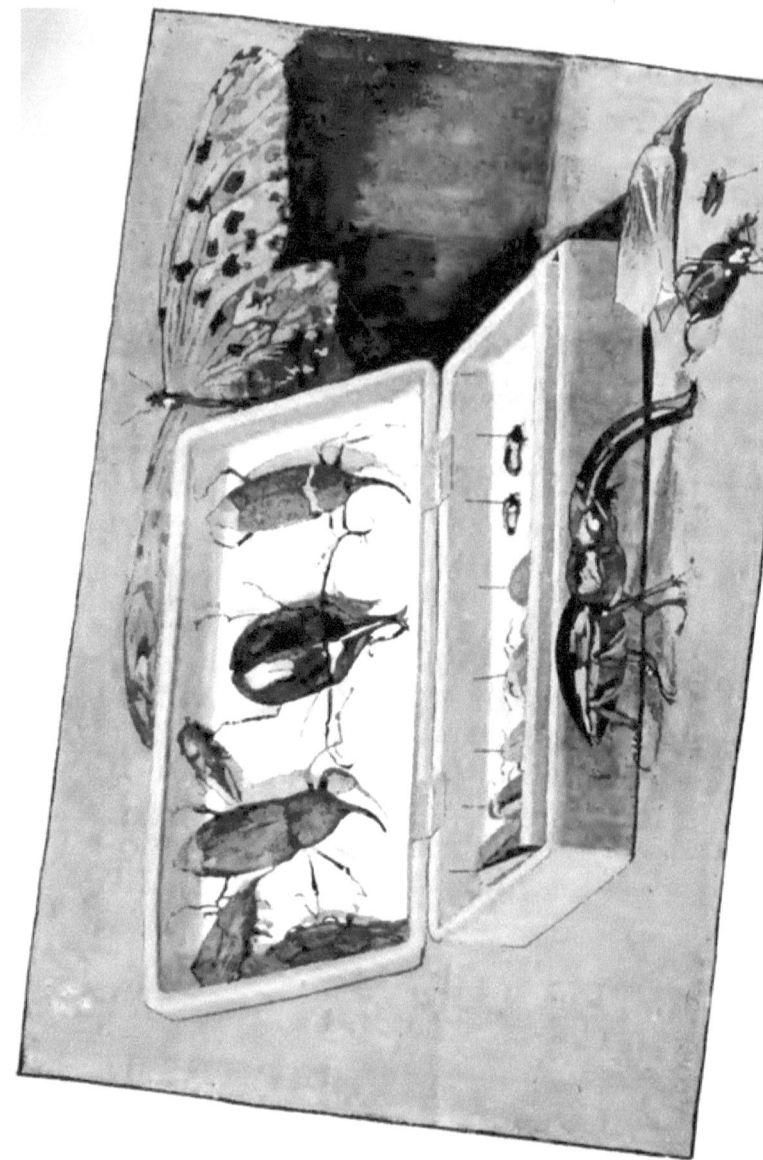

BORNEAN MOTHS AND BEETLES.

Drawn from one of Frank Hatton's collecting-boxes by Helen H. Hatton.

although the mine had, I am told, only two 14-inch lifts to combat this difficulty. It was proposed, when the pits were in full swing, to make nine miles of railway through dense jungle to Labuan, to convey the coal, instead of bringing it round the coast in lighters, as had previously been done; and, indeed, a tunnel was commenced through one of the tree-covered

THE DESERTED COLLIERY WORKS AT LABUAN.
(*From a Sketch by Frank Hatton. Drawn by Helen H. Hatton.*)

hills, and was carried within eight feet of completion, when the ruling powers at home sent out orders to abandon the works. Traction engines were also tried along roads on which there was no possibility or probability of their ever running. It is a melancholy thing to see a deserted pit at any time; but here, in these out-of-the-way regions, where labour is so scarce and transport so expensive, it is very depressing to see thousands and thousands of pounds' worth of gear rusting and decaying away, with tall ferns and great weeds growing out of long-silent boilers and disused cylinders.[6]

### III.

Of course Coal Point pits have their "presiding genius." An old workman,[7] who used to be foreman when the mines were at work, remains to "keep things in order." He takes a melancholy pleasure in cutting down a few of the weeds, which are fast concealing the railway metals; and now and then he cleans down the locomotive—his special care. He spends all his day wandering about the pits, just as if they were at work, and comes home to his house at night, after "putting things to rights," as he used to do. He is very glad to take one round the works, and will point out where some European workmen were housed, where the manager lived in "that there house on the hill." He has lived among Malays so long that he has forgotten a great deal of his own language. He lives like a native, and speaks Malay like one. I was taking one or two photographs of Coal Point, and I took his picture; he said I was the first sun-artist that had ever visited the place.

There is a great deal of "wild pig shooting" to be had round Coal Point. Recently I went out for the first time on a very dark night after pigs. Captain H., the "genius of the pit," and I crept quietly towards some uncleared jungle at about eight o'clock with our rifles ready loaded. As we came up to a noted "pig

---

[6] Colonel Harington appends this note: "I never saw so sad a sight of *days gone by and wasted work* as Coal Point presented the day Frank and I went over there on our first visit."

[7] This was Mr. Smith, who afterwards joined the Company and accompanied Frank on his first expeditions.

run," we heard the grunters tearing away the grass and routing about the ground. The utmost caution and silence is necessary on these expeditions, as the pigs can scent any one approaching a long way off, and, when once startled, they run at a great pace. When we had crawled within seventy or eighty yards of the place, we stretched ourselves flat on the grass, and waited with our rifles full cock. The mosquitoes worried me dreadfully. I managed, after a time, however, to get into a pretty comfortable position, and eventually I went to sleep. I had been dozing I suppose half an hour, when the report of rifles woke me up. My two friends had just fired, and the pig, a huge brute, almost as big as a donkey, and covered with white mud, lay struggling in the road. We had good bacon for a long time afterwards, and in honour of the active part I did *not* take in the work I was awarded the tusks as trophies.

Birds are plentiful in Labuan. Green and grey pigeon, together with an enormous fruit pigeon and the gaudy-feathered nicobar pigeon; snipe, golden plover, sand-pipers, rails, hornbills, white cranes or "padi-birds," frigate birds, several kinds of hawk, starlings, and hundreds of other birds are to be got in quantities. The most characteristic day-bird is the Java sparrow, a pretty little light grey fellow, with a red beak and a black ring round his neck. At night a peculiar bird with a "chuck-chuck," very like that of a lizard, comes out. It is called the goat-sucker, and the natives are much afraid of it; they look upon it, as we do on a raven, as a bird of ill-luck.[a]

---

[a] "The wonderful king-fisher," writes Colonel Harington, "deserves a place in this list of birds. There are, I believe, about thirteen different sorts—some quite gorgeous in their splendour of plumage."

Snakes and alligators are the most dangerous of our local specimens of animated nature. I was walking on the beach with my gun at Coal Point a short time back, and being tired I sat down under a great banyan-tree. A group of monkeys were chattering at me about fifty yards away. It is surprising how familiar monkeys will become with you, if you take no notice of them, and remain quiet. They seem to be daring each other to approach you, and grin and chatter at you. One knowing little fellow came within ten yards of me, showed his teeth, grinned, and then ran back, screaming, to his companions. I was watching this little comedy, when, happening to look up into the tree under which I was sitting, I saw a large boa constrictor, about eight or ten feet long, coiled up above my head. It was the first time I had ever seen a big snake outside the Zoological Gardens in London. I raised my gun and fired. The shot took effect in the middle of the reptile's body, and it uncoiled itself. I pulled the second trigger of my shot gun, and then reloaded. The snake dropped on the sand, twisting and twining itself about, evidently, poor wretch, in pain. It still, however, had life enough left to make for me. I took steady aim at its head, and fired both charges, one after the other. The monster was now almost torn in two; but still both the head and tail continued to twist and move for ten minutes afterwards, and the mouth opened and shut for even a longer time.

Labuan was once a very unhealthy place. Fever carried off a man a day here, but since the jungle has been cleared, the climate has much improved, and fever is very rare now. The jungle was all burned down some few years ago during a very long drought. The devastated portion presents a weird and miserable sight, enormous trunks rising eighty or one hundred feet perfectly bare, some even without a branch on them. These tree-pillars cover the interior of the island. The undergrowth has struggled up again now; it consists of tall ferns and bushes, in which the big brown jungle-hen finds a congenial retreat.

The natives are very fond of music. They make large tambourines by stretching sheep or pig skin very tightly over a wooden frame. The sound given out by one of these resembles both in tone and volume that of a kettle-drum. Each tambourine has a different note. The other favourite instrument is a series of eight or ten strips of glass, supported at each end; these are struck with a wooden hammer. Although the natives have no idea of tune, their music is not destitute of melody, and they keep time capitally. They will sometimes sit up all night playing their two instruments, and producing on them their one tune. Sound is carried an immense distance in Bornean waters, and it is quite strange and wild to hear these monotonous strains of Malay music when wending your way homewards over some lonely path at night.

Three steamers constantly visit Labuan. The *Cleator* runs between Singapore, Labuan, and Brunei, the "city of lake dwellings." She is a vessel of about 300 tons, and at present this forms the only regular communication between the world and Labuan, though the expected requirements of British North Borneo will, it is said, soon see other steamers plying to and fro. The *Royalist*, a vessel of about 250 tons, runs between Singapore, Labuan, Sandakan (on the east coast of Borneo), and the distant and little-known islands of Sulu. This ship is, however, not at all regular, and is sometimes away for months together. The *Far East* is a little vessel which has steamed about these little-known and less-frequented seas for many years, making Labuan her headquarters. She runs from that island up to Borneo, sometimes to Sulu and Celebes, and sometimes goes far inland up one of those grand rivers whose sources have still to be discovered and described. It is surprising how few vessels come into Bornean waters. I stayed a week at Coal Point a short time back, and during that time not a single sail came in sight. Months sometimes elapse without even a sail appearing between "the vast expanse of sea and sky.

There are often very brilliant sunsets in the far East. I noticed a most impressive effect at Labuan. The sun was setting in the west. The sky was tinted with brilliant lines of gold, and blue, and green; the moon pale, and giving apparently no light, had risen in the south-east. Right under the moon appeared a cloud illuminated with a silvery light. In singular contrast to the hot red glow in the west was this cool yellow light, which showed in the east. The sea was a deep green from the reflected sunset, and on the distant coast of Borneo a dark cloud hung heavily; lightning was visible at intervals, and the far-off thunder rumblings gave signal of an approaching storm.[9]

[9] Colonel Harington adds, "The sunsets were peculiarly wonderful in those regions—not the monotonous regulation sunsets one sees in India, but veritable transformation scenes, each evening producing a different effect. The most remarkable exhibition of light I ever saw out there was one evening in Gaya Bay, watching the '*sunset-light*' on Kina Balu. An artist would be amply repaid by visiting that wonderful land."

## II.

## ON THE SEQUATI AND KURINA RIVERS.[1]

First impressions of exploration—A novel experience—Making a Malay house—Working and watching—Digging for oil—" Orang Dusuns "—Astonishing the natives—Flying foxes—Exploring and sporting—Tropical vegetation—Lost in the jungle—Pangeran Brunei—A sick chief—Trading with the Dusuns—" Never seen a white man before "—Searching for coal—Christmas-Day on the equator—The slave question—Protecting a fugitive—An anxious night—The New Year and a dark outlook—A Dusun house—" I was simply a nine days' wonder "—Keeping away evil spirits—" Well, well, sir ! "—Native women at work—Strange and picturesque scenes—Discoveries of coal and iron—Riding on buffaloes—Tropical floods—A perilous situation—Geology of the Binkoka district.

I.

*Nov. 19th*, 1881.—Started from Abai with Captain Harington and Mr. Witti, in the steam-launch *Enter-*

[1] Only two of Frank Hatton's original diaries have reached England. They are the first and last, and neither of them is complete. The first is written evidently from notes, and is reprinted here as far as it goes, the last entry being January 2nd, 1882. I take the remainder of the record from the author's report to the Company. The last diary is in pencil, and contains memoranda, which shows that he was in the habit of perfecting his diaries when he returned to his station, wherever it might be. The personal details in the first diary prove that there were many things entered in his diaries which he did not, of course, report to the Governor, and this was part of the material which he would have worked up in the volume he intended to write on his

*prise*, at six o'clock; with Singapore sampan, Sarawak prahu, and Residential boat in tow.

Arrived at Sequati River at twelve o'clock, and after some difficulty in getting the goods landed, owing to a heavy sea on the bar, we unloaded everything on the sand-reef at the junction of the Sequati and Kurina

return home. This first diary I received after his death. It was found in the house he occupied at Kudat. I am convinced that other diaries exist, and there is some little hope that they may yet be forthcoming. The reports sent to the Company were in the shape of long and comprehensive extracts from his diaries, and were all written in his own hand. I give them complete as they stand. If they lack colour here and there, the reason is that they were intended to have a semi-official character. Mere personal reflections, notes of home, wayside incidents of travel and such like details would therefore be eliminated. These details would be left for publication in the book. I have endeavoured to at least suggest some of these outside incidents in the special information which I have obtained from his first comrade, Colonel Harington (see footnote, p. 120), and from the traveller who saw him on his last expedition. So far as the notes of the four expeditions herein described are concerned, I have not interfered with the text, except to give headings to the chapters, take out some of the dates, so as to carry on the narrative without the formality of the day-to-day entries, and to omit in the first and last diaries masses of mere technical figures, solar observations, and chemical and other dry scientific notes which the publishers regard as details rather for the archives of the Bornean Government than for a book of biography and travel. I remember going up to the offices in the City to see Frank's first report and being keenly touched with the perfection of the work. It was a chapter of exploration and diplomacy, a scientific and geological essay, illustrated with a careful map, sections of an oil-well, and other notable data. The slave incident (described at page 159) was regarded by the Governor and the Company as one which reflected highly upon the sound and cool judgment of the young explorer. Indeed, from first to last, I never visited the headquarters of the Company in London without being met with some compliment, official and otherwise, that had been paid to Frank, both in the public and private letters of the Governor, or in messages from travellers or officials who had seen or heard of him.

rivers. It rained in torrents all the afternoon, and getting my tent up on a piece of high ground was a matter of great discomfort and trouble.[2] The men,

[2] Colonel Harington writes to me his recollections of this trip to Sequati and the opening of Frank's work in Borneo. Prefacing his notes with a tribute to his companion's bravery and "philosophic cheerfulness" under all circumstances, he says:—

"During the time I was at Abai inspecting the place as to its suitability for the headquarters of the constabulary, Frank Hatton arrived in the *Royalist* on the 19th of November, 1881, and disembarked. His object was to consult with Witti, and then go on to the Sequati River to inspect and report on the spring of petroleum discovered there by Witti. During the few days before starting for the Sequati we made several excursions into the surrounding country, which, unlike many other parts of North Borneo, is open, free from jungle, and covered in places with the luxuriant Lalang grass. Frank was delighted with the beauty of the scenery, and my favourite view from the hill opposite the station across the valley and river up to the crowning heights of Kina Balu especially delighted him. We said that it was worth while for any good landscape artist to come out and paint a few of the views—sunrise and sunset in particular being perfect, and I strongly recommend it to some man with a 'worthy brush.' Frank was very keen to get to 'work,' however, and so having finished all necessary preparations, we set off in the launch *Enterprise* for the scene of his investigations—our party being Witti, Frank, and I, with Smith, the man of 'underground knowledge,' and a squad of some dozen natives to act as guards and labourers. A fine day and smooth sea, and we quickly steamed the thirty odd miles to the mouth of the Sequati River from Abai. We landed in the Abai station-boat, and set to work to pick a camping-ground and land all the stores, tents, and gear, and then at noon got our breakfasts. To our disgust, about half-way through the meal, down came the rain in the determined way it has in those regions, and continued off and on all day; and what was worse, a strong wind set in from the west, kicking up a heavy sea that didn't promise a pleasant return passage for Witti and me. We all 'worked like blacks,' and by the afternoon had set up Frank's tent, put up a shelter for Smith and the men, and managed to arrange a protection and covering for the stores, &c. Witti, Smith, and I, being old stagers, "growled" a good deal over the ill-luck of getting such an inoppor-

after the steam-launch left, managed to fix up themselves well with "kajangs," and to light a good fire.

tune soaking ; but to Frank, in his 'gay' youth, the whole adventure was what might be called a 'lark,' and in spite of dripping garments and soaked tent and stores, he was beaming with delight on his first step of 'life in the bush.' I got his canteen out and cooked him a 'Gold Coast' stew. I used to superintend the kitchen of our 'three-officer-company mess' on the march to Coomassie in 1874, and remembered what a good thing a camp stew used to be. To Frank this was intensely interesting and amusing, and I found him a ready pupil in the art. In spite of the pouring rain, which seemed determined to spoil all our cooking, we prepared quite a nice little feast, to which we all did full justice, as any one can fancy—a real ducking being a tremendous appetizer. Having finished our dinner, and wound up the repast with a 'dhrop of the crathur,' just to keep off the damp, Witti and I prepared to return to our ship, and after a hard row got off to her, waving adieux to the 'petroleurs' we had left dripping, but cheery, on shore. By this time a heavy sea was running, and we had to steam against it in the teeth of the wind, and very bad weather we made of it. At times the little launch positively stood still, and seemed to shake her head at the opposing elements. It was close on 3 a.m. before we got back to Abai, for besides making the very slowest way against wind and sea, we unluckily, in the dark, ran past the mouth of the Abai harbour, and did not discover our mistake until we had gone on over two miles. Luckily, Witti was an excellent sailor in every sense, and we got in without mishap. Anything like the knocking about we had I have never experienced. Amidst the whistling wind and drenching rain I wondered how the Sequati party was getting on, and whether the tent had given in, and if Frank and company were searching the neighbouring bush for their scattered properties and seeking shelter there from the elements. However, we afterwards heard that they had had a fair night, and had made much better weather of it on shore than we had at sea. The bush at the mouth of the Sequati River is of the low mangrove order, backed up farther inland by the regular forest jungle and the low hills, covered with Lalang grass, that stretch right away to the mountain range. The mouth of the river is protected from the westerly weather by a small *red-earthed* point jutting out into the sea, the entrance to the river being covered by a bar. The passage in, winds through rocks, making

There was a tremendous sea at the time on the bar, and, as night drew on, this sea increased. My sensations on camping out for the first time on a wild coast, far from all civilization, were very curious. The picturesque natives, with their swarthy complexions, seated round their fires, the wild breakers roaring on the beach fifty yards away from my tent, the sound of insects in the adjacent jungle, all these things made up an impressive and, to me, novel experience. My policemen killed two centipedes, and the insects were rather a nuisance. The strata on the beach, I noticed, dipped at a very high angle. I was rather disappointed with the quantity of petroleum floating on the river, but a good quantity of gas seemed to be bubbling up at the spring (? $CO_2$ c$H_4$ s$H_2$). Smith found oil extending from strata just above the oil in the river. This night the men did not want to watch. I made them take two hours apiece, and after a little difficulty they acquiesced.

The next day was Sunday. I got up at five o'clock; the morning very fine. I felt most uncomfortable in my tent. All the canvas was hanging down, owing to the ropes giving way. Started Smith and the men making a house the first thing in the morning. The men were felling wood all day. The heat was intense, and at noon the thermometer stood at 92° in my tent. The men worked well, and by two o'clock I had a good

a rather picturesque spot,'the break of the sea over the bar and rocks varying the eternal monotony of the lone sea-shore, and, in spite of all the disagreeables, I felt sure Frank would be pleased. Shortly after this little excursion, I returned to Labuan, having been summoned to meet Colonel Crossman, R.E., who was expected out to report on the coast defences of Borneo."

"atap" roofed, "kajanged" walled house up. It was interesting to watch the way the men built it. Two large stakes, twenty feet long, were driven firmly into the ground, and then four shorter ones, one on each side of the main poles. At the top of the two short poles a cross-pole was fixed, and tied firmly in its place with split rattans. Two more cross-poles were then fixed on, and some split bamboos tied on the outside of the kajangs and fixed on with rattans. With ataps roofed on well, the house was quite home-like and comfortable away out in the wilds of Borneo. I had a flagstaff fixed up close to the house, and the "Sabah flag" run up. The men managed to make themselves very comfortable by six o'clock, and after this I went for a stroll along the beach. I noticed numerous tracks of very large monkeys, which Smith said were "orang-utan" tracks; a large flock of brown eagles flew over us at sundown. I had the "head man" up, and gave him some sardines, tea, and milk, at which he was much pleased. But he pointed out to me that it was impossible for the men to work at night (i.e. watch) and in the day also. On thinking over the matter, I determined to dispense with the sentinel, as all hands would be required to make the "oil dock." I therefore told him that it did not matter watching. On coming back from a stroll, however, at eight o'clock, I found "Tulis," one of the best of the coolies I got from Labuan, had put a fellow, one of the Tampassuk policemen, on guard, and he was standing under the flagstaff with his Snider rifle. He saluted me, and I told him that I did not want any one to sit up and watch. "Tulis," however, said that this was a new country, filled with

"Muruts," "Dusuns," "Bajows," that the point was frequented by "Sulu Pirates," and that the men were afraid of people coming in the night. I showed him my pistols, guns, &c., and told him we would watch, and after this the men quieted down. The utter loneliness of the sea-shore for miles and miles was depressing, although we sighted three prahus to-day on the extreme horizon.

*Nov.* 21.—Got up at six o'clock and started Smith and all the men cutting trees to make a dock round the main oil spring.[3] The tide was quite out, and it was raining a little. I had a hole dug, one foot deep by two feet wide and long, at the main oil spring. Oil bubbled up freely. There was a thickness of four inches of oil floating on mud and water saturated with oil, in a few minutes. In five hours a double row of stakes was planted all round the oil, but as it was raining in torrents, and as the tide was coming in, I stopped the men working at eleven o'clock. I gave them a dose of quinine all round. It rained heavily all day, so that nothing could be done in the afternoon. I went up into the jungle above the oil spring, but was unsuccessful in finding a spring or any section. The whole place is densely wooded, and it was with the greatest difficulty I made my way along. There is about four feet of superficial yellow clay overlying the sandstone. The sandstone itself I should think was of recent origin, as it contains bands of blue clay in which fossils of tertiary age have been found. It is also veined through and through with oxide of iron, in bands and in concretionary nodules.

[3] At this place a plan for investigating the oil was drawn in detail and explained.

In many places the weathering of this ferric oxide has stained the sand yellow and red. "Pockets" of blue clay also occur. The sandstone is quite destitute of organic remains: perhaps the fossils have been destroyed by oxide of iron. I took samples of the rock along the Kurina to-day, for about 100 yards on the left bank; and in doing so I came upon a very thin seam of impure coal (about an inch thick). I also observed that the shale (at the foot of the rocks on the left bank of the Kurina) for about 20 feet, contained oil. The length of the dock round the "Sequati" main oil spring is 20 feet by 18 feet 3 inches. This is the richest portion of the shale.

It rained up till eight o'clock to-day, so no work could be done. The tide was very high. If it rains much more, I am afraid the river will swell and overflow its banks. The boring machine was got in order, oiled and covered up to-day, and some more kajangs put on my house as the rain was coming in heavily. Just before dinner there was an alarm, "a prahu is coming," but on looking out with my glass I made it out to be a Nipa palm floating ashore.

II.

There was a large crane standing out in the sea when I left my hut at six the next morning. It rained most of the day, but towards evening it cleared up. I told Smith to make a square dock round the main oil spring, and when he had puddled with clay up to high-water mark, to sink a pit. This was begun to-day. The stakes are in and well filled up with green boughs. The clay is near at hand, a ferruginous clay very fit for the purpose. The pit is now three feet deep and the oil is bubbling up very freely. I propose to tap the shale, that is strike the shale, and then run a level under the water to the other springs close at hand. It is very difficult and hard work, as everything must be done at low water in the morning.

I had a hole drilled at the outcrop of the seam of lignite on the left bank of the so-called Kurina River. [I learnt to-day that both of these rivers are called Sequati. Two hours' rowing takes one to the swamp in which the Sequati proper rises; that is the Sequati in which the oil occurs. I rowed up this river for about two miles to-day. The whole country is a gigantic swamp. Plenty of Nipa palms. Met with no people, but there were stakes for fishing fixed up, showing that the inhabitants do come down the river on fishing excursions.] I put a charge of powder in. On exploding with the magnetic-electro exploder I found that the seam is of no account. Only three small veins of half an inch thick. The sandstone is full of this black carbonaceous matter, which indeed is neither a true coal nor a true lignite. Pockets of this substance are to be found in the sandstone, as also pockets of a blue plastic clay, and nodules of oxide of iron. Wherever water runs out of the sandstone from the side of a hill or elsewhere, stalactites of oxide of iron are found, which consist of almost pure Fer. Ox. I took a set of specimens of the local rock to-day, and two photographs of the place[1]—one of my hut and one of the boring machine. Everything gets very mouldy, and living on a sand-heap is not pleasant.

---

[1] These and other photographs have not yet been found.

This evening one of the men shot a large bat, called "flying fox," or Cubong, by the natives.

The pit is now eight feet down. The dock is eighteen feet by twenty feet, all of which had to be puddled with clay and leaves. The pit is six feet square and eight feet deep, timbered with what few planks we have, and the rest with trees. The rock is now a grey sandstone saturated with oil, and we have only one pick and one shovel, as the men cannot use my boring picks and shovels. The work is therefore very difficult, although good progress is made. The oil bubbles up well now, water and a little sulphurated hydrogen come up. Smith took a few pieces of coal out to-day. I think we shall shortly strike coal. I made a blow-pipe examination of the chloritic mineral that Witti gave me, and found it to be anhydrous silicate of magnesia and iron, with much carbonate of lime. Therefore olivine with calcic carbonate. Smith also took some hard pieces of rock out of the pit, which I shall examine to-morrow. I went up the so-called "Kurina" river to-day for about a mile and a half. It is a fine wide river lined with trees. Not very deep.

When we were all over at the pit to-day, about four o'clock, my boy Abdul cried out, "Orang Dusuns," seized his rifle, and rushed out. All I could see from over the water was two spears outside the door of our hut. Smith and two or three of our men jumped into a sampan and pushed for the other side. I seized an oar and ran up. Two inoffensive Dusuns were standing trembling outside my door with their spears leant up against the wall. We asked them what they wanted. They said they were out fishing, and where was the Captain? After a little I made friends with them, showed them some pictures, photographs, a looking-glass, my guns, Winchester rifle, and gave them a shock from my magnetic electro machine, which astonished them very much. They talked together, examined my clothes, and the constant repetition of "Orang puti" (white men) told us how astonished they were to find us here. They said they would come back in two days with eggs, fowls, &c. I gave them some buttons and a box of matches, which they liked very much. They were dressed in coarse blue "Dusun" cloth breeches and jacket; a basket slung at their backs, a parong round their waists, and a spear, with a wooden point protector, in their hands. They shook hands with me a long time, and seemed very sorry to go. My boy told me afterwards that there were three men, only one ran away on seeing a man with a gun ready to fire.

Thursday, the 24th, was a heavy, cloudy day. It cleared up after a time, but still remained all day heavy, cloudy, and showery. This is the fourth day's work, and the pit is now eight feet deep. The oil is coming out in little streams from the sandstone. There is no iron in the rock through which the pit is being sunk, nor any iron concretions. Pockets of "Brown coal" or lignite are found at intervals. I examined a specimen to-day. It was saturated with oil; it also gave off much oil and gas itself. It burns without smoke. I secured specimens of the "oil shale or sandstone" to-day, and intend to examine them to-morrow. The strata through which we are digging dips at the same angle (i.e. 40°) as that exposed at the mouth of the Sequati River. One of the men brought me a very fine

L

beetle to-day. The oil is coming out of the sandstone at I should say five gallons in twelve hours now, and each foot of increased depth increases the supply of oil.

### III.

I shot three "flying foxes" this evening. The men from Tampassuk said they would not work to-morrow (Friday) as they regard this as a holiday or Sunday in Tampassuk. Smith and I utilized the day therefore for an exploring and sporting expedition. Two men came with us, one carried my rifle and some lunch. Altogether we were a formidable party. Four men, each with his gun, two large Colt's revolvers, and two swords, made up our list of arms. All the men came out to see us start, and about half-past six we trudged merrily out of camp. The weather was charming, and as we walked along the smooth sandy beach the fast-rising sun cast long shadows across our path. The beach for six miles is unequalled. About 100 yards, at low water, of perfectly smooth firm sand without an obstacle or obstruction of any kind. Tall cazurina trees, something like Scotch firs, line the shore, and just behind these the dense untravelled jungle stretches away inland. The waves break with a splendid roar along the beach, and this is the only sound to be heard on these lonely coasts. As we walked along we saw numerous tracks of wild cattle, wild boars, deer, and tortoise, but never caught sight of any game at all. The native with us said that night was the time to come out, so we promised ourselves good sport on the morrow. There was one old grey crane that kept standing in the water in front of us about half a mile away and letting us get within 500 yards of him, and then flying away. He was an awfully sharp old bird; it was impossible to get a shot at him, so after several unsuccessful stalks we paid no further attention to him. We crossed several small streams, and on one of

ELK'S-HORN FERN, AND NATIVE DUSUNS.

these there were half a dozen huts thatched with nipa palm leaves roughly plaited together. The hovels were about four feet high in front from top to ground; the roof was supported on stakes, and the floor of tree trunks cut in half. The houses were open in front and at the sides, and the natives (Dusuns) had evidently been engaged in salt-making. Their "boiling-pans," made of the bark of a palm-tree, lay strewn about, but the place had been deserted for some time. We continued our walk along towards a point which we had seen in the dim distance at starting. It is down on the map Kaliga Point; there is a good-sized river here not marked on the map. Smith reminded me that we were walking now where "white men had probably never trod before," and of course I was suitably impressed. Just at the point the rock changes, the sandstone no longer containing oxide of iron, which extends from Labuan all up the coasts of Borneo to the Sequati River; at Kaliga Point the rock is a grey limestone containing veins of quartz, and overlaid by a ferruginous, yellow clay. This rock extends to the base of the promontory which ends in Sampanmangio Point. There is another good-sized river here, and across this river the rock appeared to be sandstone again. A regular series of sandstones and limestones, the sandstones being of more recent origin than the limestones, would seem to be the geological condition of things. Both these rocks contain much oxide of iron, the sandstone being interstratified with a compact blue clay.

### IV.

At the point we met two men and a woman who were making salt. On our approach they all made off, but after much coaxing they screwed up courage enough to come and talk with us. They spoke in Dusun to our man, and he asked them who was their chief, and where he lived. They pointed round the Limestone Point (Kaliga?), and said that Pangeran Brunei was their head man. We made up our minds to see Pangeran

Brunei, so off we set again. Instead of keeping to the coast, we made a "short cut" over the hill, through a native jungle path, which is, as a rule, the bed of some mountain stream, with here and there a tree cut down. In our case it was not even so good as this. It was a long climb through tangled jungle; great leaves hitting one in the face, and thorns running into one's clothes and tearing one's flesh; everything dripping with water, and the sun only finding its way in here and there through the dense mass of foliage overhead. The soil was soft clay, covered with wet, dead leaves; for tropical vegetation, instead of shedding its leaves decently once a year, sheds them in small portions all the year round, and their place is supplied by new ones as the old ones drop off. Of course we got lost in the jungle; I knew we should before we went in, and, of course, no one had brought a compass. After a consultation on the best plan to be adopted for getting out, I thought I could just hear the waves breaking on the beach below us. We walked in the direction of the sound, and three quarters of an hour's climbing, slipping, and sliding brought us out on a coral beach, strewn with limestone boulders. I was surprised to see so little life in a tropical jungle. Where were the gorgeous birds, the parrots, the deer, the snakes of which I had so often read? I saw nothing at all in our jungle; and with the exception of a few monkeys and some sea birds, we saw no animal of any kind the whole day. We now sat down on a piece of driftwood on the "coral strand of Borneo," and partook of biscuits and potted meat, spreading the meat on the biscuits with our bowie knives in true backwoodsmanlike style. After a short rest and a drink, " not of water from the crystal brook," but of brandy from a flask, we started for the Pangeran's "palace." We found the place at the mouth of the river I mentioned above. It was only three Malay houses built on wooden piles, each tide washing right under the place. We went up into the Pangeran's house. The old man was ill, his son told us. But after a time the mosquito curtains in which he was lying were drawn aside, and we saw a thin, pale yellow, haggard man stretched on a bed. Two women, his wife (or at least one of them), were attending on him, and his sons and servants occupied the other parts of the room. The Pangeran was a broken-down man, a debauchee, old before his time, and evidently dying. He showed us two large swellings on his legs (which I think were tumours), and asked us if we could give him some medicine. I told him we would send him some. He spoke Malay very well, and was once, when he lived up-country, in the habit of visiting the Tampassuk Residency. The Pangeran's house was in reality only one large room; the floor made of split bamboos or rattans. Native matting was put over this; but, still, walking about was very dangerous, not only dangerous from holes through which one might drop through into the river below, but also from the low roof. I hit my head once or twice against the beams supporting the roof, and so I gave up trying to walk upright, and sat down Turkish fashion, as the people of the house were doing. The room was full of a motley collection of things. Several dozen large cakes of beeswax about a foot in diameter, stones arranged in squares for cooking, and cooking utensils of the most primitive pattern, four or five old Tower muskets, two coats of chain and plate armour, made by the Sulus, and of surprising good workmanship. Two looms for making native cloth occupied one portion of the room, and the Pangeran's daughter sat down at one of these and worked a while for our amusement. The cloth when finished is very strong, but not at all æsthetic. The colours are red, white, yellow, and black, and the cotton is grown here and dyed here also.

I now thought it was time to come to the true object of our visit, which was to borrow a prahu to sail back ten miles (the distance we had walked) to the Sequati River. At first the old man was not inclined to let us have it, but we told him that if he helped the white man, the white man would help him; and after a little talk he told us we could have a big prahu which was beached a short distance from the house. We then took our leave, and invited the Pangeran to come to Sequati. He said his son should come, but that they had only lived in their present quarters four months. They used to live inland, and they had come down here from some cause or other which we could not get out of him. It was after superhuman exertions for more than half an hour that we managed to get the heavy prahu launched, and then we only made very slow progress, as she leaked, and there was no wind. However, we rounded the point at last, and then the Pangeran's son said he would land us and let us walk back to Sequati, a walk of about six miles along a sandy beach at one o'clock in the day, with the sun blazing down upon us; loaded as we were with arms, this was not a pleasant prospect. However, nothing would induce him to bring the prahu on, as he said he would never get back. We therefore got out, waded ashore, and began our tramp. I shall never forget my sufferings. Not a drop of anything to drink, carrying a heavy rifle, walking on wet sand in which the hot sun was reflected back on one's face with twofold intensity. I trudged on steadily, the perspiration streaming from every pore. The thermometer must have been about 150° in the sun. At length I saw our flag at the station, and I arrived home at half-past three, quite tired out. Shortly after five, just as it was getting dark, the head man of the tribe of Dusuns, living up the Luru River (the river at the mouth of which Pangeran Brunei is now living), arrived with about forty of his men. They were all eager to trade. They brought eggs (of ancient date), fowls born, I should say, ten years ago, kaladi, ginger, camphor, betel, and other things which we exchanged for an old coat, brass buttons, empty bottles, and preserved meat tins. These latter articles went best, although "kain" (cloth) was what they wanted most. All the men were armed with spears, and they refused to take anything in exchange for their weapons. They were dressed in Dusun cloth, and they crowded round my hut, peeping in and examining everything with envious eyes. I invited the chief in, and Smith fed him with jam and biscuits and tea. I think he would have eaten a tin of biscuits if we had let him. He seemed also to relish tea very much. He said he had never seen a white man before; and, considering this, he did not seem much astonished. I think he was disappointed with our colour, for after our walk in the sun both Smith and I were rather brown. I had a man on guard all night, as the Dusuns seemed to take more interest than was quite necessary in our tea-things and cooking utensils. They went away and left us alone about eight o'clock, and I was not sorry to see the last of them. Several of the men went out wild-cattle shooting. They saw two cattle and a deer, but missed all three. Smith and I are going out tomorrow. It was a splendid day all day. The pit is getting on well, four men only were at work to-day, but by to-morrow I think we shall lie above high-water mark. This is the great difficulty; when we are sure of the tides we can get on quite well. I am sure we shall find coal in the hill, or at least below the oil. The point before the Luru river is composed of limestone, very impure, containing much silica and iron. Mr. Witti's green chloritic mineral, which I found out to be anhydrous silicate of magnesia and iron, also occurs there in limestone. It is a decomposing chrysolite.

*Nov.* 25.—The pit was timbered to-day up to above high-water mark. It is now ten feet deep, and eight feet high. The puddling still goes on. Much oil and water comes up through the bottom now, and I am afraid that without proper machinery we will not be able to do much. Smith and I went out wild-cattle shooting to-night. The lonely beach, with the wild breakers thundering down, the tall, gaunt trees, the silence unbroken except by the steady roll of the waves, and the whole effect was very impressive. We shot nothing, however, which was rather disappointing. The heavy tropical dew fell upon us and wet us to the skin, although the sky was quite clear and the moon shining.

*Sunday, Nov.* 26.—I am now confident that the petroleum exudes from coal seams in the clay in the sandstone. A few pieces more of first-rate coal (pockets) were taken out to-day. We had a great disappointment to-day, as the pit was again full of water. Impossible to say at present whether the tide got in, or whether the water came from below. The men I have divided into two shifts, one night and one day.

The rock from the point this side of the Ruru River is really a "calcareous sandstone," that is a quartz and ore sandstone having a cement of carbonate of lime, that is a very impure limestone.

The pit was sunk two and a half feet to-day. Three shots were tried; my machine failed twice. Why, I don't know. Some more coal was taken up to-day. There is but little water and a great deal of oil coming up, so the tide did get in last night. It has been showery to-day, and the monsoon is blowing strong. The insects and the sand are a great trouble in our little house.

v.

I went down the pit on Monday. It is about sixteen feet deep, and very dry. Timber is being put in. The shale was all laid bare to-day. It is a bed of true shale (i.e. hardened clay) saturated with petroleum. The oil is coming out of the sides of the pit in streams. The shale is about a yard wide, and is interstratified with the sandstone of the district, which is itself full of oil. All the beds down the shaft dip at the same angle as those exposed on the surface (i.e. 40° N.W. and S.W.). The "blower" which we followed down is now two or three feet up the side of the pit. It yields little oil now, as the oil is coming out all round the sides; but much gas. The gas is inflammable, burns with a slightly luminous, not smoky, flame, which is yellow on the top and blue at the base. It has but little smell. I therefore conclude that it is marsh gas ($CH_4$), $CO_2$(?), $CO$(?), and perhaps some little oil carried up mechanically. This gas probably comes from a seam of coal not far distant.

Mr. Witti, in his diary, speaking of the oil, says he went down two yards (i.e. six feet), and yet he says that he "cannot say on what that formation" (i.e. the superficial red clay) "may rest." Now at the place where Mr. Witti dug his "improvised well," there is about a foot thickness of soft river mud resting on the grey (non-ferruginous) sandstone. Had Mr. Witti sunk a hole as far as he thinks, he could not have failed to come upon this rock. Again he says, "in digging we now and then came on pieces of very massive lignite." Now we dug down ten feet and found one pocket of lignite; and at fourteen feet a small "pocket" of true coal; the whole weighing about *one ounce*. Mr. Witti says, "the clayey soil itself was then found highly bituminous for a surface extent of eighty square yards." . . . "Outside those eighty square yards no bitumen could be found." The real state of the case is that for about 100 yards the river mud on the right-hand bank contains indications of petroleum. This has probably been washed by the tides from the portion where my pit was sunk. This would not therefore give any idea of the true outcrop of the shale, which in reality has no outcrop at all. The soil in the shale has found its way up through the overlying sandstone, which has gradually become saturated. The ascent of the petroleum has also been assisted by gas, which probably finding its way up from some coal seam, carried up the petroleum mechanically. I took samples of the shale to-day, and also the sandstone for analysis. *Curious*, the absence of oxide of iron in the pit. The heading will be begun to-morrow. Had a bother with the man in the prahu to-day. He refused to give up Kajangs, he was ill also. Gave him $SO_2M_8$. Made compass survey of river to-day; finish it to-morrow. Heading going to be cut through the dip of the strata following the gas blower.

On the next day I had door-heads of mine partly put in. Sandstone and shale still yield much oil. Searching for coal, every prospect of finding it. Another pocket of lignite taken out to-day. Heading driven in three feet. I made a map of the district and got it coloured in. Prahu passed, went out to her in the Singapore Sampan. She was twenty days away from Sandakan. No rain at all; fine day and night.

*Saturday, Dec. 2nd.*—Went down the pit, the heading of which was four feet square. I stopped as the picks had cut through two feet of blue clay and come upon the bed rock again. The bed rock here is the non-ferruginous sandstone, full of oil and containing innumerable little veins of lignite. This may be the coal-seam "thinning out." I ordered the pit to be sunk ten feet deeper, or at least until we have got through the oil-bearing rock. With proper machinery to get out the shale I should think that 100 gallons of oil could be turned out daily. However, this can only be ascertained by distillation of the shale in Labuan. Both shale and oil-bearing sandstone must be tested quantitatively for percentage of petroleum. I collected some test tubes of gas which comes up in bubbles from the river-bed in the immediate neighbourhood of the shaft. The gas does (as I expected) carry up oil mechanically. It is itself a colourless, tasteless, and inodorous gas. It is inflammable, is not to any extent absorbed by potash, or bichromate of potash. It burns with a blue flame, slightly tinged with yellow. I therefore conclude that the gas is $CH_4$, ($CO_2$?) with perhaps some higher gaseous compounds of the marsh gas series, such as $C_2H_6$ or $C_3H_8$, which often exist in connection with petroleum. Marsh gas itself is a very common gas of coal-beds and bituminous deposits, so that this gas may be rising from some thick coal seam, or from the oil-bearing stratum. It rained heavily in the night, but cleared towards the morning.

*Sunday, Dec. 3rd.*—The high tide comes in to-night, and as there was water in the pit last night all hands were taken getting clay to-day. It rained heavily all the afternoon and the whole of the night. Water about five feet deep got into the pit. Everything was done to get it out, and at five o'clock this morning the pit was dry. A piece of one of the mineral resins was found to-day in the sandstone at a depth of twenty-four feet. I shall examine it at leisure. It is in a tin and marked No. 1. A most interesting thing, perhaps a new mineral; if so, call it Hattonite. One of the black men was very sick to-day, and I think he is down with fever.

## VI.

### SECOND VISIT TO SEQUATI.

*Saturday, Dec. 24th.*—Christmas Eve. It rained only a little, nothing happened. My leg was a little worse. Sighted two prahus.

*Sunday, Dec. 25th.*—Christmas Day. Very hot. I sat all day tormented with heat, bad foot, bad mouth, insects, &c. Curious sensations of a hot Christmas Day; the sun blazing down, not a breath of wind. The pit is down twenty-five feet now, and much more oil is coming up; but I am sorry to say no coal.

*Monday, Dec. 26th.*—Boxing Day. Pit down twenty-six feet. It rained in the morning. Two men went out shooting, they hit a deer, but he got away. The Dusuns came down to trade. "Kain" was again the cry, and I gave a little cloth for some eggs. Kaladi, red vegetables, in appearance something like pumpkins, they called labu; they taste like carrots and are rather pleasant. Kaladi is a root something like an artichoke, and tastes like starch. They also brought long sugar-canes, Indian corn, some sugar melons, but nothing really of any value. We took them over to the pit, and one of the boldest went down on the bucket. Most of them took pieces of stone away as mementoes.

I examined that piece of mineral from Papar. It is only *iron pyrites*. It may contain a little gold and silver, but very little. I will try it to-morrow.

I took to wearing a sarong to-day;[5] they are very comfortable and nice. A few pieces of coal were found

---

[5] The sarong is an oblong cloth; the ends sewn together make it a sort of very broad skirt or kilt. It is tightened round the waist by a few ingenious twists which practically make a belt; so that the sarong is a skirt and belt in one. The natives carry their knives in this belt. The sarong reaches below the knees. The cloth is a native production among the Dusuns. The Dyaks and Malays often have silk sarongs from China.

to-day, and the whole aspect of things looks more encouraging.

*Tuesday, Dec. 27th.*—It rained all the morning, but was very hot towards the middle of the day. Thoughts of home (provoked perhaps by the flies) possessed me for a long time. The pit is now being squared down prior to putting in timber. The sea is very calm. I must take what photos I want to-morrow, as I propose to start on Saturday. The time flies here in the East; perhaps it is monotony, although monotony should make time leaden wings.

*Wednesday, Dec. 28th.*—About the middle of the day a woman slave from Pangeran Brunei came in a pitiful state to seek refuge. She was wounded and bruised in several places, and she said that if we gave her back she would be killed. What could I do? I could not send her back to a brutal Pangeran to be killed, so I decided to keep her, and send her to Tampassuk. There was also a general petition for me to keep her, as the men said she would be killed if she were given back. We await the men coming to fetch her. Shortly after four o'clock two men came along the beach, armed with finely-made krisses. I called to them, and they came into my hut. One was Pangeran Brunei's son, an Ilaum. Pangeran Brunei is from Brunei; but his wife is an Ilaum. They said the runaway woman was their father's slave, and that she had been stealing beeswax. I asked the woman if she had; of course she said no. One never knows whom to believe, as truthfulness does not form a part of a native's character. I had it explained to them that white men would not harbour thieves, but that I was not in a position to send the woman away as I did not know the facts of the case. I would consult the woman's own wishes. If she wanted to go back I was perfectly willing, but I would not allow her to be taken away by force. The woman was very much afraid she would be given back. She said she would rather stay with us if we cut her up, than go back with the Pangeran's son. The truth was, I believe, that as soon as they got the poor creature out of sight, they would have cut her head off, and thrown her body either into the jungle or into the sea. Who would ever have heard of it again? No one! Not a soul ever comes this way, and many atrocities must be committed by despotic and tyrannical chiefs. The chief in question is he we went to see during our last stay at Siquati, and who lent us the prahu. I thought of this, and so gave the son some yards of cloth and a tin of Swiss milk. His father is very ill, and I advised the son to take him to Labuan. The man seemed to have but a very vague idea of where Labuan was, so I suppose the old fellow without medicine will die. The men went away about eight o'clock; they said if the woman would stay they supposed she must. Our people were afraid that they had a lot of men in ambush, and that they would come along in the middle of the night and carry the woman off. I was tormented all night with this, and, as I lay with my hand on my revolver, I fell asleep, and had the most awful dreams of rivers of blood, murders, battles, all curiously linked together by a strange story of adventures in the Sulu Islands.

*Saturday, Dec. 31st.*—Started from Siquati at halfpast eight, and arrived at Luru at eleven o'clock. It rained a good deal; but at Luru it began to rain in torrents. We had nothing to eat, as I had sent everything on in the sampan, and it had not yet arrived. We found some turtles' eggs on the beach, about 200. I ate of these and drank weak whisky and water all that wretched day. At six o'clock the sampan arrived, in the midst of pouring rain. Oh! what a wretched night I spent in a wet tent, everything damp and getting spoilt. It rained all night, and I felt very wretched. Pangeran Brunei was rather kind to us on the whole, but I could not sleep in his horrible house, the dirt and stench being something too much. If ever I get home again I will never go camping out in a wet climate again. The natives were very curious about my tent.

## VII.

*Jan. 1st*, 1882.—If all beginnings of future new years are as black as this one, I never wish to see another.[6] Rain! That's not the word for it. Abdul unable to cook, everything wet and spoiling. What I am to do if this continues I don't quite know. Go back to Siquati I think. The rain, however, cleared a little about ten o'clock, and we started away up the Luru River in the Pangeran's prahu. After about an hour and a half we were unable to get further up the river. It is simply a creek like Siquati and Kurina, flowing through immense mangrove swamps. I got a sample of the river's bottom, but it consisted simply of siliceous and argillaceous mud.

[6] Nothing of this appears in the report to the Company, nor in his private letters home; they are evidently notes intended to be read to the family circle when he should have returned home.

I was carried some distance on the back of Housin, my mandore, over swamps and mud, until we got to the Hadji's house. He, the Hadji, lives on a high hill, and I think he is rather a scamp. He knows too much. He tried to intimidate me, I think, for he said the jungle path was very bad, up to one's waist in mud, rain, and slush; also that there are many snakes, and some very big ones. We soon, however, found out the truth of the mud part of his warnings. (He also said that he had heard that silver had been found somewhere in the country.) The discomforts of the afternoon were very great. For miles through swamp, walking with clay over one's boot-tops, and often sinking up to one's knees in mud and water. Wet grass coming up to one's shoulders, and rain falling all the way, added to the other miseries of the journey. I got two Dusuns at the Hadji's, who helped to carry my things. It was curious to see the rate they got along at, barefooted and loaded as they were with heavy burthens. At three o'clock we arrived at a large Dusun house, like the one figured in Wallace's "Australasia,"—exterior of a Dyak village. I should think a hundred men lived there, with their wives and families. The headman was kind to us; he brought eggs, bananas, sugar-cane for the men, water, and other things. The house is really an immense dormitory, there being one long passage with all the rooms opening out on it, the other side being occupied by a kind of verandah, which was given to us. I was simply a nine-days' wonder. My boots, my socks, clothes, hammock, my beer, biscuits, and the way I ate with a knife and fork and plate, all were objects of extreme curiosity. When I slept, the whole

DUSUNS AT A STREAM.

village came and watched, and sat laughing to each other, and indeed they could not make me out. As night came on they struck up a strange kind of music on metal tambourines. A mysterious rhythm and tune was apparent in it, and when I asked if this was "*main main*" (i.e. larking), they said no, but a man was sick, and they must play all night to keep away evil spirits. I asked to see him, and after a time they took me along to the other end of the house, where, in a room intensely hot from a fire, which was kept up in the centre, and which they said would also scare away ghosts, was a fellow who I saw had a little fever. I felt his pulse, and looked at his tongue, and to do the latter I was obliged to hold the candle a little near his face. His children, wife, and all the women screamed for fear, and the children were obliged to be taken away. I gave him a Cockle's pill and some quinine, and in the morning he was well, and I was very popular; so much so that the whole village came running to be doctored for sore feet, sore hands, skin diseases, coughs, and what not. I advised the skin-disease people to wash themselves, but they said they did not like water. On the whole I was not sorry to get to sleep, or rather to blow the candle out and lie down. To sleep was impossible, for the noise of pigs underneath the house, dogs howling all night, now and then metal drums beating, and the hard boards to lie on, all these things effectually banished Morpheus.

*Jan.* 2*nd*, 1882.—In the morning the curiosity of the natives, instead of abating, seemed to increase; they crowded around me, and watched every operation of my toilette with wonder and astonishment. The headman could only say two words of Malay (i.e. *baik, baik, tuan*—" Well, well, sir "); but these he repeated to me over and over again with great delight, laughing the while to himself in excess of good nature. Some empty tins and bottles, and a few yards (six) of cloth, made us tremendous friends, and I left with my men at nine o'clock, shaking hands all round, and getting four men to carry my things. We walked for a long way up hill and down dale. The land was mostly under cultivation with paddy (rice) and Indian corn, which latter was very good eating. Now and then we passed through a wood with but little undergrowth; the trees, however, were very high, with long thin stems. Stopped at twelve o'clock, as it was very hot, at a house, and I drank a bottle of porter and ate a pomolo (something like an enormous orange) with much gusto. The natives were eager after the seeds of the pomolo, and seemed to value them very much. At 12.30 we continued our way, and arrived at the Kudat Dusuns at one o'clock, a wretched house, the dirt underneath the piles being only equalled by the dirt under the roof. The Dusun women do all the labour. All day long and far into the night the work of threshing paddy and grinding Indian corn was continued by these thrifty housewives. They thresh paddy in a wooden bowl, being simply a log of wood with a hollow made in it. Three women work at this. One stamps the corn with a long stick of heavy wood, and then hands the broken grains to the next worker, who separates the chaff from the rice in a shallow pan made of nipa-leaves and rattans. The third takes the mixture of rice and paddy (i.e. rice with the husk) which results from the last operation,

BUSUN WOMEN THRESHING RICE.

Drawn by W. H. Margetson, from a sketch by Frank Hatton.

and puts it in a similar shallow pan, where she separates the rice from the husk by a peculiar movement of the pan, accompanied with a jerk. Long practice has made the women perfect at this, and the men are equally perfect at doing nothing. The women use their left hand with equal facility to their right, and indeed make no distinction. They are covered with brass wire, the legs from the ankles to the knees, and from the wrists to the elbows, also wearing a collar of brass wire round the neck.⁷

Every time they hammer the bracelets jingle, and at night by the light of the burning resin (damar), which casts a lurid glare round the rooms and passages of the curious long low house, the whole scene was peculiarly picturesque and fascinating. I had to bend almost double to walk about, as the house is built for Dusuns and not for white men. The roof was covered with the smoke and dust of ages, there being no chimneys or any attempt to conduct the smoke from the cooking-fires away. It therefore curls up and hangs about the house, and finds its way out through holes in the roof. Here a man died during the night, and the grief of the friends was very genuine and deep. I wonder some epidemic does not break out amongst these people, as the dirt beneath the house is terrible. Pigs, fowls, cattle, dogs, and other animals all accumulate their filth below the

---

⁷ Here the original diary finishes. The remainder of the notes are part of an official report and "extracts from diary" furnished to the Governor. The original diary, so far as it goes, is written in an ordinary folio half-bound book, and it was evidently continued in a similar volume, which is not forthcoming.

house, and the smell which rises is anything but pleasant.

## VIII.

*Jan. 3rd.*—We procured some fresh men from the Dusuns, and started for Kudat in the pouring rain at eight o'clock. The direction was N.E. to E.N.E., and the whole way through dense jungle. The Dusuns quite missed their way many times, and no wonder, as days of rain had converted all the valleys into swamps, in which we waded up to our waists, through wet undergrowth and amid pouring rain. The thorns and the spines in the jungle caught my clothes, and I even felt the weight of my pistol and my gun was a dreadful nuisance. We struck the coast at a point about seven miles south of the extreme point of Sampanmangio at 1.30, and arrived at Kudat at 3.30, tired out, wet through, covered with mud, lank and hungry.

*Jan. 4th and 5th.*—I remained at Kudat preparing for my trip round Marudu Bay. While staying here I found a very rich ironstone in the hill from where the Kudat workmen get their drinking-water—I should think fifty to sixty per cent. of iron, or even more. If coal is discovered in the bay, this may at some future date be worth working. It is at all events worth noting. The ore is a hard dark oxide of iron, and occurs in the tertiary sandstone.

*Jan. 6th.*—We left Kudat at 9.30 in the Sarawak prahu from Abai, *en route* for Tertipan, in the extreme S.S.E. of Marudu Bay. There the natives say there is good coal. After a brisk sail over the green waters of the bay, we arrived at Sheriff Ali's Kampong at the mouth of the Tertipan River. The Sheriff did not treat us with any show of friendship, and asked me what I wanted and where I was going. I explained that I required guides to go up to the source of the Tertipan River, as I had learned there was coal there. The Sheriff asked me what the Company would give him as compensation if they worked minerals in *his country*. I evaded this by saying I would like to see whether the mineral in question was any good or not, and so Sheriff Ali agreed to wait my inspection

THE ENTERPRISE IN ABAI HARBOUR.
(*Drawn by Helen H. Hatton. From a sketch by Col. Harington.*)

before he fixed the amount he would require. Altogether I don't think Sheriff Ali is a great friend of the Company.

*Jan. 7th.*—I started away early in the morning with some native guides, and three of my own men, to the source of the Tertipan River. After about two hours' walking along a cattle-track we arrived at the foot of the hill where the river rises. This hill is about 700 feet high, and there is a capital section exposed at the stream. The Tertipan River rises near the top and rushes down the thickly-wooded side of the hill, over a very rocky bed. "Here is the coal," said my guide, when we had got nearly to the top, pointing to some large black boulders in the middle of the stream. I saw at once that the mineral was not coal, and on breaking a piece and examining with the glass, I recognized *serpentine*. A little higher up the river I found the rock *in situ*, occurring with a funginous dolomite which weathers brown. The serpentine is brined very much with *quartz*, and the stream was full of rolled pebbles of this mineral.

## IX.

AT a future date it will be advisable to clear some jungle here and search this district with the boring-machine. I found no other minerals, save *iron pyrites*, in the quartz in the stream. We retraced our steps and got back to Sheriff Ali's house at 12.30, when I told him his minerals were "no good." At one o'clock we left in the prahu and arrived at the mouth of the Bongon River at three.

Arrived at Sheriff Ibea's town of Bongon at ten o'clock at night.

*Jan. 8th.*—I spent the day in paying visits to the various Sheriffs. Sheriff Shea, Sheriff Mohameb, and Sheriff "Hamid" all received me very kindly. I procured four buffaloes and intend to start for Timbong Batu to-morrow to take a preliminary view of the country before going into the interior, which I shall do in the dry season.

*Jan. 9th.*—Left Bongon at 10 a.m. My party consisted of myself and five men. We arrived at Datu Malunad's kampong at twelve after a hard ride on buffaloes, sinking often up to our knees in mud, although seated on the top of our "steeds." Datu Malunad is a son of Datu Malunad of Tamemisan, on the south-west of Marudu Bay. The rain began very soon after we left Datu Malunad's, and continued to fall in torrents all the way to Timpong Batu, where we arrived at four o'clock wet through and covered with mud. Riding on buffaloes is picturesque but not pleasant, trying all the time to keep one's seat, avoid fallen trees, and the constant danger of having one's head taken off by overhanging branches with one's feet hanging down without support, and altogether in a most precarious situation.

*Jan.* 10*th.*—The Timbong Batu Dusuns treated us very kindly, and this morning, as it was fine, for two hours I went out to examine the river bed. This was the only opportunity I had during my stay of examining the district for minerals. I picked up some rolled pebbles of serpentine, and some schistose pebbles from metamorphic rocks in the interior. Also quartz, both pure and ferruginous, containing iron pyrites, and it may perhaps on assay yield some gold and silver. I found a piece of a hard bituminous mineral, which can hardly be classed either as a coal or a brown coal. I send home a sample (No. 1 Bongon). I shall shortly make an analysis, and shall enclose results in my next reports.

*Jan.* 11*th.*—It commenced to rain again at twelve o'clock yesterday, and rained all day and night, and it is still raining without any sign of stopping. We are shut up at the Dusuns', and the Bongon has become an impassable torrent.

*Jan.* 12*th.*—Impossible, the Dusuns say, to get back

to Bongon, as a little stream which we crossed in coming is now a rushing river. The whole country is flooded, and still the rain is pouring down in torrents. The Dusuns are in fear of their houses being washed away, as the river has risen to within a few feet of the piles. Early this morning a large buffalo passed down the stream drowning amid *débris* of jungle, driftwood, &c. He was going at ten or twelve miles an hour I should think. I thought matters might only get worse if we remained, so at 1.30 we packed our goods on the three remaining buffaloes (one having escaped), and left Timbong Batu. We found the jungle almost impassable. The rain had washed over many trees, and heavy growths of creepers and thorny weeds, rendered " limp " by the wet, hung about our way. In many places the cattle-track was entirely wiped out by the river, and we were obliged to cut a path through the jungle. Twice the animals swam in streams through which we had previously passed, with the water not above our knees. At 5.30 we arrived at Datu Ower's house, quarter-way to Bongon.

## X.

*Jan. 13th.*—Left Datu Ower's at ten o'clock in a little prahu with two men and a guide, leaving my other three men to bring the Karbaus (buffaloes) back to Bongon overland.

The boat we obtained was small and leaky, and the stream was rushing along with great violence. We went down at eight or ten miles an hour; one man was on the look-out all the time for floating timber and overhanging trees, which every moment we encountered.

THROUGH STORM AND FLOOD IN THE JUNGLE.
From a drawing by W. H. Margetson.

To face page 170.

Evidence of the great floods were apparent all down the stream, and in about half an hour we came to a stop before two immense trees which had fallen across the stream. Bamboos and driftwood had stuck there and formed an effectual barrier to our further progress. The water was here thirty or forty feet deep, and roaring along, one vast rapid for miles. We at first tried to cut our way through the obstacle, and while standing with precarious foothold on fallen trees with the water roaring underneath, the rain came on again in torrents, and really matters looked serious. It was impossible to go on, and seemed equally impossible to go back, as we could not have made a mile in a day against such a current. We had no axe, only a parong, and a week would not be time enough to cut through one of the trees which barred our progress. On the right dense jungle, with not a house for miles, and the country flooded. The left bank was a tall grass swamp, and this was the best chance. We tried to drag our boat through, but found it was too heavy for us. Now an unlooked-for help arrived in the shape of four Sarawak men (in a little prahu) who, more bold than their fellows, were coming down trading to Bongon. With their help, after an hour's stiff pulling, we got our boat past the obstacle and into the river on the other side. We arrived at Bongon in safety at four o'clock, and I learnt there that the people had not experienced such floods for ten years. The men have not yet arrived.

*Jan. 14th.*—The men arrived at 10.30. They told a serious story of the great difficulties they had met with in the jungle, and how they had lost another buffalo.

We left Bongon at twelve, and arrived at the mouth

of the river at four o'clock. As I had found metamorphic rocks in the river-bed at Timbong Batu, and the same at Tertipan, I thought it would be as well to see an exposure north of Tertipan, between that place and Binkoka. My guide told me that there was a section exposed at a stream called Merrisinsing, a place almost half-way between Binkoka and Tertipan, on the eastern shores of Marudu Bay.

*Jan.* 15*th.*—I therefore went to Merrisinsing, and followed up the river there for some distance, finding, as I expected, plenty of evidence of metamorphic rock (serpentine) in the river-bed. The coast is composed of sandstone inclined at rather a high angle. It is therefore evidence that metamorphic rocks extend over a great portion of this part of Borneo. Probably the chain of hills running from the Binkoka district and having their culminating point in Mount Mentapose (12,000 feet high, according to Mr. Witti) are composed of metamorphic and igneous rocks, and this will perhaps be a good mineral field. I intend to devote my first systematic mineral exploration to this district.

*Jan.* 16*th.*—I returned with my party to Kudat.

*Jan.* 17*th and* 18*th.*—Remained at Kudat.

*Jan.* 19*th.*—I went in the boat with four men to Terminissan, on the north-west shore of Marudu Bay, in order to see what formation prevailed on that side of the Bay. The Datu Malunad received me very kindly, and said he would like to hoist the Company's flag and bring his people and his cattle down to Kudat to live. He lives near the source of the Temernissan River, which flows throughout its whole course through a tertiary sandstone district. All this west coast of Marudu must be examined for coal, which is the only useful mineral likely to occur there.

*Jan. 20th.*—I left Kudat in the *Enterprise*, as my provisions had run short some days ago. We called in at Sequati, landed provisions, and took away the slave from Mr. Smith. The pit I found was thirty-eight feet deep, and thirteen feet of beading had been cut. They were working in a hard blue clay, which is an admirable fire-clay, and I should think almost equal to Stornbridge clay. Many pieces of coal and mineral resin (similar to that which occurs at Coal Point, Labuan) had been found, and the pit is now quite dry.

## III.

## UP THE LABUK RIVER AND OVERLAND TO KUDAT.

Tropical forests—A mysterious chief—Native ideas of gold—
—Discovery of a hill of pure talc—Leeches and rattans—Sin-
Dyaks—A river accident—Head-hunters on the watch—"Like
men with tails"—Omens—"Terrible news"—A strange ceremony luckily concluded—A lovely scene—"The giant hills
of Borneo"—Collecting upas juice—Mineral prospects—Initiated into the brotherhood of the Bendowen Dusuns—"Oh,
Kinarringan, hear us!"—Talking to a dead man's ghost—
Tattooed heroes, and marks denoting a coward—Rice harvests
—"Only iron pyrites"—More brotherhood ceremonies—A
model kampong—Hardships—Inhospitable Ghanaghana or Tunfoul men—A ghastly scene—Not head-hunting, but head-
stealing—Pig-killing, and a dead man—Promise of minerals
in the Sugut rivers—Lost in the jungle—An angry native and
a churlish tribe—The end of the journey—"In the Bornean
bush from March 1 to June 15."

### I.

HAVING been instructed by the Governor to proceed to the Labuk River in order to investigate "the antimony find," which had been reported from that district, I left Sandakan for the Labuk on March 1st, 1882, at 6.30, in the steam launch *Boyah*. Before leaving I received two small pieces of sulphide of antimony, weighing respectively 11·325 grms. and 13·726 grms., and upon which I have already written a note to the Company. This ore was reported to have been brought down the river by Hadji Sedik, who was said to know of large deposits existing up the Labuk; indeed, I was told that there were " seven hills of antimony." It at once struck me as strange, if the ore existed in great quantities, that such small specimens only could be obtained.

Nothing of importance occurred on my first day's journey. It rained considerably, and on picking up the house-boat from Sandakan, which had started before us, we all put into a tree-covered sandy island called " Liborreu " to wait for the morrow.

We left Liborreu at an early hour the next day, and were glad enough to get away, as there was no fresh water there. We arrived at the mouth of the Labuk River at one o'clock. The actual mouth is about a mile wide, and the Labuk is joined at its embouchure by another stream from the S.E. Shortly after reaching the mouth we grounded on the bar, and were delayed an hour and a half before we succeeded in finding the deep channel and getting into the river. During this time I took a bearing of Tanjong Sugut, N.E. from our position. Having got well into the river, we steamed on in a W. to W.N.W. direction for about twelve miles, when our course changed to N.E. into a much smaller channel, leaving an immense swamp, looking like a lake, on the W. The Labuk winds and turns very much; a large bold stream about 300 to 500 yards wide, and having a very rapid current. The banks here are lined with magnificent nipa palms, which grow to an enormous size. These useful growths form a fringe along the river, at the back of which are trackless mangrove swamps, the homes of the Labuk crocodiles. We anchored on the left bank at 10 p.m., and it rained very heavily all night.

We got away in the early morning, and up to midday passed two small tributaries, one on the right and one on the left bank; they were respectively twenty and forty yards broad. The banks were still lined with nipa, and the stream was very deep and rapid. The weather to-day was beautiful, and nothing could be more delightful than steaming up this unknown river. Presently we left the swamps behind us, and now the banks were covered with vast forests, from whose sombre depths could be heard the cries of hornbills and the chatter of monkeys. Enormous creepers hung in pendant growths from the great dark trees, butterflies and insects of every hue and colour fluttered before us, the sun blazing out and shedding a golden radiance over the scene. On and on we went, and as we rounded a bend in the stream a charming view opened up to us. A long stretch of river for miles, ending in a bank of forest backed by lofty-peaked blue mountains. Soon afterwards a stream, some fifty yards broad, joined the Labuk on the right bank, and the river ceased to be tidal. The Labuk is here about 250 yards broad. I shortly afterwards took a bearing of the highest peak before mentioned (275°, height about 4000 feet), distance ten miles. This hill is called Tingut, and gives rise to a river of the same name, which joins the Labuk on the left bank, and is sixty yards broad at its mouth.

In the afternoon we arrived at "Lomantic," a Sulu village situated on the right bank of the river. There is a small wooden pier on which the people, the moment they saw us, ran and hoisted the Company's flag. The headman of the village is Datu Pangeran Momonko Nagara, who is a gutta trader. I learnt here that Hadji Sedik (the antimony man) had been up the river as far as Pungoh, which is close to the head-waters of the Lukan. The headquarters of the Dumpas men is at Neiot Tungal, and these people are already being complained of.

All the morning of the next day was spent cutting wood for the steamer, and we did not get away until 1.30. The Labuk is now about 150 yards wide, and the soil changes from a sandy bank to a red gravel mixed with blue clay. Stone heaps now began to make their appearance in the middle of the river, the water became shallower and shallower, and the stream swifter and swifter, until at 5.15 we made scarcely any progress at all. Shortly after this the launch got ashore on a stone bank; the stream catching her turned her on her side, and I thought she was over. All hands were put on, and by dint of much hard pulling we managed to get her free before night. It was evident, however, that the launch could not be used any further up the river, not only on account of the shallows, but also because she had started a plank and sprung a leak. The only thing to be done was to pull the house-boat up as far as Tander Batu with ropes, and then borrow the native "dugouts" ("gobangs") for further progress up the Labuk.

II.

*March 5th.*—We left our anchorage for Tander Batu this morning, dragging up the house-boat and leaving the launch behind. Just before we started, Datu Serikaya's son came down to get what he could in the shape of tobacco and rice. Rice is very dear at Tander Batu just now, as the Datu's prahus, which go down to Sandakan to buy that necessary article of food, are three weeks over due; and the people are living entirely on potatoes and what little fish they can catch in the river. A bag of rice at Tander Batu just now is worth $14.

As we journeyed up we came in sight of the Labuk hills; the first and highest hill bearing 300°, about 4000 feet high, and distant about eight miles. Hill No. 2, bearing 310°, height 4200 feet; and hill No. 3, bearing 297°, height 3500 feet.

I noticed here tufts of grass hanging on branches twenty feet over our heads, deposited there by the river during the wet season.

Tander Batu is a small village on the right bank of the river, having a population of 250 persons; only five large houses. The people were originally Sulumen, but having lived for generations in the Labuk they call themselves "Labuk men." The chief of this part of the country is Datu Serikaya, who has the Company's flag flying on a post outside his house, with two old iron cannon beside it. He received me in great style, and placed a table before me, resting himself on the other side. Some finger-glasses, half full of water, were brought, and one of these the Datu drew towards him, and used as a spittoon. I then discovered that the table was not intended for refreshments. We sat thus for nearly three hours, talking over the matter of procuring "gobangs," or dugouts, and from a Hadji trading up the river I obtained two. I got no assistance whatever from Datu Serikaya. In Bongon, Sheriff Shea told me not to eat in Datu Serikaya's house, as dark stories are told of his having poisoned more than one person.

Going up the stream to-day, I noticed hills 200 to 300 feet high, composed entirely of quartz and serpentine identical with that of Tertipan, in Marudu Bay.

*March 6th.*—We stayed at Tander Batu, all hands cutting wood for the house-boat to take back to the steamer.

I had many complaints of Datu Serikaya's people from all the traders in the river. He was unjust, unfair, &c. I myself found him perfectly indifferent as to whether I (a Company's officer) got on or not, and, indeed, I think he would have preferred my not going further up the river.

As Datu Serikaya would neither lend anything nor do anything, in spite of his flying the Company's flag, I was obliged, on March 7th, to send my head policeman back to Lomantic in the hope of getting a prahu. I and half the men pushed on in the two prahus and the house-boat, which we had also brought, leaving the others to come on after us. Our progress inland was now slow, as for miles we were all out in the water dragging the boats up against the rapid current. We passed a small village on the right bank. The people were gutta traders, and their houses consisted of beached prahus covered in with "kajangs." They come up the river at the end of the wet season, trade during the dry weather, and go out to sea with the great rains. There were some fifty people living in these prahus. They were all full of complaints against the up-country people and against Datu Serikaya, their trouble being that they could not get their debts paid, and had, in short, been swindled out of their money. There were several Sarawak Malays there, but the majority of the people were Sulumen. They said that Tampias was eight days' journey up the river, and that an hour's rain was enough to flood the stream. In the wet season the Labuk must be terrible: a rise of at least twenty feet above its present level, with an irresistible current. Trees of enormous size are piled up on the banks; and even away in the jungle lie trunks of trees which have been swept there by the flood. The amount of denudation effected by these tropical rivers is enormous; vast beds of rolled pebbles, consisting of quartzite, quartz, serpentine, mica schist, porphyritic granite, &c., are to be seen all along the Labuk.

About noon the rain began, and wetted us most thoroughly. We, however, pushed on, and camped in the wet on a stone bank.

*March 8th.*—Waited until eleven o'clock for Smith and party to come up. The hills in this country are composed largely of rich clayey ironstone; and, indeed, in one place near our last night's camping-ground, where there had been a landslip, the exposure showed a bright red ironstone, which in England would have been jumped at as a source of wealth. On both banks of the river, at about a mile distant from the water, rise the Labuk hills, heights varying from 500 to 1000 and 2000 feet. To-day we passed a little village still on the right bank; all the villages seem to be built on the right bank. The population consists of forty-five people, and the headman is called Tuan Imum, being a kind of magistrate in the Labuk.

AT WORK ON THE LABUK RIVER.

From a drawing by W. H. Margetson.   To face page 180.

A DECEITFUL AND REFRACTORY GUIDE.
From a drawing by W. H. Margetson.   To face page 181.

I got bearings of three hills. Here are the figures: (1) bearing 260°, height about 4000 feet, distance about three miles; (2) bearing 275°, height 3500 feet, distance about three and a half miles; (3) bearing 235°, distance about six miles. I noted the absence of any large tributaries to the Labuk; all that we have passed as yet being very small.

Early the next morning I told off a party of men, with picks and shovels, to search some red river gravels which had attracted my attention. I used the remaining shovel myself, but unfortunately with no valuable result. I found mica and chlorite schists among the other rocks. It has rained a little ever since we left Elopura, and to-day is showery. We had to make continual halts, as the men said they could not work in the rain. Passed a small kampong on the left bank, named "Konamas," headman "Melana:" men, fourteen; women, thirty. Near this village, on the opposite bank, stands "Buis," headman "Hidal;" three men, ten women. The Dusun countries inland, but not far from the river, are called "Anosyne" and "Bokis," both, I was told, populous tribes. The people at Buis, who are half Dusun and half Sulu, call themselves "Orang Rungus." They say that near Kudat there are many more men of their kind. They complained of the Dumpas men very much, saying that they stole their goods and swindled them. The headman showed me a common pin-fire revolver, worth about $5, for which he paid forty pounds of gutta; also a string of beads, worth about twenty cents, which he had purchased for eight pounds of gutta. He complained also of the Dumpas men's scales and weights, saying that one picul of gutta in the Labuk country on arriving at Sandakan weighed two piculs.

All the prahus except mine went on ahead the next day to Pungoh. I stayed at Buis and travelled with Dusun guides two hours in a S.S.W. direction to a hill bearing 245° to 255°. A high hill in the distance bearing 317°. No. 1, distant two miles, height 700 feet; No. 2, distant twelve miles, height 2000 feet. The natives affirmed that there is gold in the bed of a stream running from the nearer hill. Arrived at the spot in question I was shown some scales and plates of mica, which were pointed out to me as gold. The bed of the stream is composed of thick, black earthy matter, on the top of which the mica was floating. We returned to the prahu, and pushed on as quickly as possible, and in the afternoon arrived at Pungoh, which is simply a gutta-working place. When all the workers come down from the woods, there are some 350 people at Pungoh. I here learned that Hadji Sedik had been up here with some men collecting gutta, and that he himself had never left Pungoh village. No one had ever heard of the antimony, and I have concluded in my own mind that those minute specimens given to me from Sandakan never came out of the Company's territory, but *were imported*.

Mr. Witti, when on his journey from Bongon to Sandakan, came down the Labuk as far as our present station, Pungoh. From here he went overland to the head-waters of the Lukan, distant from Pungoh some two hours. This is a terrible country, if the stories one hears about it are correct. I was told by Hidal, my Dusun guide, that last year it rained for seventy days without stopping. The river rose to an enormous height—trees, houses, men, boats, all were taken down the stream, and many people lost their lives. Then another year, he said, there was no rain for three months, and the river, according to him, nearly dried up. An hour's sharp rain up country in the hills will make the river rise several feet.

Leaving Pungoh, we pushed on past a deserted kampong, called by Mr. Witti, Liposu, and at evening we sought our usual camping-ground on a stone bank.

I started away at an early hour in the morning up a tributary on the right bank, direction S.W., about fifty yards wide, very deep, and flowing through forest primeval. In places there were placid green pools with but little current, into whose green depths one could see down for three or four fathoms to the pebbles gleaming and shining on the bottom. After an hour's journey we came to a waterfall, and as we could go up no further, I stopped and examined the river-bed for minerals. Among the boulders I observed syenite, greenstone, serpentine, oxide of iron boulders, and mica schist half decomposed. Having satisfied myself with regard to the minerals in the river-bed, I returned to the Labuk, and continued my journey towards "Tampolon" country, or, as the people call it, "Tanah Dumpas."

I waited at Tanah Dumpas, in the Tampolon country, on the 13th, to give the men a rest, as the constant walking in the water, dragging the prahus up against the rapids, has made their feet sore. It rained heavily to-day, and I got a hut run up, and made myself as comfortable as possible. A Dusun brought a fine specimen of talc from a small hill on the left bank of the Labuk, near a Dusun kampong called Sasapong. I took all my men over to the hill, and we ran a hole some six or eight feet in. No change of strata was noted, nothing but a solid hill of the purest talc.

The Tanah Dumpas men number: Sulus, 30; Dusuns, 40. Headman: Seribangsah Tongu. All these people are poor, and in great want of rice.

The next day I sent the Sandakan police back with notes and lists of provisions required. It was arranged that on the 3rd of April they should be at Tanah Dumpas with the things, and that Smith should be there to take the stores. Smith and nearly all the men went on up stream towards Sogolitan, at which place he was to stay until I came up. I thought it advisable to explore the country on the right bank, in the direction of some hills which the natives said were not far from the Kinabatangan. In order to do this Dusun guides must be procured, and it was arranged to start to-morrow. The people here are rather grasping, and are continually begging rice.

I left Tanah Dumpas with my Dusun guides on the 16th, and ran down the river as far as a small island, into whose right passage flows a tributary called the Telupid. Entered the river at 9.30, course being S. to S.S.E. We passed a beautiful waterfall on the left bank, and our course changed to E.S.E. This river is very like the last one I ascended, deep, dark, and placid at its mouth, and becoming a rushing torrent a little way up. The country is thickly wooded with enormous trees and rattans, and surrounded by high hills. I carefully examined the rolled pebbles in the river; they were identical with the stones found in the other river, previously noted.

## III.

Not being able to find traces of any useful mineral in the Telupid, I left this river and followed up one of the tributaries, going overland to do so. Had the greatest mineral treasure imaginable lain in the hills, nature had taken effectual means to conceal it. I was never in a jungle with so many leeches as well as other flying and crawling pests.[1] The rattans also were a great obstacle, stretched as they were across the path at heights varying from one inch to 30 feet. These catch the feet and trip up the traveller, while the rattan leaves hang down from above, armed with hundreds of thorns, each one strong enough to catch a fish with; and indeed they are used for this purpose.

The tributary we were following was called the Timbalas, it runs into the Telupid on the right bank, and both rivers rise in the Gempis hills. The whole country from here to the Kinabatangan is called Pomodanyoun. The rock at the head of the Timbalas was a decomposing quartz, containing plates of mica, but all in a very pulverulent and decomposed state.

*March 17th.*—Left our camp at Tanah Dumpas and passed through the N. channel of a large island which

---

[1] "The land leech is a troublesome pest to those travelling in the jungle, both from their large numbers and from the fact that besides the weakening effect from the loss of blood, bites occasionally give rise to troublesome sores. I have heard of no real case of injury from poisonous snakes and have seen few such snakes. Centipedes occur frequently in the houses, but their bite is painful only for an hour or two. Scorpions are found occasionally in dead wood, &c. Fish with poisonous spines occur frequently and sometimes give rather troublesome wounds."—*Medical Aspect of North Borneo, by T. H. Walker, A.M., M.B., Principal Medical Officer of the Company, Nov., 1883.*

here divides the Labuk into two. Nothing but going up rapids to-day; we ascended one 4 feet high in 20 yards, and shortly afterwards got up one 8 feet high in 15 yards, and passed a veritable whirlpool. The water rushing round a sharp bend was met by some vertical rocks, and the stream striking on these had created a dangerous whirlpool. Just above this pool there is a small Dumpas village, on the left bank, called "Kabuan." The population numbers thirty persons, and none of them dare go further up the river than they are at present, as the men of Sogolitan have closed the river against them. We passed a splendid waterfall on the right bank, the mouth of the Bombolie, which is some eight yards wide, and falls from a height of fifty feet into the Labuk. We camped to-night just below a rattan, which was stretched across the river marking the frontier of the Sogolitan and Delarnass countries.[2] To our camp to-night came two small

[2] A rattan slung across a river is in some districts called a bintang-marrow station, for raising which a heavy tax or fine is levied. Occasionally the tax is taken out in blood, though in the neighbourhood of the coast the bintang-marrow is not maintained with the severity that obtains inland. Mr. Resident Pryer in his account of a trip on the Kinabatangan was accompanied by a native, named Banjer, who spun many yarns about this rattan business. Banjer was a sultan's man, and had once been put on a "bintang-marrow" station. The man in charge of it thought the time had come to take a little duty in blood, just to let people see that the sultan didn't keep "bintang-marrow" stations for nothing. So they caught a trader, accused him of evading the payment of duties, and tying a rope round his wrists fastened him to a post with his feet off the ground, and left him hanging there. He cried continually all day long: "I have committed no fault, I have committed no fault." They returned in the evening with their krises and hewed him to bits. Banjer went on to tell Mr. Pryer that he was present when the Tunbumohas "semunguped" a man who was a bought slave. The Tunbumohas tied him up

prahus containing two Sarawak gutta traders and four Dumpas men whom they had engaged to take them up the river. The head of the party asked permission to accompany us, as he was afraid of the Sin-Dyaks of Sogolitan. I agreed, and so we all went to sleep under three enormous fig-trees, from which we were unpleasantly moved in the middle of the night by a sudden rise of the river.

There was a heavy stream running the next morning as we moved onwards, and our only way of progress for miles was by hugging the bank and dragging ourselves up by trees, rocks, or anything that was possible to catch hold of. We soon, however, passed the Sogolitan river on the left bank. Opposite this is another tributary ending its course in a splendid cascade, some sixty or seventy feet high.

I was informed that in this district there are several thousand people calling themselves Sin-Dyaks. They are painted and tattooed in a peculiar way. On the other side of the rattan, which my Malays were not at all willing to go under, there was a guard of three Dyaks in a native dugout. Their boat was of capital workmanship, being carved at the bow. The men were tattooed with blue all down the arms, breasts, and legs, and had pieces of wood in their ears. They wore

with his arms outstretched (crucified in fact), and they danced round him. At last the headman approached, and wishing him a pleasant journey to Kina Balu, stuck his spear about an inch deep, and no more, in the man's body; and another then said, "Bear my kind remembrances to my brother at Kina Balu," and did the same; and in this way, with messages to deceased relatives at Kina Balu, all those present slightly wounded the man. When the dance was over they unbound him, but he was dead. This custom is known as "semungup," and is practised by the far inland tribes to this day.

a head-cloth of common blue calico fastened on by a plaited rattan, which was passed over the top of the head-cloth and under the chin. They were armed with spears and native-made short swords, and looked very formidable savages.

We arrived at Smith's camp before noon. He was well posted below a bend in the river, at the foot of a hill about 3500 feet high. Potatoes, kaladi, melons, cucumbers, &c., were now in plenty, and my famished men got a feed of something more than rice, for which they were very thankful. The country here is very mountainous, and as the river is confined by high banks the current is tremendous, and I was advised by the Dyak chief not to try and go up further by water. It was, however, impossible to carry our things up any other way, and the dangers ahead could not, I thought, be much worse than the dangers we had already passed.

It was 11.30 when we started on again, the whole party together. My prahu was leading, a little prahu with Datu Mahmad (my guide when we get to Kinoram) followed. Then came Smith and the police, and lastly the mandore and coolies, in a large prahu full of things. We had passed rather a difficult bit of river when I heard a shriek, and looking round I saw several heads bobbing in the rushing water and a prahu, bottom upwards, floating down and dashing among the boulders in the distance. I jumped from my gobang and rushed to the spot; but before I arrived the prahu had gone out of sight, and most of the men had got ashore, some with great difficulty and many narrow escapes. The Dumpas men, who swim like fishes, were of great help in getting the people ashore, and

THE PERILS OF AN UNKNOWN RIVER.

had it not been for them I think the accident would have been a fatal one. The missing goods were many, the severest losses being two bags of rice, three rifles, six axes, and some parango, and a box of blow-pipe apparatus; while all the men's clothes, blankets, &c., had gone out to sea, and some poor fellows had scarcely a rag to stand in. The Dumpas and Sulu men who were following us dived all day trying to recover goods, and by their means two guns and half a bag of rice were got up. The Dyaks here gave us no help, and indeed their prahus were on the watch at a bend of the river some way down, for blankets, kaglangs, or other things which might float down, and which they would very quickly clear up. These people are indeed head-hunters. Only seven days ago a head was taken at a tree bridge over a torrent. A Dumpas man was walking over a felled tree (which in this country always constitutes a bridge), when four Sogolitan men set on him, pushed him down the steep bank, and jumping down after him, took his head and hand and made away. I saw the victim's head and his hand in a house not far from the scene of the murder. Some four or five weeks ago the Sogolitan chiefs, Iamboune and Pongout, admitted that seven heads had been taken from slaughtered men of Tingara (a country near the Kinabatangan). He (Iamboune) said there was a blood-feud going on between the men of "Loundat" in Sogolitan and the Tingara tribes.

Having got our things together, we crossed the river and made our camp for the night. It was useless to expect anything from the Sogolitan people. They had already requested us not to go up to their houses, as their women were afraid. The Dyaks here all eat monkeys and preserve the skins, which they fasten round their waists, letting the tails hang down behind, so that in the distance they look like men with tails.[3]

[3] Mr. Carl Bock, in his interesting narrative of travel up the Mahakkam and down the Barito, published under the title of "*The Head-Hunters of Borneo*," heard of people with tails at the village of Dassa, a settlement of the Beona Dayaks. Carl Bock wonders if "Mr. Darwin received the first suggestion of his theory of man's simian descent from the fables concerning the existence of tailed men which obtained credence among so many uncivilized people." Such definite statements were made to the traveller in this village that he ultimately, with the consent of the ruling authority, sent one Tjiropon, who had seen the tailed people in an adjacent country, on an expedition to bring two of them safely to Dutch territory. The messenger was well paid, and credited with letters from his chief to the Sultan of Passir, in whose territories the tailed people were said to exist. Some time afterwards Carl Bock returned to Passir. Tjiropon gave a meagre account of his mission. He had seen the Sultan of Passir, and had delivered to him the letter of his Highness of Koetei, but he had seen no tailed people this time, though "before Allah" he swore he had long ago. With great difficulty Mr. Bock organized another party of inquiry, with the following result:—

"After twenty-five days' absence the party returned with an interesting communication from the Sultan of Passir. It appeared that Tjiropon had after all delivered the letter from the Sultan of Koetei, in which the latter potentate asked his royal cousin to send him two of the *Orang boentoet*, or 'tailed people;' but the letter had been misunderstood by the Sultan of Passir. The suite in attendance upon him were known collectively as the *Orang boentoet di Sultan di Passir* —literally the 'tail people of the Sultan of Passir;' and his Highness, taking offence at the supposed request of his brother ruler that two of his personal attendants—in fact, his confidential men—should be sent to him, had waxed exceedingly wroth, and, calling Tjiropon before him, he ordered him to depart immediately. 'If the Sultan of Koetei wants my *Orang boentoet*,' said he, 'let him fetch them himself.' And so the Sultan of Passir, expecting an attack from the Sultan of Koetei in response to his challenge, had been arming himself ever since, erecting fortifications, and preparing for war. The

I left Sogolitan with the remaining prahus, it having been arranged that Smith should take the men from the prahu and walk overland as far as Tampias, which was my rendezvous. The Dyak chief, Iamboune, had offered guides, for one fathom of cloth, to be paid beforehand. We had got some little distance up stream when I heard a gun fired, and on going back I found that the Dyak would no longer give men as guides, and I learnt that the truth was that the Sogolitan men dare not go to Tampias, as they were in feud with the Dusuns there. The Dyaks were now coming down in numbers, and the chief asked me whether I would allow his men to "rampass" the goods of the Dumpas men who, as I mentioned before, were coming up with us, and who were now just leaving to catch us up. I made no direct answer to this, but said I would think first; and having distributed the men, who could no longer go overland, among the various prahus, I sprang on board my gobang, and ordered every one to clear out as fast as possible, as I wished, at all risks, to come into no collision with the people. The Dyaks, when they saw us going away, became rather excited

letter from Mr. Meijer had satisfactorily explained matters, and put his Highness at his ease. His mistake was, perhaps, pardonable, for he sent word that the only *Orang boentoet* he had ever heard of were those, so called, forming his suite."

It seems to me that the author of "The Head-Hunters of Borneo" unconsciously offers in his illustrations a possible explanation of the current fiction. His Bornean hunter wears an outer skin in such a way that the tail of it might in the distance be mistaken for a human dorsal appendage; while the scant toilette of the Dayak boys lends itself to the same idea. Natives of tribes not cultivating this kind of dress might naturally enough speak of others as *Orang boentoet*, and native travellers desiring to exalt their own importance may have invented the living tail out of the ornamental one.

on shore ; but they made no effort to stop us, and I really think they were afraid of the black men who were with me.

Progress up the river is very difficult and dangerous. I think we ascended not more than fifty yards to-day, divided in three rapids. After this we passed under a second rattan stretched across the river between Kananap, a district of Sogolitan, and Sogolitan proper. These two rattans form one "key" to the country, and if one is cut down, in defiance, the Dyaks never leave the war-path until the offenders' heads are at rest with the others in their head-store. All these people are very superstitious. The "bad bird" is a great trouble, for it causes trading parties to turn and go back, even when within sight of the end of their journey. On head raids there are several special birds, and great attention is paid to their warnings. If the bird flies from left to right and does not again return, the whole war party sits down and waits, and if nothing comes of the waiting every one goes home. This evening I caught a first sight of Mentapók, stated by Mr. Witti to be 8000, but which I should think is at least 9000 feet high. It is a fine, bold peak, with exposures of white rock near the summit, and is not unlike the Matterhorn.

IV.

On the 20th we passed into the "Miruru" country. Mentapom was bearing 345°. I noticed an extensive landslip on the right bank of the river, and curiously enough the rock exposed was sandstone. It seems that we have passed a great range of hills, composed of plutonic and metamorphic rock, and have now got into a sandstone formation once more. I should think, however, that this inland sandstone is of much more ancient origin than the coast formation, which is very recent. Further on another big landslip was passed, disclosing strata dipping at 80° S.S.W.

## V.

We camped to-night almost at the foot of Mentapom, and I fired my gun several times as a signal to a prahu which had not yet come up. Some Dusuns, who were catching fish, asked us not to fire, as it made the spirits on Mentapom angry, and we should sure to get rain. I cannot tell how they got hold of this curious superstition, but, sure enough, half an hour afterwards the rain came down in torrents.

*March* 21*st*.—At about nine o'clock the missing go-bang came up. Terrible news! She had gone over, and all our things were lost. A gun and sword-bayonet, a box of tinned provisions, four or five blankets, half a bag of rice (being all the rice we had to feed twenty hungry men), and all the biscuit, besides endless things belonging to the Datu and the unfortunates in the boat. This is a most terrible business for us. The men have not a grain of rice to eat. I was thinking over the situation, when one of them said he could see a house on the top of a hill near the base of the Mentapom. He pointed it out to me, and I determined to go up and try and get food. Taking some cloth and four men, I went forward. At our approach all the people ran away and shouted, "Take the paddy; there it is, there it is!" They were in the midst of cutting paddy. When they saw that we did not intend to rob and murder them, they came back, and, gaining confidence by degrees, they at last did not want to sell us any rice. When told that my men had nothing to eat, and that if they did not get rice they must starve, the people merely laughed, and said they could not let us have any, as it was not yet time. They have a superstition connected with the beginning of harvest. However, we frightened them a little, and eventually succeeded in getting some rice at one fathom of cloth per gantang. We left these inhospitable shores at four o'clock. Coming down I noticed tracks of rhinoceros, and a stream flowing from Mentapom contained nothing but quartz boulders. When we arrived at the prahus I learnt that Smith and party had gone on. He had nothing to eat. What the men will do I cannot say. I am but little better off than he, as all my day's work only produced a quarter of a sack of rice.

Left our camp for Tampias as early as possible on the 22nd. At one o'clock we passed the Labuk's most important tributary, the Kagibangan, which is as large as the Labuk itself. It flows in on the right bank. It occurred to me, when passing, that perhaps Smith might have mistaken the river and gone up the Kagibangan. This river comes from the Lebu (mount) country, and is quite unknown. Smith has no food with him, so I am rather anxious about him. We arrived at Tampias at dusk, to find as I expected, that Smith *has* gone up the Kagibangan. The people here are Sulu gutta traders.

I had a hut put up the next day for storing provisions, and sent a prahu after Smith. I also sent some men up to the nearest Dusun kampong to get food, and in the morning Smith arrived, all well; and, what is still more important, he brought a little rice. He said he had gone up the Kagibangan about a day's journey, and arrived at a large Dyak kampong containing several hundred men.

Up to the present time the greatest difficulty has been to get guides. The Dusuns always make some poor excuses; and, indeed, the only aim of Dyaks, Dusuns, Sulus, and Labuk men, whom I have met up to the present, is to get as much as possible out of one. I tried to persuade a Mentapôk Dusun to go up the mountain with me, but he said there were man-eating ghosts, rhinoceros, snakes, &c., and he was afraid. My two men came down from the Dusuns to-day, bringing potatoes, kaladis, and a little rice. They told me that the chief desired to go through the ceremony of cutting a fowl's head off.

On arriving at the Dusun kampong, I was received by the headman, "Degadong" (a name given to him by Datu Serikaya), who said he had never before seen a white man, although he had heard of Mr. Witti. His house is called "Ghanah" and the country "Tonao-rum." It is situated on a hill to the south, and on the right bank of the Labuk river. To-morrow was fixed for "the cutting ceremony," which is to take place at my hut. Afterwards Degadong promises guides and porters. I told him I wanted to keep on the right bank, and he said, "Oh, yes, I could do that."

At about twelve o'clock on the following day the Dusuns commenced arriving, boat-load after boat-load, until some hundred men had collected, all armed with spears and swords. The chief now came up, and we at once proceeded with the ceremony. First the chief cut two long sticks, and then, sitting down, he had a space of ground cleared before him, and began a discourse. When he came to any special point in his discourse he thrust a stick into the ground and cut it off at a height of half a foot from the earth, leaving the piece sticking in. This went on until he had made two little armies of sticks half a foot high, with a stick in the middle of each army much higher than the rest, and representing the two leaders. These two armies were himself and his followers and myself and my men. Having called in a loud voice to his god, or Kinarringan, to be present, he and I took hold of the head and legs of the fowl, while a third person cut its head off with a knife. We then dropped our respective halves, and the movements of the dying fowl were watched. If it jumps towards the chief his heart is not true, if towards the person to be sworn in his heart is not true ; it must, to be satisfactory, go in some other direction. Luckily, in my case, the fowl hopped away into the jungle and died. All my men now fired three volleys at the request of the chief, and I gave some little presents all round and sent the people away pleased and delighted.

Smith and a party of men went down the river the next day to fetch up the provisions which are coming from Sandakan. I and ten men pushed on for Kinoram by land. We left Tampias and arrived at Degadong's kampong just as a torrent of rain came on. The direction was S.W., and the distance about four miles.

The Dusun headman, "Degadong," was very kind. He presented me with a spear and I gave him a long knife. This exchange of weapons is customary after the fowl ceremony. The two black policemen I have with me are a great nuisance. They are strict Mohammedans, and refuse to eat in a Dusun house on account

FRANK HATTON IS MADE A "BLOOD BROTHER" OF THE DUSUN CHIEF DEGADONG.
From a drawing by W. H. Margetson.
To face page 196.

of the pigs, dogs, and dirt. Their manner also offends the people, and to-morrow I shall send them back to Sandakan.

*March* 29*th*.—I got the black men away as early as possible. They were very troublesome, and had I taken them on they would most likely have created some disturbance with the natives. Two chiefs of " Touaorum," Degadong and his brother, accompanied us on our first day's tramp overland. The road lay over a high ridge, and we had often to climb heights of 2000 and in one case upwards of 3000 feet. From the summit of one of these, where there was no high jungle, I had a splendid view of the country. To the north lay the Kinabatangan valley, with the Silam hills in the distance; eastwards stretched the Labuk, girded by hills rising one above the other up to the noble crags of Mentapok. In the distance again was the Sugut vale, with range upon range of tree-capped mountains rising right away to Kina Balu, which, seemingly near, towered like a fairy castle up into the blue sky. I shall never forget this lovely scene, but more especially shall I remember the wonderful tints and shades presented by the distant " giant hills of Borneo." A blue sky showed up every crag of the principal mountain, which stood out purple and black. The setting sun shed its rays on rock and tree, and the water streaming down the time-worn sides glinted and flashed, while all the nearer hills were clothed in every shade of green. A few white clouds appeared in the distance, and as I neared the Dusun kampong of Toadilah night clouds were closing in the glorious landscape. It was a most exceptional view, and one which this season of the tropical year can alone afford.

I took some bearings of Kina Balu from Toadilah; they were as follows:—

  Highest peak . . . 327°
  Right extremity . . . 334°
  Left extremity . . . 323°

## VI.

The spot where we put up to-night is a small house belonging to Degadong. The place is very hot and dirty, and the people very primitive and frightened. Pigs, dogs, and dirt are the great drawbacks to a Dusun house, but one can get used even to these discomforts in the jungle. The headman of Toadilah was called "Khuai." He told me that from all this country as far as Moroh the whole of the gutta is taken to Menkabong. It thus escapes the Company's customs. This jungle is full of gutta, and I think a considerable trade goes on, as I saw two Dusun parties, one of fifteen and one of twenty men, going to the coast with their baskets full. A tree was pointed out to me which would yield twelve catties, without killing it.

I paused at "Toadilah" twenty-four hours, as Degadong's brother wanted to go a day's journey and fetch a stone for me to see, which he had obtained from Silam Hills. Orang Kaya Degadong took his leave, with many protestations of friendship. He told me that his only troubles were with the people of Lobn, with whom he was in feud.

*March 31st.*—To-day some men came in from collecting upas juice. I asked how it was obtained, and they said they make a long bamboo spear, and, tying a rattan to one end, throw it at the soft bark of the upas-tree, then, pulling it out by means of the rattan, a little of the black juice will have collected in the bamboo, and the experiment is repeated until sufficient is collected. I cannot tell what truth there is in this story, but the people had no reason for deceiving me. The Dusuns at "Toadilah" all wear brass collars, bracelets, and anklets, a black piece of cloth round the head, kept on by a band of red rattans. The women wear a short sarong of native cloth, which is fixed on tightly at the upper part by brass wire. They also wear collars and anklets of brass wire.

Early in the morning Degadong's brother came back, bringing with him a capital specimen of sulphide of antimony, weighing, I should think, about fifty grms. He said that he got it in a river in the country at the "back" of Silam. It was three and a half days to there from Toadilah; thus it would be eight days before we got back. My provisions were running low, and I had, I could not tell how long a journey before me. On thinking it over I gave up going after the antimony at present, but its search shall be prosecuted from Kinoram at a future day. I tried to get Degadong to part with his specimen, but he would not, although he offered to go with me to find more whenever I liked.

We left Toadilah and proceeded on our journey, following a high ridge of hills in a S.S.W. direction. The whole way lay through vast primeval forests, in which I noticed many tree-ferns twenty and more feet high. The general character of the forest was almost Australian, judging from the solitude and unbroken silence which reign in the depths of these trackless woods. The only sounds come from insects. Parrots, monkeys, wild cats, bears, deer, and other usual denizens of tropical jungle are here entirely absent. The tracks of a large animal were seen; they appeared to me to be those of a tapir. I got a bearing of Mentapok. It was 75°.

The Dusuns at Toadilah were afraid to receive a note which I wanted to leave for Smith, should he come in this direction. They were afraid there was a charm in it. After much persuasion, however, they took it in, and placed it carefully away in a bamboo.

It is impossible to reach any house to-night, as the next place is too far, and there is no water; we therefore prepared to camp in the jungle. There was a small stream called "Tadjum" in our vicinity, and as it did not rain, a night in the woods was not at all unpleasant. (To-day, six miles in four and a half hours. Direction, S.S.W.)

*April 2nd.*—A beautiful day broke upon us in our forest beds. We awoke early, and our friends the Dusuns soon came up. Away we went in a W.S.W. direction, the path as usual leading over ridges and hills varying from 1000 to 2000 feet, "Tadjum" and Labuk vales away in the distance. At 2.30 we descended into the Bendowen vale. The place was surrounded by hills, some rising as high as 4000 feet. We shortly after arrived at the banks of the Bendowen river, a rushing stream about forty yards broad; in the wet season more than 100. It comes down from the Bendowen hills, which are about three days' journey away, if one follows the river. To-day we have been travelling over a clayey country, the clays getting harder and harder, until here at Bendowen the transition into slate is complete. The cause of metamorphism is also at hand in the shape of vast masses of quartz. The slate at Bendowen is excellent, and an extended search for minerals is advisable all up the river. (To-day, ten miles in five and a half hours.)

We left Bendowen in the morning after a splendid bath in the stream. The temperature down to 60°, a thing which I never observed before. It was, indeed, quite cold, and the moisture in the breath condensed as it issued from one's mouth. Degadong's people turned out rather sneaks. There was plenty of time to come to Bendowen village yesterday instead of camping out on the stones near the river. They had stated we should not get there before dark, whereas we could get there in half an hour. They also disputed over every inch of cloth (their wages as guides and baggage bearers), would not accept black, must have blue, &c. The Bendowen people received us very kindly. The people gave me some pieces of iron pyrites, which they thought was "Sarring" (copper).

*April 4th.*—To-day I was initiated into the brotherhood of the Bendowen Dusuns. The old men and all the tribe having assembled, the ceremonies began. First the jungle was cleared for about twenty yards, and then a hole dug about a foot deep, in which was placed a large water-jar. In this country these jars are of enormous value: $30, $40, and even $100 of gutta being given for a single jar. The bottom of the jar in question was knocked out so as to render it useless in future. The clay taken out to make the hole was thrown into the jar, and now the "old men" commenced declaiming, "Oh, Kinarringan, hear us!" —a loud shout to the Kinarringan. The sound echoed away down the valleys, and as it died, a stone was placed near the jar. Then for half an hour the old men declared that by fire (which was represented by a burning stick), by water (which was brought in a bamboo and poured into the jar), and by earth, that they would be true to all white men. A sumpitan was then fetched, and an arrow shot into the air to summon the Kinarringan. We now placed our four guns, which were all the arms my party of eight mustered, on the mouth of the jar, and each put a hand in and took a little clay out, and put it away. Finally several volleys were shot over the place, and the ceremony terminated.

It was now noon, so we got away as quick as possible. Our journey lay over a hill, which was at least 4500 feet high; we crossed the "Nobow," "Peringan," and "Gopie" streams, all tributaries of the "Kalagion," which itself is a tributary of the Labuk. We forded the latter stream, and followed its course for some little distance. Its banks give capital exposures of slate and quartz, but I observed no other mineral. In the evening we arrived at "Senendan." Four houses, seventy men, eighty women, headmen or "Orang Kaya," "Gitan" and "Geusonar." In all we did about seven miles in five and a half hours. Direction, N.N.W.

I stayed at "Senendan" the next day to rest and recruit the men, who threatened to break down. Orang Kaya, Pindar, of Bendowen, when we went through the "fowl-cutting ceremony," gave me the name of Datu Tomongong; he being Orang Kaya, Tomongong, and his brother chief, Orang Kaya, Sibandar. Both these chiefs had accompanied me as far as Senendan, and they left to-day with many protestations of friendship. The people are all in the midst of their rice harvests, and it is splendid weather. If we only had enough provisions nothing could be pleasanter than our journey. I am anxiously expecting Smith. The Dusuns at Senendan want to cut a fowl's head with me to-morrow; I would rather not, as it delays our journey so much; but to refuse would perhaps be dangerous, and we are such a small party. The people here are very thrifty and very dirty; they seldom bathe, but they pick up every grain of rice which falls as they are husking it. They call me pinai; had never seen a rifle, paper, matches, or a candle. I explained and showed them my Winchester rifle, and, instead of being afraid, as was the case with Mr. Witti, the Senendan people wished to buy all our guns. The price offered was one gong for one gun.

Before leaving the next morning I was again obliged to go through the fowl-cutting ceremony. This time two water-jars were buried. Water and fire were not used, but were replaced by spear-heads and sumpitan darts. These were carefully placed in the jars, into which I also dropped a note for the ghosts. Then followed the usual harangue and placing a stone. The whole proceedings were this time very serious, and the place was chosen near a footpath in order to let people see where the first white man in Senendan made friends with the tribe. All being over, volleys were fired, and away we went in great good humour, and with half the people in Senendan at our backs.

On our way we passed a solitary grave, marked by a rough stone; the rank grass grew high and green upon it. When I noticed it, one of the headmen was on his knees busily tearing away the grass and talking to the dead man's " ghost." He was telling him that the white man had come, and was friends with the

TALKING TO THE DEAD MAN'S GHOST.
(*From a Drawing by W. H. Margetson.*)

Senendan people. The dead man was the brother of the chief. The Muruts' here are much tattooed.

¹ "The Muruts are head-takers, but do not preserve the heads as do the Dyaks; they keep the skulls, or will even divide the skull of an enemy into several shares. They take also the finger-nails of their enemies, which they display as trophies outside their houses. In the case above alluded to, where Basilan was killed, the Muruts seized a poor old Paluan woman who had long lived among them, bound her and set her on a bamboo grating over the open grave of the murdered man. Then the brother of the deceased stabbed her, and any one of the bystanders who wished did the same, her blood falling on the

Those men who have fought, or have gone on bold or risky expeditions, are tattooed from the shoulders to the pit of the stomach, and all down the arms in three broad parallel stripes to the wrists. A head-man, or rather a sometime headman of Senendan, had two square tattoo marks on his back. This was because he ran away in fight, and showed his back to the enemy. Another and a braver chief was elected in his place.

A gentle incline brought us to the top of a hill, where we waited a short time to enjoy the splendid view. Nalalu, which is not far away, was bearing 337°. From Byag, the kampong where we are to spend the night, the people go to the foot of the final precipice in three days. The "Dendagong" hills, near Menkabong, lay in the distance bearing 215°. We now descended into Byag, which is a curious little mountain village, no long houses, but all small ones, built on a steep incline. There are ten houses containing sixty men and fifty women. Headman, Caronne. The people cannot tell how long since they settled at Byag, but more than 100 harvests ago.

There is a large pool at Byag, forty yards in diameter. The old man says there is a lake at "Longat," two days' journey from here. The people have a splendid harvest, and all the rice-fields are full of cucumbers, melons, pumpkins, &c. The soil seems capital. (Three miles in two hours. Direction, N.N.W.)

corpse. After this her skull was divided among the chiefs; and I saw the principal chief decorate the plot of ground before his house with a part of the skull, having the long hair attached, and the ten finger-nails, five on a pole, as supporters, the pole being decorated with ribands of the skin of the banana plant:"—L. E. de Crespigny in the *Sarawak Gazette*, quoted in *Borneo Herald*, April, 1885.

## VII.

*April 7th.*—Left Byag for the purpose of examining the river which flows along the valley. We forded the "Aona" stream running into the "Tympac," a tributary of the Labuk, and at 9.30 arrived at the "Lilompatic," which is an important tributary of the Labuk, running E. This stream is now only thirty yards wide, but in the wet season it must be 100, and deep enough to float the biggest ships, although it can now be crossed with the water no higher than one's waist in places. We walked up this stream with immense difficulty, climbing over enormous boulders and fallen trees, where a slip would have ensured a broken leg, if not something worse. At 10.0 we arrived at the "Kinang-Konang," a rapid little tributary of the Lilompatic on the right bank. The natives said there was copper here. There were two capital sections of the river exposed; the formation still consists of grey slate and quartz. From the quartz at its junction with the slate were running small streams of water, coloured red from the presence of oxide of iron. This told a sad tale of *only iron pyrites*. I soon had the men at work with pick and spade, and we got some quartz containing unmistakable iron pyrites. I took a sample, and as it was raining heavily, we made the best of our way back to Byag.

We resumed our journey in the morning, and shortly after leaving Byag arrived at the banks of the Lilompatic. The road lay as usual over high hills. Having waded through the river up to our middles, we stopped on the opposite side to go through the ceremony of brotherhood with the headman of Byag, who accompanies me to the next village, and also with "Orang

Kaya Dorrok," the chief of "Niasanne," our resting-place for to-night. No water-jars were buried, but three stones were placed in a triangular fashion, and two fowls were slaughtered. The spot selected was close to the woodland path; this is an important point. We fired three volleys, and I held the feet of the two fowls, whose bodies were left to rot. The ceremony over, we marched on to Niasanne, which is a beautiful little village high up in the hills; and yet surrounded on all sides by mountains stretching away in the distance to Labuk. These mountains are composed entirely of quartz, and the soil is excellent. The people are well-made, and I particularly noticed the absence of skin diseases among them, and also of smallpox-marked persons. This I have noted since leaving Bendowen. They are very simple; eagerly snatch up empty cartridge-cases and tins without contents, for which they will carry my baggage for miles. They shave their heads like the Chinese, leaving a patch at the back and two small tufts at the ears. All the men and women wear much brass, but earrings are not at all popular. "Niasanne" headman, "Dorrok;" 14 houses; men, 47; women, 35. The people here have cocoanuts, limes, oranges, mangosteen, plantain, jack-fruit, sago (which they use only for making ataps), betel, durian, rice, Indian corn, cotton, tobacco, melons, cucumbers, sweet potatoes, lemon-grass, kaladiums, a kind of onion, rope-tree, &c. The soil is very fertile, and the tobacco plant growing out in the open reaches a height of three to four feet. Their livestock includes goats, karubas, pigs, and fowls. Niasanne is the most favoured kampong I have yet seen or am likely to see, I expect. They have a good fence round their village, and have capital paths.

*April 9th.*—Amid the adieus of all the tribe we left Niasanne, and crossing a small tributary of the Labuk, which was full of boulders of a blackish rock containing iron pyrites, we proceeded on our N.N.W. course. The road lay as usual over hills and down dales; one moment we were crawling like flies up a slippery hill, at another shooting down a mountain side towards the valley. The Muruts know their own country well, but out of their district little or nothing. I remember, at Mentapok, asking how long it would take to get to Nabalu; the answer was three months; at Datu Serikaya's a year was mentioned as a probable time.

On our journey we passed "Gerass" village; 13 houses, headman, "Gompian;" men, 34; women, 25; and a little distance further we arrived at Gompian's second village, "Mereganan;" houses, 10; men, 40; women, 27. At these kampongs there are extensive clearings on the hillside, and orange-trees, lemon-trees, mangortun, durian, plantain are plentiful. We regaled ourselves with oranges, which, though very sour, were very acceptable. Although the "dry season," it has rained heavily, and yesterday was showery. We were all thoroughly wet as we trudged along in a N.N.E. direction. At 11.30 we sighted a great grass plain, which is Danao. If this were only a lake the view would be complete. At one time the place may have been covered with water; the hills rising out of it tend to convey that idea. All this country is very hot in the day and cold at night. I notice the contents of my phenol bottle are always solid at night and liquid in the daytime; 63° is a nightly temperature, while 90° is frequent in the shade during the day. Headman Gompian accompanied us a little way, and would present me with a spear. Shortly after he left us I had a narrow escape of being caught like a pig in a trap. The trap was set right across the footpath, and I struck the stick with my foot, when a sharp bamboo swept round and only just missed my leg.

At 12.25 sighted Habalu, bearing 335°, and soon after caught sight of the Labuk or Liogon, which we had not seen for so long. The country is all cleared here, and ancient paddy-fields with long cutting grass six feet high for miles and miles was our road. In the afternoon we arrived at Ghanaghana, on the right bank of the Labuk. We were wet through, tired, and dirty; and on taking off my boots I found my socks literally drenched with blood from leeches. The leech is the worst pest of the traveller in Borneo; but just now I feel the constant staring of the people rather oppressive. Wherever I go and whatever I do, a crowd of some eight or ten follow to stare and wonder. At Ghanaghana the people received us rather churlishly, but Durrok of Niasanne left us with friendly farewells and the gift of a spear. At Ghanaghana the natives are all in the middle of their paddy harvests. Men, women, and children are busily engaged in storing the rice which had been cut during the day. At six o'clock they all begin drinking a kind of "arrak." They prepare it by placing cooked rice and water with cocoanut milk in a bamboo, which they then seal up; fermentation commences, and in a week or so a spirit is produced, which smells very much of ethylic acetate. At seven o'clock the whole household was drunk; men, women, and children rolling on the floor, laughing and shouting.

I have one man who has broken down; he can scarcely drag himself along; so we are very short-handed—only seven in all.

Got but little sleep for the noise and shouting, which was going on all night. Ghanaghana boasts 70 men; women, 55; houses, 12; headman, "Pindar." We had some difficulty in procuring men to carry the things, and all wanted a fathom each and their wages beforehand. There were strings of human heads in all the houses in Ghanaghana. I was not sorry to cross the Labuk and leave the place. Crossed the stream Kinarang, flowing W., and descended from the tableland Batokan. This tableland is elevated about 400 feet above the Danao plain. Leaving it, we struck the Labuk River again. The stream is now about forty yards wide and some two feet deep. In the wet season it always overflows and floods the whole surrounding district. We followed the Labuk for some distance, crossing and recrossing several times. The boulders of phosphyrite granite in the river are large, and are washed, I expect, from Nabalu, which, from our present position, bears 335°. At length we left the Labuk to the south of us, and followed a tributary, the "Todongon," for some distance, leaving it eventually behind us, and going up to Tuntoul. The Ghanaghana men here refused to carry our things any further, and as five men out of the nine had already got their wages (a fathom of red cloth for a whole day), and it was now only 11.50 o'clock, I told them that if they persisted in deserting me the other four would get nothing. Finally I had them sent away and would hear no more from them. They talked a good deal and loudly, but did nothing, and presently disappeared. The Ghanaghana men have a general bad character. I noticed that scarcely a man of them was untattooed. Their enemies are the Loba Muruts, and the Menkabong Dusuns and Badjows.

The "Tuntoul" people are not very hospitable either, and as our Ghanaghana "friends" told them that they (the Ghanaghana men) got two fathoms of cloth for carrying our things a couple of hours, the Tuntoul people requested similar wages before they would work. I talked the question over with them for a long time, but to no purpose. I was anxious to get the wages reduced, as I was afraid the store of cloth would not hold out. At length I thought of empty tins. They took them at once, and liked them better than cloth. In the meantime food is getting shorter and shorter. I ate my last biscuit yesterday; milk and sugar have long since been finished; fowls, salt, and potatoes form my food, with tea, of which there is a little left. Half a bottle of brandy is all I have in the shape of liquor, and Smith not yet heard of.

Ghanaghana to Tuntoul, about five miles, in three hours; main direction, N.E. Tuntoul, Orang Kaya, Goukolat; men, 49; women, 33; houses, 10.

## VIII.

*April* 11*th*.—Left Tuntoul in a northerly direction, and crossed the "Pasabau" River, Kina Balu bearing 318°. Again following the Labuk for an hour, we left the river, I think, for good. We marched across Danao Plain,[5] with the tall rank grass on both sides of

[5] Mr. Witti's first great expedition was from Marudu Bay to Pappar, and he finishes his diary report of it in terms of congratulation which may be quoted here with interest as illustrative of the work of his young scientific colleague. Closing his record of a brief trip of four

us, and arrived at "Sinoront." Headman, Indadtong; houses, 13; men, 30; women, 55. This is not five minutes' walk from Danao village. Had I known, we ought to have gone on to Koligan to-day, but the Dusuns will never take us past the first village.

The people of Sinoront Mr. Witti speaks of as having formerly been head-hunters; I think they not only were so, but are so. I saw the three dozen skulls taken in former times, which Mr. Witti mentions, and also on the same row a very new one. The fresh addition was taken some four months ago from a Suluman. The unfortunate was a slave of Datu Serikaya, of Tanda Batu, in the Labuk. This man was sold to "Degadong," the Dusun chief of Tonaorunn, for gutta, paddy, and a gong. Degadong getting tired of his slave, sold him to some travelling men of Sinoront, who took him home to their village and made him work in the fields. He tried to escape, and so the savages took his head; and his skull, still white, hangs in the house on a line with those which were taken ten years ago. It is new and fresh now, but beginning to get smoked and black, and in a few

weeks, Mr. Witti writes to the Company :—" I cannot conclude without expressing an earnest hope that my missing companions will reach the coast as safely as we four did. Then only dare I look back to our trip with a tiny bit of satisfaction. I shall then repeat to myself what I heard my faithful dozen talk over when we had emerged on Danao Plain. They questioned one another: *What will our old men at Tamposuk say?* 'What will my employers say' is the query with me. . . . Whenever we came to a place for the first time there we dare show our faces again. To make sure of this required a good deal of attention, for the natives are rather mixed in their temper; genial in some villages, churlish in others. . . . A gracious Providence let me carry the drug against sumpitan-dart and snake poison in my vest pocket, from Bongon to Pappar, without making me resort to it."

months' time will not be distinguishable from its grim companions.[6]

We stayed to-night at Danao, which is distant only 200 yards from Sinoront. Danao: men, 40; women, 35. When Mr. Witti was here the population was much larger. A great many people have left, owing to fright of the Muruts, who made a raid here about seven months ago. The people from Lebu came down on Danao at night, and firing a volley from their sumpitans into the sleeping-house, they rushed in, took seven heads from one house and three from another, one a woman's. During the fight one of the Lebu men fell, and his head, still new, hangs in the Danao house. The method of attack of these Muruts,[7] and indeed of all the tribes, is cowardly in the extreme. It ought to be called *head-stealing*, not *head-hunting*. They wait in the bush watching the house all day, and about three o'clock in the morning, when every one is asleep, they enter the house, take as many heads as possible, and decamp at full speed.

The Danao people have a kind of second storey to their houses, to which they climb in the wet season,

---

[6] Formerly the Danao Dusuns were head-hunters. In the house of the headman here there are still preserved three dozen skulls, forming no doubt an heirloom. Among the skulls in question, Witti noticed two which were taken from children, "and it is remarkable how firmly set and how white the teeth in all of them are." Previous travellers have shown that in the head-hunting districts of Borneo small heads, those of women and children, are considered most honourable, as evincing especial courage in the captors, it being understood that the tribes attacked would fight hard for their women and children.—*The New Ceylon.*

[7] It was a company of Muruts who massacred poor Witti and his followers about a year after these diary notes were written.

when all the lower part is under water. They told me that in the wet season the whole of the plain was a sheet of water for sometimes more than a month. Tuntoul to Danao, three miles, in two and a half hours; direction, N.

*April* 12*th*.—Pushing on early this morning, we soon left Danao Plain behind us, and entered the woods again. The rice-fields on the plain are all fenced round, and windmills set to frighten birds away. Crossing the Meusaban and Nogorass streams, we arrived without incident at Koligan. We have had bad weather lately; the rain always begins in the middle of the day with thunder, and lasts until evening.

Koligan: 3 houses; men, 21; women, 25; old man, Sabong. Danao to Koligan, seven miles, in three and a half hours; main direction, N.N.W.

The people were engaged in killing pigs here, and the noise was very great. They fasten the animal's legs and then thrust a sharp bamboo right up to the animal's heart. The curious part of the operation is that from the moment the bamboo enters the body the animal makes no more noise.

There was a dead man in one of the houses here, and I went to see him. He was placed in a sitting posture dressed in all the things he had; a cigarette was being held to his mouth; and a brass box containing betel, &c., was open before him. His friends were seated around, and were telling the dead man not to go to the right or left, as they were the wrong roads, but to keep straight ahead, "and that is the way to Kina Balu." This ceremony lasts one day and one night, and the next day the man is buried with most of his material belongings.

*April* 13*th*.—Our path from Koligan lay over a level country, watered by numerous streams and rivers. One important river, the "Lukan," running E.S.E. into the Sugut, was crossed this morning. It evidently rises in or near Kina Balu, as boulders of porphyritic granite are plentiful. Had I means and food I should like to examine the Sugut rivers, and this is a work that must be done in the near future. Another member of the Sugut system, the Silam-silam, was crossed soon after, course N. by E. Presently we arrived at Bonkud: old man, Gunsanad; men, 22; women, 30; houses, 5. We crossed the Pangkatan, where the Bonkud people get their water, and arrived at a large village, Limaousse, at eleven o'clock. Limaousse: old men, Garanter and Gendiong; men, 31; women, 37; houses, 7. Arrived at Marang-Parang at 3.30: old man, Egongad; men, 10; women, 15; houses, 2. The country is called Gophon. In the afternoon we arrived at the Lunganan, and crossed into Lasas tired to death at 3.30.

## IX.

Our Koligan baggage-bearers, following the same plan as the Danao, Tuntoul, and Ghanaghana people, lingered behind, and tried in every way to make us lose time. Getting tired of this, I told every one that they must get to Lasas to-night, and pushed on alone. For hours we went up hill and down dale, until all at once the path lost itself in a rice-field. About two miles back we had passed a rice hut, from which all the people ran at our approach. Being quite lost, I thought the best thing would be to get back there. This was, however, easier said than done, and shortly afterwards we were wandering at random in a bamboo jungle. It was about an hour before one of my men found the path from a Dusun rice reaper, who, however, refused to tell us the way without we gave him a "cigarre," which is not a smoke, but the Dusun for "three feet of cloth." So we paid the fellow and he showed us the way, our course being N. by E. We hurried on now quicker than ever, as rain-clouds were gathering and the rumble of distant thunder warned us of the approach of the daily storms. On arriving at Marang-Parang I found that only two men had kept up with me, the others being miles behind. We pushed on, however, for our rendezvous at Lasas, fording a large river, the Lunganan, one of the heads of the Sugut. Lasas is situated on the left bank of this river. It rained in torrents; and wet us through before we got to Lasas, which we did at 3.30, quite tired out. In vain I waited for my baggage-bearers to come up, and night came without them. They carry all my food, my hammock, rugs, table-chair, canteen, everything in fact. I at Lasas to-night have nothing to eat, nowhere to sleep, and what is more important, no change of dry clothes. However, I manage to sup off sweet potatoes and melons, and being very tired go to sleep.

*April* 14*th*.—Lasas : old men, Lingie and Linkapan ; houses, 8; men, 170; women, 200. I got up feeling hot and tired from the effects of yesterday. About eleven o'clock all my baggage-bearers came up. They had slept in the jungle all night, the Dusuns from Koligan refusing to bring the things along. Soon afterwards who should come up but Smith, with all his men and plenty of provisions from Sandakan. To-day was a great day for me, as my food was finished, and I had been living on Dusun fowls for a long time past. Smith had travelled overland from Tampias, partly following Mr. Witti's route, *via* Mirowandei, Beyaon, and Lausat.

The next day I left Lasas, twenty-three men in all; crossed the Lungalan; took from the bank a bearing of Kina Balu, 280°. At seven we arrived at the village of Banter; headman, Linkapan, of Lasas; men, 30; women, 35; houses, 5. We soon crossed the Mokodar, which is the Sugut proper. (D. N.) Kina Balu now bearing 265°. Having again crossed, we left the Sugut and proceeded over "Garass" hill (misprinted, in Mr. Witti's diary, Paras). The hill, as well as much of the surrounding country, is composed entirely of steatite, massive, olive green, and much less pure than that of Tanah Dumpas. Mr. Witti speaks of this hill as follows: "We came, on its southern slope, to an outcrop of the same mineral as Sheriff Shea had given me a sample . . . should the mineral prove of industrial importance the water-carriage will be at hand."

The mineral is of no value whatever, neither is there a trace of any surface outcrop of any mineral of commercial importance, although borings and careful mineral search below the surface would be advisable in this region, and when fixed up in "Kinoram" I intend to come here and make the necessary investigations.

Lassas to Mituo, about twelve miles, in five hours; direction, N.N.E. Mituo, first village: headman, Dinkol; men, 12; women, 15; houses, 2. Second village: old man, Brontei; men, 12; women, 22; houses, 3.

Pushing N. we left Mituo and went on to the Bundo

country; Kina Balu bearing 250° from the first village in Bundo, which consisted only of three houses. Crossing the Kaponakan for the first time, we arrived at the third and last village in Bundo, which is some six miles from Mituo, a distance we performed in three hours.

All the Dusuns now, ever since we left Ghanaghana, have behaved rather badly. They will tell any stories to get an extra inch of cloth out of us. For instance, the Lasas, Koligan, Mituo, and Bundo people say they cannot take us to Moroli, as there is a disease there, and they are afraid of catching it. I am sure we shall find at Moroli that this is untrue. Again, last night the Mituo people said we could see the lights of Bundo from their house, and they pointed to some distant lights, which I found afterwards were in a paddy hut of their own, in which, for that night, some men were staying.

Leaving Bundo, our course lay along the Kaponakan, which river we crossed five times; our direction being N.N.W. to N.W. From Moroli, at which place we arrived at 2.20, we had a splendid view. On the horizon Mentapok was distinctly visible, bearing 133°. A high hill to the S.S.W. of Mentapok must be Bolinkadus, the source of the Kagibangan in the Lobu country.

We made nine miles in four and a half hours during the day (April 17), and of course, as I expected, there is no sickness at Moroli. On the following day we go on to Munnus, which is about fourteen miles away. Travelling over some hills, we struck the Telusib, the Munnus river, which runs into the Kinoram. Arriving at Munnus we were not very well received; I cannot tell why. From Maoli to Munnus, about fourteen miles, in six and a half hours; main direction, N.W. Munnus: houses, 4; men, 100; women, 102; headman, no one. Munnus is situated at the foot of Tumboyonkon hill on the left bank of the Telusil, between that and the Kinoram River, which runs not far away. Here a Dusun gave me a small piece of pyrites, which he said he had found in the river. I ground it up and went through some reactions for copper without result, except that I used all the specimen up. I went to sleep and thought no more about it.

*April* 19*th*.—Just as we were leaving, the man asked for his stone back. I gave him some matches, and explained that I had used all his stone up. He then replied that if the stone was not forthcoming in seven days he would take a head from the first of my people he met with. I was nearly getting angry, but thought better of it, and went away as quickly as possible. This, however, only shows the spirit of the Munnus Dusuns, who are the most churlish, ill-disposed tribe I have yet seen. A tramp of six miles in a N.N.E. direction brought us to Kinoram, and practically our journey was over.

\* \* \* \* \* \*

Smith, who is ill, and nearly all the men (most of them also ill), went on to Kudat. I stayed at Kinoram until April 24th, getting material ready for making a house.

Subsequently I went down to Bongon,[3] and had a

---

[3] "While Frank Hatton was at Bongon," writes Colonel Harington, "I and Mr. Gueritz, then the Assistant Resident at Kudat, went off in the Kudat boat to visit the new station, where Frank had established himself, in order that I could report on the stationing of a police detachment there. Gueritz wished to have an interview with

tremendous struggle getting stones and kajangs to Kinoram in two prahus up the Kinoram River. The river is quite unnavigable, full of rapids and waterfalls,

a certain *sheriff* who resided in that neighbourhood. After a hard row and a pleasant sail—a favouring breeze having sprung up in the afternoon—we reached the mouth of the river, and, taking in sail, proposed to row and punt our way up. On reaching Bongon, to our surprise, we heard that Frank was much farther up in the country, and that he had gone into the bush. We determined to follow him up. However, during the night, rain commenced to fall, and by morning the river had become a torrent, and we had nothing to do but bolt, as our supplies were running short. It is wonderful the way the river filled up in the short time that elapsed from the time the rain commenced to fall. The next morning we started, but took such a long time getting to the mouth of the river that by evening, instead of being near Kudat—owing to a strong head-wind—we were not half-way across the inner portion of Marudu Bay, opposite the mouth of the Bongon River, having rowed all the way. And then night fell, and our crew began to *crack* up. They certainly at first were trying to pull, but soon we saw that they were simply 'going through the motion' of pulling—dipping the heavy oars into the water and not putting any back into the stroke. We decided to rest for the night, and having got into shoal water, we dropped our anchor and wished for day. A more miserable night I never passed, every pitch of the boat over the heavy running sea nearly sending one over the side. And then as hour after hour went by we wondered would day ever appear. Sleep was impossible for us, though the natives slumbered peacefully, as if reposing on the most comfortable of French beds. The lucky black can sleep anywhere, at any time, and in any position. At length morning broke, and we rowed to the shore, to a little village (inhabited by Bajows, I think), where we got some fowls and cooked a breakfast—luckily having a tin of cocoa and milk left. I never relished a meal more, being desperately hungry—our dinner the evening before consisting of half a tin of 'sweet biscuits, washed down by some Hollands strong waters' —not the sort of dinner one would order as a *rule*. After our breakfast we said adieu to the Bajows, and put off again; and a fair wind having sprung up, we hoisted our sail and got back to Kudat about midday, completely done up, and utterly disgusted at the failure of our attempt to visit Frank and his new station."

## Up the Labuk River and Overland to Kudat.

and subject to the most sudden floods. No prahu has ever navigated the river before, but with my usual good luck I got all the things up; nothing lost and no one hurt.

My subsequent proceedings in Kinoram will appear at length in my Kinoram report. Suffice it to say here that I have obtained an excellent specimen of native copper from the Kinoram river near Kias, and that sulphide of antimony has been brought to me from the Marudu river, to which place my steps will now be directed.

I have been in the Bornean bush from March 1st until June 15th, and travelled several hundred miles by land and river.

KINA BALU, FROM GHINUMBAUR (EVENING).

## IV.

## FOUR MONTHS IN THE DISTRICTS OF KINORAM AND THE MARUDU.[1]

Looking for antimony and copper—The Marudu valley—In the bed of the Kinoram River—Dangers and difficulties—Camping in a cave tenanted by bats and swallows—A romantic night—The horrors of leeches and ticks—Immense ravines—The natives "prayed me for rain"—Superstition obstructs the way—The "reported antimony" tracked to its "reported" hill—A treacherous guide—Sayup objects to white men—Discovery of copper—Descending a precipice—Limestone containing iron pyrites and a small percentage of copper.

### I.

I ARRIVED in Kinoram from Labuan on the 23rd of July, 1882.

#### FIRST VISIT TO THE MARUDU.

*July 25th.*—Proposing to find the source of the

---

[1] This report is marked "Kinoram, No. 1.—Report in diary form of investigations conducted in Kinoram and the surrounding districts during the months of July, August, September, and October, 1882." I have searched for "Kinoram, No. 2." The Company have no such document, and it is possible that the notes for this report may have been lost with the diaries. There is, however, the following letter to the Governor, which indicates reasons for postponing the preparation of a complete and finished report, with maps, &c.; and the house at Kinoram referred to in this chapter is mentioned in the letter as

Marudu River, in order to investigate the whole of this stream for the reported antimony, we left Kinoram in contemplation. The present diary-report therefore refers to a second visit to the Kinoram, though it chronicles the first exploration of the Marudu:—

"*Kinoram, April 20th*, 1882.

"MY DEAR MR. TREACHER,—I have arrived safely at Kinoram after some difficulty and a very long and hard journey from the mouth of the Labuk to the present country. My object was to explore the Labuk and its tributaries for antimony. I went within three days' journey of the source of the former river, and examined more than thirty tributaries, but to no purpose; and I am of opinion that for surface outcrops the Labuk district is quite wanting in useful minerals. I also think that the pieces of sulphide of antimony handed to me never came out of the Company's territory.

"I am much pleased with Kinoram, and I think it may turn out a good mineral country when properly explored. In order to do this I am now going to make a house in this country, and store food and other things. I have sent a list of things required down to Mr. Everett and Mr. Cook, and I am waiting here for them. I was unable to explore the country from Tampias on the Labuk to Kinoram, as food, trading goods, cloth, and everything were short, and our only object was quick travelling in order to get stores from Kudat. I reserve my full report and map until I have settled the copper, which I think exists at the head of the Kinoram River.

"Smith has had to endure a good many hardships, and if you deem it advisable, I think a small bonus would be well given. If you think fit, Smith returns to Sequati to finish his work there. He wants eight or ten men, and the sooner he goes the better, as I am most anxious to finish that investigation. I can get on quite well in here by myself, and am great friends with the Dusuns. I should like to make Kinoram my headquarters for mineral exploration, and from here go up the rivers Kinoram, Kapona, Kau, Sujut, Telusih, &c., all of which may yield metals, but I must have a place to fall back upon, and a place where I am sure of getting food.

"Among the Dusuns in some parts we had extreme difficulty in getting food. I want also five police and a headman, Housin, if possible, with guns, &c., as the whole country is in a most unsettled state and full of head-hunters. My mandore, Sahat, and Smith have full instructions what to bring me from Kudat, and my boy goes to

to-day, and walking some five miles, direction W.N.W., arrived at Mumus. Our course now lay along the Kinoram for about two miles, but we left the river at Kias, and struck across country in a N.W. direction, towards some high hills in the distance. Arrived towards night on the banks of the Pengopuyan, a tributary of the Marudu, we pitched our camp there under the shelter of some cocoanut-trees. We are only about three miles from Kias, and the country is called Lobah. The whole of the lower parts of the hills are, or have recently been, under cultivation. The district presents no features of interest, and is composed entirely of sandstone.

Old man, Kambigging, chief of Pengopuyan, came down last night, and goes with us to the source of the Marudu. He advised me not to go down the river, as the chief, Gensalong, very much objected to my coming. Leaving our camping-place, we continued our N.W. course, getting a fine view of the mountain in which the Kinoram has its source. This peak is called Nonohan-t-agaioh (about 8000 feet). Nonohan has no special meaning; in Dusun *t-agaioh* means *the great*,

---

Labuan to fetch clothes, provisions, &c. Smith, being ill, returns to Labuan before going to Sequati. I shall be waiting my goods and men from Kudat on the 27th of April, by which date I shall hope to hear from you.

"My route has been the following, and much of it was perfectly new, and I the first white man:—Paitan to Lamcut'e (Labuk River), Tander Batu, Punjah, Tamponlon, Sujalitan, Kajibanjan, Tampias, Tonaononin, Donalai, Bendonen, Senendan, Bejaj, Niasanne, Ehana-jhaua, Tuntaul, Danao, Sinoront, Kolijan, Lasus, Bundo, Mituo, Mirali, Mumuis, Kinoram, and I have been travelling since March 1st.

"Ever yours very sincerely,
"(Signed) FRANK HATTON."

the "t" being merely put in for the sake of euphony. It was bearing 203° from the spot above the Pengopuyan, while Tumboyonkon gave 162°. After repeatedly crossing the Pengopuyan we arrived at the foot of Madalon, which is about 4500 feet high, was distant about two miles, and the highest point bearing 305°. At noon we crossed a tributary of the Toaran, or Marudu River, called the Sorab. The boulders of sandstone here were mixed with some huge masses of conglomerate, the cementing material in the latter rock being silica. We shortly afterwards arrived at Pudi, a Dusun village on the slopes of Madalon, and here we put up for the night. Pudi: old man, Lounsah; houses, 3; men, 12; women, 16; the place being about eight miles from our last night's camp.

From Pudi our route to the head-waters of the Marudu lay over a huge ridge, from the top of which we had a splendid view of the whole of the mountainous part of Borneo. The principal peaks were bearing as follows: Tumboyonkon, 147°; Nonohan-t-agaioh, 170°; Waleigh-waleigh (i.e. a house), 185°; Nabalu, 195°; Sayup, 200°.

Descending from the hill we came down into the Toaran, or Marudu valley. Here the river is merely a torrent rushing down from Madalon. Taking a north-north-westerly course, it flows through vast tree-covered valleys, and between high cliffs for miles and miles. Following down stream some distance, I came upon a splendid section of cliff, with contorted ferruginous clays interstratified with beds of limestone, dipping at an angle of 20°, W.N.W. The natives say that Kina Balu was, many years ago, on the sea-coast. Geologically speaking, this might have been so at a recent period, as all the strata from Madalon is of recent aqueous origin. The object of our journey being ascertained—I had satisfied myself that the Marudu rose in Madalon, and did not run from the range of igneous mountains—I determined to go back to Kinoram.

Mr. Beveridge returned from Kudat, where he had been getting stores and men. Everything was now ready for our journey up the Kinoram, which I proposed to make in order to see if the river gave any further specimens of the native copper which has been found by a Dusun on one occasion lower down the river, at the junction of a tributary called the Kias.

II.

*July 31st.—Up the Kinoram to the head-waters.—* With the intention of proceeding up the Kinoram River to the head, and exploring the whole of the bed in the height of the dry season, I left Kinoram house on the 31st of July with Mr. Beveridge, two Chinese gold-washers from Sarawak, one Malay gold-worker, and twelve Malay police and carriers. Mr. Beveridge has already made one trip up the river, which has two sources, one from the S.E., which he examined without result. He was twelve days up the stream, endured many hardships, and was at last obliged to return on account of sickness. We all arrived at Munus to-day, and put up for the night in the Dusun house there.

Travelling right up the bed of the Kinoram River, and walking over boulders, which are here only small in size, we arrived at Kias (the spot where the native copper was found) in an hour and a quarter. From here the new work of our trip begins, as the Kinoram has been thoroughly explored up to Kias, and, indeed, examined right up to the head of one of the sources by Mr. Beveridge. There remains the second source, or the one from the S.W. Tumboyonkon was bearing S., 10° W. from Kias as we commenced our journey again, and the weather charming.

As we proceeded, our road became worse and worse, and about two miles up the river we came to a very difficult place—a long stretch of deep and rapid water, with precipitous cliffs on either side. It took us until night to get past this obstacle, which, however, we managed to do by clinging on to the almost impassable face of the cliff by roots, trees, or any other hold we could get. The men with heavy loads had a very hard time getting past. The moment we were over, we pitched our camp on the first place which offered, and got some huts made as quickly as possible. I noticed that the rock along the lower portions of Tumboyonkon is limestone, of which there are many boulders in the river, together with pieces of a dark, fine-grained syenite, which must come from above.

Terrific work all the next day (August 2nd), climbing over immense boulders, where a slip would simply be fatal. Great landslips have occurred all along the stream, and enormous boulders have consequently blocked up the bed. The river flows along the spur from Kina Balu, which, running N.N.E., culminates in two peaks, Nonohan-t-agaioh, 8000 feet, and Tumboyonkon, 6000 feet—the terminal mountain of the spur. One branch of the river runs through a rugged ravine from Nonohan-t-agaioh, and this is the true Kinoram.

The western, or south-western source comes down from a mountain named Waleigh-waleigh (house), a part of the northern Kina Balu spur. As we travelled along, I noticed in a small cave in the rock some twenty or thirty swallows' nests. They were greenish-white below, and fixed to the rock by a white glutinous substance. They are said to be worth about $1 per catty.

Any description could not do justice to the difficulty of our road; and the dangers and troubles we passed through could only have been compensated by a great mineral find. It commenced to rain in torrents about one o'clock, and continued until about four. All this time we were making our way slowly ahead, clinging by hands and feet to the slippery moss, and trying to prevent ourselves from being precipitated over the falls, or breaking our necks and heads on enormous stones. At four, being quite wet through, we camped in a cave, or rather a hole formed of gigantic fallen rocks, one fifty feet and one forty feet high, with eight or ten of fifteen feet and upwards in height, forming sides to the cave, which also ran some ten or twenty feet into the living rock. The outer apartment was filled with swallows, while the inner one was tenanted by bats, whose guano covered the floor to a depth of about eighteen inches—there being the same thickness of birds' guano in the outer cave. A very rank, mouldy, badger-like smell pervaded the place, and on the roof were about 100 of the same nests previously noted. It was a romantic night sleeping there, with the men stowed away in crevices and holes in the cliffs, the vast nature of the latter being most impressive. The roar of the water outside, as it dashed over fall after fall, the glare of the campfire on rock and tree, the uncertainty of ever being able to get back or forwards, with provisions for only a few days, and not a living soul in the whole country round! The true primeval forest of Borneo reigns supreme in these hilly fastnesses; and the camphor and gutta trees near the source of the Kinoram have yet to feel the axe of the trader and the pioneer. We are now up the river about seven miles, D. S.W. Seven miles of very hard travelling, and if rain should flood the stream, retreat will be quite impossible.

The rocks in the river-bed consist of boulders of limestone, sandstone, syenites, serpentine greenstone, and a conglomerate which rapidly decomposes.

*Aug. 3rd.*—Our direction to-day varied with the turns of the river, at first W.N.W., but afterwards W.S.W., this being the true course. Leeches and ticks (the latter especially) added horrors to our way. When Mr. Beveridge was up here before, a tick got into his arm, and the operation of removing it was very painful. We passed through immense ravines, with cliffs in one case rising 500 and 600 feet from the river-bed. Vast boulders fallen from these enormous "walls" lay strewn all around us, some of them of great height. Over these the men had to climb, with packs on their backs, and it was with the greatest difficulty that they got along. In the afternoon we arrived at a level spot between the hills, where a small island divides the river. Here we camped for the night. The chiefs of Marak-Parak and Pengopuyan were down on the river on a fishing expedition, having come over the hills to the north of us, where they say there is an easy pass into Lobah.

Our course up the river the next day was S.S.E., and we left our camp in the early morning, so as to get on as far as possible. As our rice was very low, I sent two men over with Durahman, of Marak-Parak, to buy rice in Lobah. Many of the men are down with fever, five in all. Mr. Beveridge, four Malays, myself, and the Chinamen pushed on up the river, leaving the sick men behind at the camp with two days' rice per man. We again had to contend with immense boulders, mostly now consisting of igneous and metamorphic rocks. Further up the banks consist of the same conglomerate, which has been noted in a former report as forming the banks at Kinoram, and the tableland as far as Pamaitan. Mr. Beveridge and the Chinamen continually washed samples from the banks and samples taken from various parts of the bed for minerals, but found no trace of anything. At 11.30 we arrived at the spot where the river is joined by its largest tributary, which is about one-third the size of the Kinoram proper; also got a sight of Nonohan-t-agaioh. The Kinoram from here takes a S.S.E. direction, while the tributary is followed in a S.W. Taking the S.W. branch of the Kinoram, we followed up some distance, searching almost step by step all along the river for indications or traces of minerals. We had not gone more than four miles when we came to the foot of a fall some forty feet high, and pouring into a pool some seven or eight fathoms deep, with perpendicular cliffs on either hand. Standing on the brink of this pool, one could see down fathoms deep. The roar of the water, the dash of the spray on the rocks, and the pleasant breeze which always blows down stream in these mountain regions, were very agreeable, but I thought for a time that our further progress up the stream was effectually stopped. Another consideration was, that all along the stream we had not seen any convenient place to camp, and it was already getting dusk. We tried the left bank, which had a somewhat less steep slope than the right, and after an hour's sharp climb we stood above the fall. A mile further up we found a camping-ground, and here we rested for the night. I had a great fire made at once, as the nights are very cold up in these regions. Temperature early morning noted 24·5° C.

We were on the move at a very early hour next morning, and proceeding in a westerly direction. We soon came upon the junction of a tributary, and a little distance further up, the main stream again divided, one branch coming from the S.S.E. and one from the S.S.W. We followed the latter until it became a mere brook. All these tropical rivers are made up of networks of streams, draining considerable extents of land. It is probable that even the largest does not rise in any deep-seated spring, as in the dry season very little water comes down the rivers, while in the rainy weather they become boiling floods, which are quite impassable. As none of our searching yielded even the minutest trace of any mineral, I thought it as well to return, as we have only rice enough for two more meals. We reached a point about thirty miles from Mumus—that is, following the windings of the river. At evening we got back to our previous camp, rather cast down with our continued want of success.

On the next day we ate our last meal, and finished the rice this morning, after which we retraced our steps to the camp where our sick men had been left, and where, luckily, my men from Lobah had already arrived with a good quantity of rice.

### III.

*Aug. 7th.—All down the Marudu.*—As the Kinoram had given no further specimens of copper, I now decided to leave the river, and crossing over the country strike the head of the Marudu, and work down this stream to somewhere near Bongon. It is not far in a straight line across from the Kinoram at Bongon to the Marudu. Leaving camp, therefore, we took a N. to N.N.E. course, our road leading us over a high hill, where the jungle was remarkable for the almost total absence of undergrowth and the great size of the timber. Dead leaves covered the ground to a thickness of nearly one foot, and nowhere was there any exposed outcrop of rock. Leaving the ridge, we descended by a steep slope into Kias, and pushing on, soon put our camp up at the cocoanut-trees on the Penyopnyan previously mentioned. Kambigging, the chief, and a lot of Kias people came down with vegetables and fowls to sell, which was lucky, as our stores of tins had been exhausted while on the Kinoram.

I was up very early the next morning, a pain in my knee having kept me from sleeping. Not a soul was stirring as I walked about the camp. The last embers of the watch-fire were smouldering away. All the grass and leaves were wet with the morning dew. The men, stretched around in every conceivable position, were huddled together in their blankets, for the mornings here are damp and chill. Later on I found that a regular breakdown of the health of our party had occurred, perhaps owing to the sudden change of climate. Out of fifteen, seven were down with fever, including Mr. Beveridge and the two Chinamen. I employed the morning dosing all hands with enormous portions of quinine and Epsom salts. I waited here all day in hopes of a change, but in the morning I found the Chinamen and two Malays so ill that I sent them back to Kinoram in charge of Dusuns. Mr. Beveridge was better, so we started away on our trip to Marudu. Our direction was at first N.W., which afterwards changed to N., and we arrived at Pudi shortly after one o'clock, having travelled only six miles. Every one, however, was quite done up, so we made a stop at Pudi. I think the "roughing it" up the Kinoram had tired out all the men. The house at Pudi is a wretched, dirty place, and the people more miserable and poor than most Dusuns. They "prayed me for rain," saying that if the heat continued, their crops would wither and they would perish. All their potatoes and Kaladis are almost dead for want of rain, and, indeed, the drought is rather severe. I told them to ask their " Kinarahingan " (God) for rain; but they said it would be much better for me to ask the Kinarahingan, as my prayers would surely be answered.

It is a curious superstition this of the Dusuns, to attribute anything—whether good or bad, lucky or unlucky—that happens to them to something novel which has arrived in their country. For instance, my living in Kinoram has caused the intensely hot weather we have experienced of late. This is attributed to me by all the Dusuns of Kinoram, Mumno, Kias, Lobah—in fact, everywhere. I can only conclude that the natives have the most imperfect idea of time, for just now is the close of the dry season, and therefore very hot and dry.

*Aug.* 10*th.*—Leaving Pudi for the Marudu, we took a N.N.W. direction; Madalon, the source of the river, bearing 295° from Pudi. Curious rumours about the Marudu native chiefs had been current ever since we left Kinoram. Kambigging, a very friendly chief, asked me not to go there. " I took heat; and Gensalong (the Marudu chief) did not want either heat or me." After some difficulty, however, we persuaded a guide to come with us, and pushed on in earnest.

Having crossed several streams, we got a splendid view of the Bornean highlands, with Nabalu towering far away above all the others; although Waleighwaleigh, Nonohan, and Tumboyonkon are of no inconsiderable height. Shortly afterwards we crossed the Tonaran, running E.N.E. into the Marudu, which it enters on the right bank, rising to the east of Madalon, while the Marudu rises on the west. Madalon is about 4500 feet, a long high ridge, separated by a wide valley from the igneous mountains of Borneo; and composed, judging from the rivers, entirely of limestones and sandstones. Our course being still N., we crossed several tributaries of the Tonaran; one of these, which entered the Tonaran on the left bank, we followed for some distance, but at length left it to the south, and climbing a high hill, we descended, and once more struck the Tonaran, running N.N.W.

Our road now lay right in the bed of the river, and we had many opportunities of examining the boulders in the bed, and of seeing capital sections of strata exposed by the river. The boulders consisted exclusively of limestone and sandstone. The former was a hard, blue stone, similar in appearance to the mountain limestone of England; the latter a coarse-grained, lightish-yellow rock, hard, and but slightly ferruginous. The limestone in places contained veins of the crystallized carbonate of lime, and often interbedded clays of a reddish and sometimes greenish colour, evidently altered by pressure, as the cleavage of these clays was quite slaty in character.

Travelling down the river-bed we soon arrived at the junction of the two sources of the Marudu, the Tonaran rising to the west, and the Nonohashan, or true Marudu, rising to the east of Madalon. The course of the Marudu from Madalon is N.N.E., while the Tonaran runs N.N.W.; from the junction of the two streams Madalon bears S.S.W. At four we arrived at Pampang, the first of the chief Gensalong's villages. Pampang: 1 house; old man, Lounahaigne, but under Gensalong; 10 families, 26 men, and 30 women. Pudi to Pampang about twelve miles.

The people here were also "praying me for rain," and would not be convinced that it was not in my power to alter the state of the weather.

Leaving Pampang we still continued down the river, passing the village of Moligo, arrived at Gensalong's country, Madanao or Kombaione, early in the afternoon. I explained to Gensalong, who received me in a very friendly way, that I did not intend to damage his country, but that I had been informed that there existed both birds'-nests and antimony in the neighbourhood. He said he did not know of any, and, indeed, could say certainly that there were none, and he pointed out that had such things existed in his country, they would long ago have been used as articles of trade. Pampang to Madanao seven miles.

*Aug.* 12*th.*—From Kombaione to Bongon. This morning our party split up; Mr. Beveridge returns to Kinoram by the road we came, while I return *viâ* Bongon and Timbang Batu, as stores have to be got at Bongon. Kombarone: headman, Gensalong; men, 300; women, 350; but, when all collected, about 1700 people in Lobah. From Gensalong's house we took an E.N.E. direction. We travelled through flat land all the way to Bongon, passing the villages of Ghoure, 3 houses; Tandok, 3 houses; headmen, Irasam and Lomad; men, 40; women, 55: then Talentang, 4 houses; headman, Engaioh; men, 50; women, 65. Our course changed as we left the Dusun countries to the N.N.E., and we passed the Badjow kampongs of Ranao, Sembilingan, 7 houses, and at length arrived at Bongon at five, having done sixteen miles.

The next two days were occupied in Bongon, and on the 15th I was back at the house in Kinoram.

Mr. Beveridge went down to Kudat for stores, a fresh house was built in Kinoram, and a mining-hut at Kias for prospecting.

*Sept.* 1*st.*—The men and Mr. Beveridge having arrived, we all got away to Kias, where the work of examining the Kias old and new river-beds had already begun. Sokaug, a Dusun, was going with me as guide up the Upper Pengopuyan, from which place he had brought a specimen of *iron pyrites*.

IV.

*Sept.* 2*nd.*—*Up the Pengopuyan.*—Left Kias for the

Pengopuyan, arriving at the "Cocoanuts," struck the stream, and travelled up this river for some distance. The road reminded me of the Upper Kinoram, and it was a great struggle to get up the rock; at the spot where the iron pyrites were taken is a compact bluish limestone, containing veins of quartz. The pyrites occurred in the limestone in concretionary nodules distributed through the mass. Having examined the district, we left the river to the north, and climbing a steep hill arrived at Pelandimbon—2 houses, 25 people. A hill about 4000 feet high, near Tumboyonkon, was bearing 193°. Extreme point reached on the Kinoram exploring trip 220°. In the evening returned to Kias.

*Sept. 3rd.—Search the Marudu.*—Mr. Beveridge has now started work at Kias, and as there was nothing for me to do in assisting the work there, I thought it a good opportunity to go to Madanao, and explore for the antimony reported by Sheriff Shea. I therefore collected a small party, and left Kias for Kinoram.

*Sept. 5th.*—The Dusuns are all very anxious about the sickness at Kudat. Left Timbang Batu and arrived at Bongon; the buffaloes, which started from Kinoram before us, have not yet arrived. They carry all the blasting tools and a lot of provisions. Towards night the two men in charge of the buffaloes came up with the news that both animals had broken down, and had been left at a place about four hours' journey from Bongon. This will evidently delay us a day at least. On the next day I had a sharp attack of fever, and did not get away again until the 8th.

We got away to-day and arrived at Madanao in good time. The old chief was very kind, and made us presents of fowls, tarrap, and other fruit, rice, sugar-cane, &c.

*Sept. 9th.*—The specimen of sulphide of antimony shown to me by Sheriff Shea in Bongon, was reported to have come from the hill at the back of Gensalong's house, which was said to be composed entirely of

PORTRAIT OF MR. VON DONOP.

antimony. There was also, I was informed, a Chinese-made brass cannon on the summit, through which a red deer or *kejang* could walk. This hill was to-day thoroughly explored from foot to top, and the result of all our investigations was the discovery that it was composed of barren sandstone. There was no change in the formation anywhere in the neighbourhood on this side of the river, as the adjacent hills were all examined with exactly the same result. Mr. Von Donop[2] came up from Bongon in the afternoon, and the following future journeys we made together.

Our attention on the following day was directed to the hills on the left bank, which were found to consist of limestone, with interstratified clays, all inclined at a very high angle. A torrent rushing down from the hills gave some capital exposures of strata, which about the lower parts of the hill consisted of limestone and clays, the sandstone being exposed on the ridge from where the limestone has been removed by denudation. The limestone contained veins of calcspar, but was, as far as I know, quite destitute of *organic remains*. I had several large rocks broken by blasting, in order to obtain fossils, but never a trace could we find.

The Dusuns were much alarmed at the blasting; they ran out of their houses with their hands to their ears, and the chief was not a little pleased to learn that we were leaving him on the morrow.

We followed the Marudu River the whole way to Pampang. Minute inspection of the river-bed revealed no traces of minerals. Madanao 400 feet high; Pampang 800; our general direction was S. The formations are still aqueous, consisting of alternating limestones, sandstones, and clays.

The general dip of the strata at Pampang is 35°, S.S.E. In the immediate vicinity of the Dusun house the formation consists of a ferruginous sandstone, overlain by about fourteen feet of clayey soil. We made our way to the top of the highest hill in the district—a hill from whence edible swallow-nests were

---

[2] The Company's Commissioner of Agriculture.

reported—and walking for about an hour through jungle and over sandstone, we at length arrived on the top, 1300 feet. Our blasting operations revealed a condition of things precisely similar to Madanao, the foot of the hill being composed of limestone, the sandstone appearing only on the higher parts towards the summit.

Having no encouragement to continue investigations in the Marudu, I determined to return to Kinoram, and from there make a trip to Sayup, in order to see the Tampassuk, and get a view of the positions of the mountains Tumboyonkon and Nonohant-agaioh, with regard to Kina Balu.

V.

*Sept. 14th.*—We got away to-day, and going *riâ* Ramao and Timbang Batu, arrived in Kinoram on the 16th, with two buffaloes bringing rice enough to last us our journey. We are obliged to take rice with us, as there is none to be had in any of the districts we are going to. Having had one day's rest in Kinoram, we were all ready on the evening of the 17th.

We left Kinoram at nine the next morning, and travelling on without incident passed through Kias, where Mr. Beveridge is still hard at work, and shortly arrived at our old camping-ground in the pouring rain. From here we branched away to the right, and ascending a high hill arrived at Nonak : 3 houses; headman, Kambigging. The place is situated on a high hill, from where one can get a fine view of Tumboyonkon and Nonohan, which I begin to think are only the termination of Nabalu.

From Nonak we took a W.S.W. direction, and shortly afterwards arrived at the road to Kion, which we followed, leaving the Pandassan[3] and Tampassuk path to the W. Our course now varied from S.W. to W.S.W., and we were told that we should arrive at Kion to-night; this pleased us very much, although we could hardly believe it. Crossed the stream Sorab, and then struck the river Rumalow, a tributary of the Tampassuk, which I at first mistook for that river. The Rumalow evidently rises not far from the Kinoram in Nonohan-t-agaioh, and many of the boulders consist of aqueous rock. At 11, being at fault for a road, we had to wait for our buffaloes with the guide. They, however, soon came up, and we got away again. The latter part of our way was through tall, cutting grass —twelve to fourteen feet high—and it was very difficult to make any way at all. One's hands got cut, and owing to the rain the track was extremely slippery, and we slid and tore ourselves very much during our very tedious progress.

Towards evening arrived at *Kion Gendokod* quite wet through, as we had been rained on steadily for the last two hours. We were much disappointed on finding that this Kion was not the one near Kina Balu; the true Kion is called *Kion Phome*. Nonak to Kion about thirteen miles, general direction S.W.

Having left Gendokod we crossed the Tampassuk

---

[3] Captain Mundy's narrative of the operations of H.M.S. *Iris* against the pirate retreats in the waters of this district is among the most interesting of *Rajah Brooke's Journal* (John Murray, 1848), and contains a stirring account of the defeat of the native pirates, and the burning of the picturesque "nests of the sea-robbers" at Tampassuk and Pandassan.

River, which was very rapid and came up to our waists. It was with much difficulty that some of the men got across with their loads. Passing Nahaba (ten houses) we crossed the Tampassuk twice more, the second ford being a very dangerous one. I had a long pole cut, and taking it in both hands helped myself across with it. It was, however, with great difficulty that I managed to steady myself in the rushing water, which seemed to want to tear one off one's legs every minute. The rice on the largest buffalo all got wet, which was our greatest misfortune. Just as we arrived at Trentidan, down came the rain in torrents, and further progress to Sayup was stopped for the day. Trentidan: houses, 4; men, 20; women, 24. I was told there was no more fording until we arrived at Sayup.

The people here are wretchedly poor, rice is scarce, owing to blight, and the staple food is Kaladi (sweet potato). When we opened our sacks of rice, and spread the grain out to dry, the Dusuns watched us with anxious, eager faces, and gave many hints that they would like some. Our trading goods were of no use to us, and, indeed, failed to procure for us so much as a potato, while fowls were at a premium. Madalon 27°.

*Sept. 21st.*—At an early hour we left Trentidan, and for a short time followed a S. direction, which was our true course. Our arrangements have changed since last night, as it was our purpose to go to Kion *viâ* Sayup, thus getting a good opportunity of examining the Upper Tampassuk; but a man at Trentidan informed us that there was a better and an easier route to Kion, *viâ* Bongaland Tumbotukan. At an early hour, then, we left Trentidan with this man as guide, and travelled for a short distance in a S. direction. This was the true road to Sayup and Kion, and I think that it was part of the plot to take us in the right direction at first, so as to lull any suspicions. We toiled up a ridge some 2000 feet high, and shortly afterwards climbed some hundreds of feet higher. We could now see Abai Plain, the Montenani Islands, and far out to sea. Our direction of travel was due W., and I knew something was wrong, as we were proceeding straight for Abai. Nothing came of questioning or threatening the guide, and as we were now quite in his hands, there was nothing to do but go on, which we did, and soon arrived at the village of Sokia—1 house; 12 families; headman, none.

Our course now bent round to the S.W., and after crossing a small stream called the Khorinsad, a tributary of the Jinamboure, we followed a S.S.W. direction. This was our true course, and our spirits rose considerably. The Khoribson was passed at midday. This stream is a tributary of the Nolohau, which probably belongs to the Kadamian system. From midday until evening we were lost in the jungle, and our struggles up immense precipices and over gigantic boulders were hardships enough for one trip. The guide having brought us to the summit of a high and densely wooded hill, put his bundle down on the ground, and went down the other side of the steep at a great pace, saying he was going to find the way. Fancying he had been misleading us, and now intended to desert us, I followed him, and brought him back by drawing my revolver. Seeing we were all in earnest, and being not a little frightened himself, he took us down a stream in a westerly direction, and eventually we got clear of the maze of jungle towards evening, and finding a footpath we shortly afterwards arrived at a hill kampong, called *Poduss*. This place had never before been visited by a white man. There were no less than thirty houses scattered through the hills, while the men numbered 100, and the women 125. Headman, Bonkar. I am now quite sure that the Trentidan people, at the instigation of the Sayup Dusuns, took us the wrong way on purpose, as for some reason or other the Sayup people object to white men coming to their country. Trentidan to Poduss about twelve miles.

*Sept.* 22*nd*.—It poured in torrents as we left Poduss this morning, and we had had some difficulty in getting a guide, as the Trentidan man had prejudiced the people against us. At length, by giving very high wages, and paying before starting, we secured the services of one man. Our road lay up hill and down dale, the villages about here being invariably situated on the tops of hills. Passing through Sizid (eight houses), Nabalu was bearing S.S.E. From time to time we obtained splendid views of Nabalu, and as it rains every day with us, we had grand spectacles of the water tearing down the precipitous sides of the mountain. Just after noon we arrived on the banks of the Panataran River, which is a tributary of the Kadamian. Here all further progress was effectually stopped; as, owing to the frequent rains, the river was very much flooded, and to attempt a crossing must certainly have proved fatal. We were obliged therefore to camp where we were, and finding a deserted paddy-hut with no roof, we rigged up our waterproof sheets and made ourselves as comfortable as circumstances would permit. It turned out afterwards that it would have been better had we slept on the stones near the river, as the hut was infested with ticks. From the spot on the river where we stopped, a high hill called Tohun, to the west of Nabalu, was bearing 167°, while the highest point of Nabalu itself gave 140°. Nabalu has almost the appearance of two mountains, the western end a short high ridge, separated by a terrific ravine from the eastern end, which itself trends gently away in peak after peak, each peak, as one goes east, getting smaller and smaller, until the spur of the mountain becomes a low ridge which again leads up and ascends to Nonohan-t-agaioh, and the terminal cone Tumbo-yonkon.

At the spot on the river where we camped there entered the Panataran, a small tributary from the east called the Peramad, about fifteen yards wide, and rising in Nabalu, or its neighbourhood, as evinced by the quantities of porphyritic granite boulders in the bed of the stream. However, even where we were the granite was already *in situ;* of other boulders, the most numerous a dark, somewhat coarse-grained syenite, ferruginous sandstone and limestone.

Poduro to the Panataran, about seven miles; D. S.W. We passed a most wretched night in the hut, as it came on to rain at eight, and never ceased until two in the morning, by which time we were quite wet through, as our water-proof sheets were the worse for wear, and in fact almost useless; added to this, a strong wind blew the rain right in upon us, and wet us most thoroughly. By morning we could wring the water out of our rugs, and, indeed, we were in a very wretched condition. Short of food, bad weather, a continued run of ill-luck, and no rice to be had, our own supply running low, with flooded rivers to cross, we determined to return to Kinoram on the morrow.

Leaving Panataran, we passed through the villages of Sisid and Bongal, from which latter place we travelled due east. Our route was quite new from Sisid and much shorter. Without incident we arrived at Nahaba in the evening. Panataran to Nahaba about sixteen miles.

*Sept. 24th.*—From Nahaba to Upper Kias *viâ* Kion Gendokod. The men never turned up at the Dusun house, where we arrived at night, so we had to sleep in our wet things and go supperless to bed on the floor.

Before daylight the next morning Mr. Von Donop and myself got away down to Kias River, to see what Mr. Beveridge could do for us in the way of food. Shortly after we had satisfied our appetites, our men arrived; some of them appeared quite exhausted with the journey.

In my next report I will enclose a plan of Kias with the works that have been made there. Exhaustive searching in the Kias River, both in the ancient and modern beds, has not given even the smallest trace, although the specimen of copper obtained by the Dusun does not appear to have travelled any distance. The next thing to do is to examine all the hills in the neighbourhood of the Kinoram, and Mr. Beveridge starts on a preliminary trip in a few days.

VI.

*Sept. 29th.*—*Search for edible nests.*—Having had three days' rest, I felt ready to-day to accompany the chief of Pamaitan, called Bonkal, to Pinowanter, where he stated there was a cave containing quantities of edible swallows'-nests. I put some faith in what he said, as he is a chief of considerable standing, and not inclined, like many Dusuns, to tell stories for the sake of talking.

Leaving Kinoram, therefore, in company with Bonkal, our direction was E.S.E., and our road lay through young jungle at first. This, however, being passed, we walked through a stretch of primeval forest, and shortly afterwards we came to the banks of the Tinandokan, flowing E.N.E.; and said to rise in a hill called Dogohoh to the east of Tumboyonkon. This stream and the Telidusan, which we passed shortly afterwards, are both tributaries of the Pamaitan, which itself runs into the Kinoram somewhere near Timbang Batu. The table-land to the east of the mineral exploring station, Kinoram, is for some little distance from the river composed of the old river-bed conglomerate. The Kinoram must at one time have been a much more considerable river than it is at present. Kinoram to Pamaitan about five miles; D. E.S.E.

With the dawn on the last day of the month we started for Moroli, taking a S.W. direction; crossed the Pamaitan several times, and passed through the villages of Melankup (six houses) and Lauk-lank-en-Sayup (three houses). Our course changed to S.S.W., and our road lay through primeval forest, which is said to be well stocked with gutta and camphor. Arrived on the banks of the Tendahouran stream, a tributary of the Pamaita. After a tremendous pull up a very steep hill, we arrived at *Moroli in the vale*. When coming from the Labuk, I stayed at the houses on the hill-top. Pamaitan to Moroli twelve miles.

*Oct. 1st.*—Got away to Pinowanter to-day, taking the old man from Moroli to assist in the bichara with the Pinowanter people.

Leaving Moroli in an E. to E.S.E. direction [Moroli: old man, Sidik; men, 100; women, 120; houses, 15; but dispersed among the hills], we followed down the Alowakie, which is a tributary of the Kaponakan; it received a small tributary called the Solokanmomanon. Leaving the Alowakie, we passed through Tiput (two houses), and shortly afterwards struck the Kaponakan, which river we followed for some considerable distance. Our course was now S.S.E. with the river, but on leaving the Kaponakan we followed a S. course. Climbing some small hills, and crossing the streamlet Tionkon, we arrived on the banks of the Kondironkan River, running E.N.E. to the Kaponakan, close to Pinowanter, and up near the head of which the edible nest cave is said to be.

Pinowanter consists of 5 houses; old man, Sakhong; men, 30; women, 35. Two high hills about two miles away; one Barrambangan hill gave the following bearings from Pinowanter: western end, 263°; eastern end, 230°. The other hill, separated from Barrambangan by a deep ravine, was called MolongKolong, and is about 4500 feet high. It gave bearings:—highest point, 286°.

After some trouble with the Pinowanter people, who much objected to show us the cave, and any amount of bichara between the chiefs, we at length got a guide and left Pinowanter in a W. direction. We passed a small saline spring, through the water of which small bubbles of gas were rising. The temperature of the salt spring also was higher than that of the neighbouring streams. Arrived on the banks of the Kondorikan, the river noted yesterday; our course now lay right in the bed of the stream. After immense difficulty in getting up, and climbing up over large boulders and up steep banks, we at length arrived at a place where the Dusuns pointed out a hole in the rock to us. We had brought no candle, and, in fact, had no means of obtaining a light; this was a mistake, but it would not prevent us exploring the cave. The hole was on a level with a deep pool, and there was evidently water inside, of what depth one could not say. The pool had to be crossed first, which was quickly managed by swimming across. The Dusun chief from Pamaitan, myself, and a Malay entered the cave, which, luckily for us, only had about a foot of water on the floor. It was very low, so that we could feel all over the roof with our hands. Every inch of the place was examined, and not a shadow of a nest could be found, nor was the rank smell which always pervades guano-caves present. Thoroughly disgusted with the Pinowanter Dusuns, whom we suspect of having taken us to the wrong place, we retraced our steps, and so angered was Bonkal that he drew his parang on the Pinowanter men, and there would have been a fight but for the old man of Moroli, who acted as peacemaker.

We arrived back in Kinoram on the 4th of October, and Mr. Beveridge was down from the hills with a small box of specimens. One of these was a piece of quartz, containing what struck me at first sight to be copper pyrites. On obtaining a little of the substance free from gangue, and boiling in nitric acid, it all dissolved except the sulphur; on the addition of ammonia a quantity of ferric-hydrate was thrown down, the liquid above the precipitate assuming a *strong blue colour*, and therefore showing the presence of copper in considerable quantities. I told Mr. Beveridge of my discovery, and said he had better go back at once to the spot where that specimen had been found. I would come up after him.

VII.

*Oct. 7th.—Trip to Tumboyonkon.*—Left Kinoram, and, passing Muruns, mounted a hill some 1500 feet high, being a fort hill of Tumboyonkon. We slept in a paddy hut on the top. The ravine where the copper pyrites has been found is on the other side of the ridge on whose side we now are. There is no Dusun name to the place where Mr. Beveridge is, so I will call it *Ravine Palupalu*, which in Dusun means little torrent.

From our hut on the hill the next day we took a direction by the compass S.S.W., and, cutting our way through the thick jungle, we toiled up the saddle of a ridge trending north from Tumboyonkon. Arrived on the top, we stood at a height of about 3000 feet, and at once commenced our descent down the almost precipitous face of a cliff into the ravine Palupalu. But for the trees, travel in such a country would be impossible, as the slopes are so extremely steep. The danger of falling stones from above was very great; one of my men had his foot badly bruised by a big piece of rock; he, however, managed to drag himself into camp, although he did not walk for a week afterwards. Before noon we arrived at Mr. Beveridge's camp, the distance from Kinoram being about nine miles. Every one was away at work, and as we descended we had heard shots fired several times. Mr. Beveridge was at work down stream, so I went down about three-quarters of a mile to him, at a spot where an immense landslip of thousands of tons of rock had fallen into the torrent. The road was of the worst description. I can only say that in places where we were coming down waterfalls, our lives hung, not exactly " on a thread," but on a twig the size of one's finger, or on the hold of a root or a tuft of grass. Had any of these frail supports given way, not only broken heads but broken necks would certainly have been the result. The rock consists of a green limestone matrix, veined through and through with calc-spar, and containing much iron pyrites, which latter, on testing, gives a slight *copper reaction*. This is quite distinct from the quartz containing copper pyrites, of which only one small specimen has up to the present been found. We can therefore report considerable quantities of limestone containing iron pyrites and a *very small* percentage of copper.

[Assays for gold and silver have not yet been made.]

The jungle about here is quite destitute of any of the essentials for making the usual jungle huts. Bamboo, any kind of large leaves, bark of trees, all are absent; the only things to be got are rattans and vegetable resin or dammar. Even the timber is small, moss-covered, and of little use.

*Oct. 9th.*—I have had a very bad leg for some days past, which is getting worse every day, which I am afraid will oblige me to go down to Kudat. I had to send to Bongon and Kinoram to fetch rice to-day, and to

Muruns to get fowls. Up stream to day, Mr. Beveridge obtained a piece of quartz containing iron pyrites and copper in small quantities, and also some quartz which evidently comes from a vein running through serpentine. In the afternoon specimens of quartz containing iron pyrites with traces of copper sulphide were brought from the next ravine.

In our ravine the sun climbs over our ridge at about 9 a.m., and sets behind the other ridge at 3.30 p.m. Even in the middle of the day it is cold, and the men were always huddled up in their blankets. The thick foliage prevents any warmth getting down to us, while the torrent, from whose banks we are only a few yards distant, creates a cool breeze. The roar of this stream reminds one of two or three locomotives at very high pressure blowing off steam, and any conversation has to be carried on in very loud tones. To-night it rained in torrents, and everything got very wet, as my waterproof sheets are useless, and we have no big leaves. As night drew on the pitchy darkness reminded one of a coal-mine heading.

*Oct. 10th.*—Men returned from Muruns with a very little rice; nothing else to be had. The Muruns people threaten to fell trees across the path between this and Kinoram, making their excuse the sickness at Bongon; but if they do so, it will be out of mere spite. Blasting towards the top of Tumboyonkon revealed limestone cropping out there. Mr. Beveridge had an attack of fever, and my leg is now so bad that I cannot walk.

*Oct. 12th.*—How I got back to Kinoram I can hardly tell, but I know that I was in great pain all the way. A buffalo took me to Bongon on the 13th, and on the 15th I arrived at Kudat quite done up.

The elevations which appear in this report are only approximations, but I am now in a position to determine the various altitudes by observation, and in my second Kinoram report I shall give the observed heights.

THE HOUSE AT PAMPANG, MARUDU RIVER.[4]
From a Sketch by Frank Hatton. (See page 235.)

[4] This is taken from a sketch-book that came home in Frank's boxes. It contained several other water-colour drawings, but the Pampang house was the only finished one. The mountain of Tumboyonkon had evidently a great charm for him. His sketch-book contains the commencement of a careful drawing of it from the river, and the beginning of a close study of the highest elevations of Kina-Balu, with a suggestion of sunset in the sky.

## V.

## EXTRACTS FROM DIARY OF THE LAST EXPEDITION.[1]

Difficult operations—An ancient clearing—The fable of the Kinabatangan Cave—Dangers present and to come—Fever and leeches—The future coal-fields of Borneo—Durian—Fighting the torrent—Outcrops of coal—Lost—Expecting to prospect for gold—Relics of a murder believed to have been committed by the natives who killed Witti—Among the Muruts—A misunderstanding that nearly led to a fight—An offer to go out against Witti's murderers—Shooting rapids—Swamped—"Rain, rain, nothing but rain"—Narrow escapes—Dismal wastes—From the river to the sea—Thunder and rain—The last entry in the last diary—"River swift and deep."

*Jan. 6th.*—Left Sandakan at 6 a.m. in the steam-launch *Sabine*, and arrived at the Muruyan mouth of the Kinabatangan at 9. Fine entrance: cazurina-trees at mouth, afterwards mangroves. Anchored not far from mouth, and went on up stream at 11.30. Evidences of freshet as one proceeds. 12.5, main stream on the left; still enormous mangrove-swamps. We slowly passed on at 1, forest and rattans now replacing the nipa and mangroves. Current heavy,

[1] It has been thought well in the interest of the reader to condense these extracts, seeing that many pages of the diary are simply notes of observations, important to the geographer and to the Government of Sabah, but not of general interest.

soundings varying from four fathoms to six and seven. At 6.30 arrived at Malapi.

*Sunday, Jan. 7th.*—Tenegang one day up in a prahu. Bought a gobang for $26; rather a swindle. Stayed at Malapi, making all ready. The agent at Malapi is a Banjermassing man, and, like all natives, a fraud. Ward stayed here three days. Country all densely jungled and very flat; while all clearings are quickly hidden by thick, tangled grass. Could not sleep for mosquitoes and sandflies. Sulu *main*[2] going on here; the people speak a mixture of Sulu and Paitan.

\* \* \* \* \*

*Jan. 8th.*—At Tenegang was an elephant's tooth for holding the fishing-nets down. People half-Dusun, half-Sulu, like Orang Rungus in the Labuk. At 12 waited for sixty minutes at an ancient clearing, where the remains of two houses, long since deserted, were found. A small clearing in the immense jungle, and three wooden spears (tanda) protecting the property of the people is all that remains of old Tenegang. . . . At 2.45, turning round to the S. to 160°, i.e. near S.S.E, and eventually at 2.50 to S.E. 130°. At 3.15, 160° S., 10° E. At 3.20, S. At 3.35, 170° S., 10° E. At 3.40, 160°, about S.S.E. At 4 due S., 180°. . . . The river being flooded, and the country also for a great distance inland, we could not get ashore. This at any time would be difficult on account of the vegetation. At 5 stopped on a mudbank to cook; immense difficulty.

*Jan. 9th.*—After a dreadful night, and very little sleep on account of sandflies, started away up the flooded river at 8 in W.S.W., D. 260°. . . . As we proceeded, came on an immense swamp, much overgrown

[2] Malay for "a play."

by trees of the nature of the mangroves. At 11.40 still on through dense swamp, D. 240° (W.S.W.); 11.45, 206° (S.S.W.). At 11.50 arrived at another immense swamp, or inland lake, and turned back. A rise of ten feet only between this and yesterday's campingplace. Absolutely no place to land, although went up the river twenty-one miles. ——, a yellow clay covered with six or eight feet of black slime at the inland lake or swamp. Temp. 30° 5′, 12.30. It being quite impossible to get on further, we turned back, and got back in three hours and a half, making the distance twenty miles. At the mouth stopped, and decided to send Beveridge to Silam, while self go up Kinabatangan to head. Got everything ready to-night. D. to Silam, S.E.; distance thirty miles; gave Beveridge a compass. At 8 p.m. temp. 29°, bar. 30.1. To-day it rained at intervals all the time, and there were several showers yesterday.

*Jan. 10th.*—Left our station at 8.15. Temp. 27°, bar. 30.2. Beveridge left for overland.

At 8.35 got back into the Kinabatangan. At 9.35 took sample of siliceous sand of river-bed. . . . At 12 made a halt, temp. 32° 5′, and landed at Bilet, where got a fowl, some sugar-cane, and a specimen of meerschaum, which the man said he had got from Sindyak, near Pinungah. Left again at 1.20 in a S.W. D. 230°.

Here heard of the Tingguluns, who some three or four years ago were always coming down here. The man was using the meerschaum for polishing his betel-nut box, and often asked how much per catti. 1.50, 320° N.W., through 360° N. to 10° (N. 10° E.); a hill ahead bearing N. 13° E. At 1.55, 30°, near N.E.;

through N. 360°. 2.40 to 2.45, 260° (W.S.W.). 3.15, 300° near W.N.W. 3.20, 320° N.W.

At 3.30 made a halt, in order to let prahu get up. Here we were informed that, to avoid fever, it was a good thing to wash with the clay from the river.

Elevation from mouth Tenegang, 120 feet. Distance to-day, eleven miles.

*Jan.* 11*th.*—Left at 7.20, D. 320° N.W. 7.20, temp. 39°, bar. 30.2. 7.35, 230°. At 7.40, 220°, i.e. near S.W. At 8, 160°. 8.20, 210°. At 8.25, 190°. 8.30, 180° S.

### The Buli Dupie's Story of the Kinabatangan Cave.

There was once a powerful Panjeran in the Kinabatangan who had seven sons (about thirty generations ago). This chief was famous for his fighting powers and for his bravery. One day he said to his eldest son, "Go and conquer some islands near Sulu," where a powerful chief, the enemy of the Kinabatangan people, lived. Accordingly, therefore, the brothers started on their expedition with seven large prahus. After a severe fight they proved victorious, and with a large booty they returned to their country. Night found them pulling up against the strong current near Malapi, and as darkness set in they were just opposite a cave in the limestone cliff on the banks of the river. "Let us," said the eldest brother, "sleep in that cave; it is easier, and we shall enjoy more comfort than in the prahus." "Oh, go not there," said the youngest brother; "I fear, if you do, some harm will come to us." "Do not be stupid," replied the elder, and his voice ruled the others; so they went into the large cave by a big opening. Having slept the night, the youngest brother got up with the morn, and rousing his brothers, said, "Oh, brothers, let us go out. I fear the cave is closing upon us; see, oh! see, the opening is very small." And, indeed, this was the fact; but the eldest brother, who was sleepy, said, "You speak that which is not," and his speech again ruled the rest. In vain the youngest son reiterated his warning, and when the hole was getting smaller and smaller, and there was only just time for escape, he got out, leaving his six brothers in the cave. The hole was still closing, and as the youngest looked in again, he saw his brothers each in the arms of a fairy-like damsel, who led them away into the cave. The hole shut with a bang on the brothers and their fairy ladies for ever, and to this day ladders are kept hanging outside, and rice is thrown in by the passing Sulumen to feed the long-lost brethren.

I was informed at Bilet that Sin Dyaks are Dyaks who wear trousers, while real Dyaks only wear the waistcloth. . . . It rained to-day several times. One terrific shower and thunderstorm. We, in fact, get very unsettled weather every day. Rain, in showers, begins, as a rule, about eleven to twelve o'clock, and continues at intervals until four or five o'clock. One storm sent the temperature down $2°$ C. 1.30, $200°$ W.N.W. 1.35, $320°$ (N.W., near). The people say it is twenty days from here to Pinungah. 1.55, $310°$; passed a house on the left bank. At 2, $298°$. 2.5, $260°$, near W. 2.10, $190°$, near S.

At 3.15 passed a high hill on left bank, with strata inclined at a high angle. The rock was a limestone, much veined with quartz. At 3.50 a heavy rainstorm came on again, making the trip very miserable. At 4.0, 190° (near S.). 4.6, 300° (N.W.). 4.25, 240° S.W. 4.35, 130° (S.E.). Distance got through to-day, sixteen miles. Stopped at 4.45 at Subak. Bar. 30.5. Elevation above Bilet, 110 feet. At 4.40 passed on right a small tributary on left bank, three fathoms wide. I was told that we came from the same stock—Adam: this by a wretched old Suluman.

*Jan.* 12*th.*—Left Subak at 8.23. D. 130° S.E. Bar. 30.1, ther. 29°. 8.40, 140° (S.E.). 8.55, 176°, near S. All through primitive forests. At 9, 250°, near W.

I hear that if we go up the Quamut we shall meet the Tinggulans and roving bands of Muruts. At Malapi the people said fifteen days would bring us to Pinungah. Here they say one month. Quamut is ten days this side of Pinungah. It is two days to Sebangan. . . . 11.35, passed a small tributary on the left (right bank), about five fathoms wide; rapid current, much overgrown by primitive jungle, and apparently uninhabited.

Met some people coming from the Lukun. They said four days would bring us to Quamut. They remembered Witti and his adventures in the Lukun. . . . Stopped at four o'clock. Distance to-day, thirteen miles. Height above Subak, 100 feet. All day through immense forests, and I had a touch of fever. Our camping-place on left bank, where a lot of driftwood was thrown up. The place was an old clearing. The sandflies are a terrible curse; so is sitting in a prahu all day.

*Jan.* 13*th.*—Left our camp at 7.15. D. 260°, bar. 30.1, ther. 28°. . . . The only things we see now are a stray pigeon and dozens of graceful cranes or storks, which I can never hit, as they are such shy birds.

320° at 1.53 (N.W.). At 1.57, 280° (W., near). At 2, 280° (S.W.). At 2.8, 200°. At 2.15, 190°. At 3, 210°. At 3.15 a high hill, bearing 240°. We are also travelling through immense jungle, which is now hilly. Met a prahu with some Javanese in it, who said that in three months we might hope to get to Pinungah. The speaker said also that Ward had not got to Pinungah yet. I don't think he spoke the truth. . . . At 3.47, 350°. 3.55, 360° (N.). Halted at 4.30., bar. 30. Distance got over, sixteen and a quarter miles ; elevation, sixty feet.

*Jan.* 14*th*.—Heavy rainstorm in the early morning prevented our cooking, so we had to go on without our breakfasts. Started at 6.15. . . . I had a terrible attack of fever and ague, and made up my mind to go back, which mind I changed as soon as the attack was over. I shall never forget the horrible sensation of shivering with cold beneath a burning sun. Temp. 33°.

*Jan.* 15*th*.—Left our camp at 7.25. D. 30° N.E. 7.45, 330°; two miles an hour. If I have fever again to-morrow, I mt go back. . . . At 1.40 made a halt to go on shore. At 2.15 started on again. . . . At 4.50 stopped. Elevation got up, 100 feet ; bar. 29.95. Got over seventeen miles.

※ ※ ※ ※ ※

*Maden, serigo, gunong, matu*—the native way for testing a kriss or their luck. (*Okor kriss.*)

[A blank is left for a note on the kriss test. . . . He went on again from his camping-ground at 5.30 in the comparative cool of the morning, while the mists were on the river, which had risen in the night and become a terrible torrent; then follow a page or two of observations; stopped at a deserted place for food, thinks it is Sebangan, " which is now deserted on account of the alligators—the reputation of the place is so bad that when bathing in the boat this morning I had a man with a full-cocked gun on guard." Everywhere the country is flooded. On the previous day there is this closing note—"take specimens strata right bank to-morrow". . . . Elevation to-day only about 60 feet. Distance got over to-day nineteen miles.]

| Distances. | | Miles. |
|---|---|---|
| From Malapi to Tenegang. | | |
| Jan. 8th | | 5 |
| ,, 10th, Tenegang up K.B. | | 11 |
| ,, 11th, up K.B. | | 10 |
| ,, 12th ,, | | 13 |
| ,, 13th ,, | | $16\frac{1}{4}$ |
| ,, 14th ,, | | 4 |
| ,, 15th ,, | | 17 |
| ,, 16th ,, | | 19 |
| ,, 17th ,, | | 19 |
| | | $120\frac{1}{4}$ |

Strata now consists of clays containing intermediate bands of sandstone, the whole dipping at an angle of 35° to the N.E. Also a ferruginous clay containing bands of—

\* \* \* \* \*

*Jan. 19th.*—Got away at 6. . . . At 8, bar. 30.5, ther. 26°. At 8.5 passed a small tributary on the left about six fathoms wide. Our course at 8, 200° S.W. To-day we passed what might be called our first rapid (*carangan*), and the river became much more winding than formerly. . . . Banks now composed of a conglomerate similar to the Kinoram, one that is igneous and metamorphic rocks cemented by silica.

The men complain very much of "Limantungs," a kind of leech. . . . At 1.30 saw houses floating down stream. We have often heard of the Americans rolling their houses, but these people fasten their prahus together, make a raft, and then build their houses on the top. When sickness prevails, this is the way the people forsake their countries. . . . Kinabatang stones, specimens of the 17th. Sandstones, ferruginous and fire clays. Also on the 18th. . . . At 4.55 halted for the night; bar. 29.9. Rained in torrents just as we wanted to cook, and miserable enough it was.

*Jan. 20th.*—Got away at 6.15, 280°. . . . At 7.25 got to our first carangan, D. 210° S.W., and one mile per hour. At 7.50 passed a tributary on the left, ten fathoms wide at mouth. Our course 260° (W.). . . . Vast deposits of mud, formed of detritus, brought down by the river, in which are imbedded canes, sticks, and other vegetable matter in regular stratifications—the future coal-beds of Borneo. Might account for sandstones, as at Siquati, containing veins of a light coal. Where river bares itself, water trickling from banks much impregnated with oxide of iron. . . . At 4.13 entered the Quamut, D. 300° N.W., and stopped at the police-station. Elevation to-day, 100 feet. The place Quamut is a miserable hole; and as it rains in torrents every day, I can't see how we can get to Silam. . . .

*Jan. 21st.*—Quamut is a lonely police-station at the junction of the Kinabatangan and Quamut rivers, but in the latter. After the wild scenes in Kinoram and around Kina Balu, this country is flat and uninteresting, and, from a mineral point of view promises, so far, nothing. Rained very heavily all day. " Lamog " stream below Lukan, straight for Segama.

*Jan.* 22*nd.*—Left Quamut at 6.50; got back to Kinabatangan at 7, and continued our course up stream, D. 28° (N.E.). Could get no prahus and no guide at Quamut, so thought it best to go on to Pinungah and try there. . . . At 3.47 passed a large tributary on the left (right bank), about twenty fathoms wide, and, indeed, the same as the Quamut; some hills 1000 feet high in the distance. D. of our course 280°, 3.47 (W.).

\*     \*     \*     \*     \*

*Jan.* 24*th.*—The river flooded; fearful state of things; nothing but rain, rain, rain; cannot get on. Bar. 29.5, ther. 26°. Left at 6.20. D. 240° W. . . . The force of the current is terrific; the river being flooded, we can only make about a mile and a half per hour all day. At 4 stopped for the night, as the force of the stream had tired the men out.

Slept in a dead man's house. Ghosts and ginger— the Malay superstition. [This is evidently a memorandum of material for future use.]

*Jan.* 25*th.*—Left dead man's house at 6.20. D. 290° (W.). Bar. 30°, ther. 27° 5'. Elevation got once yesterday, fifty feet. No rain this morning, but the river frightfully flooded. . . . At 1.30, 250° (W.). From 1 to 2 looking for Durian only. Rain in torrents. Durian yellow-skinned and red pulp.[3] . . .

---

[3] The durian grows on a large and lofty forest tree, somewhat resembling an elm in its general character, but with a more smooth

Had some capital pigeon-shooting to-day—a bag of twelve. . . . Sighted high ranges of hills. . . . Elevation 100 feet to-day.

\*     \*     \*     \*     \*

*Jan. 27th.*—Got away at 5.50, D. W.; one mile per hour, and for hours dragging the prahu up rapids and carangans. At 7.15, 160° (S.). At 6.30 passed an island. At 7.25, another island. . . . Stopped at 9.25; got away again at 10.25. . . . The people here are in the most pitiable condition of filth of all Dusuns that I have yet come across. I have never seen any so filthy, so miserable, and so abject as

and scaly bark. The fruit is round or slightly oval, about the size of a large cocoanut, of a green colour, and covered all over with short stout spines, the bases of which touch each other, and are consequently somewhat hexagonal, while the points are very strong and sharp. It is so completely armed, that if the stalk is broken off it is a difficult matter to lift one from the ground. The outer rind is so thin and tough, that from whatever height it may fall it is never broken. From the base to the apex five very faint lines may be traced, over which the spines arch a little; these are the sutures of the carpels, and show where the fruit may be divided with a heavy knife and a strong hand. The five cells are satiny-white within, and are each filled with an oval mass of cream-coloured pulp, embedded in which are two or three seeds about the size of chestnuts. This pulp is the eatable part, and its consistence and flavour are indescribable. A rich butter-like custard highly flavoured with almonds gives the best general idea of it, but intermingled with it come wafts of flavour that call to mind cream-cheese, onion-sauce, brown sherry, and other incongruities. Then there is a rich glutinous smoothness in the pulp which nothing else possesses, but which adds to its delicacy. It is neither acid, nor sweet, nor juicy, yet one feels the want of none of these qualities, for it is perfect as it is. It produces no nausea or other bad effect, and the more you eat of it the less you feel inclined to stop. In fact, to eat durians is a new sensation, worth a voyage to the East to experience."—Wallace's *Malay Archipelago.*

those above Quamut. Churlish and suspicious, envious, timid, and inhospitable.

The banks are composed of the red, recent river-gravels, containing pebbles of quartz, ferruginous sandstone, &c. All along here tried for minerals—no trace. . . . At 3.30 just escaped a fearful rapid, a place where I set my teeth and held my breath as we dashed into the terrific current. . . . Stopped at 4.20. Elevation 100 ft.

*Jan. 28th.*—Left our station at 6.25, D. 240° (S.W.). Terrific rush of water, as a fresh flood had come down during the night. Bar. 29.1, ther. 28°. At 7.15, 330° (N.W.). Very hard work to-day. . . . We go now only about half a mile per hour. At 9.15 stopped to cook. At 10.50 got away again. D. 300° (N.W.).

At 12.20, having made half a mile by fearful exertions, 230° (S.W.). The current is so swift that paddling is impossible, poling equally so, and the banks are so steep and wooded that dragging by a rope is not to be thought of. The only way to advance is for a man to push on ahead a little way by clinging to trees and half-swimming, get a foothold on a tree-branch or on the bank. A rope from the prahu is then thrown to him, and we drag ourselves up a few yards. The current, I should think, is at least twelve miles per hour in the middle of the river. . . . Engaged a man named Jabit, who is from Pinungah.

\* \* \* \* \*

*Jan. 30th.*—Got away at 5.45. D. 300° (N.W.). Bar. 29.55, ther. 29°.

At 6.30, D. 220° (S.W.). At 6.40, 260° (W.).

The natives all say that the Kinabatangan rises in Kina Balu; but no rolled pebbles of porphyritic granite, as in the Labuk. At 6.45, D. 250° (N.W.). . . . At 8.40

stopped to cook. At 10.10 got away again from the Dusun (Tambanor) house, where two coffins were set out. In these the dead remain for one or two years sealed up. D. N. 10° E. At 10.15, 300° (N.W.). Rate, one mile per hour. . . . Many landslips of ferruginous sandstone, which weathers black; vertical strata. At 4.15, 130° (S.). At 4.20, 240°, and stopped and slept. On a carangan for the first time on the Kinabatangan. Pebbles of ferruginous sandstone and quartz.

*Jan.* 31*st.*—Got away on our last day's journey at 7.20, D. 200° (S.W.). Pace, one mile per hour, and opened a fresh bag of rice. . . . At 1.40 arrived at Pinungah. Jabit twenty-three days. Spent curious night at Pinungah with Ward, who is staying here. Elevation to-day, 110 feet.

*Feb.* 1*st.*—Rain in torrents. From Tungara. Below Lukan, Lamag, Lamad. . . . Longbilang on the Segama *there is gold*.[1] ——— On the Segama. ——— Namut Bolud from the mouth seven days. [There are three blanks in this entry of Feb. 1st, as if the names of places, &c., were only set down for private guidance.]

* * * * *

[1] Mr. Crocker, the Company's manager in London, writes:—"On comparing Frank's diary with the map which shows the route of Mr. Walker, who has since discovered gold in the Segama, I find that Frank tried to cross into the Segama higher up than the point on Walker's map. Consequently the tributary Longbilang mentioned by Frank as containing gold is above the Sanguie Belang tributary where Mr. Walker has found it. There is every reason to believe that gold will be found higher up, and it is sad to think that had it not been for the swamp (see pages 277, 278) Frank would have got across country and made the discovery early in 1883, in the district noted in his diary-note of Feb. 1st." The diary has, however, been valuable as a guide to the succeeding pioneers; and, being forewarned by its useful pages, Mr. Walker (a clever young officer) was of course wise enough to avoid the swamp which Frank and his expeditionary corps of natives made heroic efforts to cross.

*Feb.* 2*nd*.—At 7.20 started up the Pinungah River. D. S. 180°. ... The head of the Segama not far from the coast. At 8.37, 260° (W.). At 8.40, 280° (N.W.). At 8.45, 160° (S.E.). Hewitt coal. Ferruginous sandstone. At 12.5, 110° (S.E.). At 12.8, 250° (S.W.). Vertical strata; on the river ferruginous sandstone.

\* \* \* \* \*

*Feb.* 3*rd*.—At 7.30 got away and left Ward. At 7.30, 200° (S.W.). ... At 9.0, 160° (S.E.). At 9.30 found coal-boulders in the stream, and stopped for lunch; also piece in situ sandstone. Curious metallic slime—2 Fe. On the right bank (left bank) coal cropping up in small seams, one-half to one foot wide, landslip sandstone. On the left bank (right bank), about 300 yards below the outcrop on the opposite bank, coal also. Outcrop only in isolated pockets in fire-clay. Outcrop N. and S., almost. Mandore having forgotten the picks, had to send prahu out to get them, as well as rice.

Enormous deposits of feoric hydrate in the water, indicating large quantities of iron below. Means at disposal not sufficient to enable me to bore, and surface outcrops are all I can go by.

220° and 40°, N.E. and S.W., line of dip of strata on right bank. Angle of dip 42° (N.E. and S.W.).

On right bank (left bank). Direction of dip, 260° and 80° (i.e. W.S.W. and E.N.E.).

Numerous tracks of wild cattle, deer, and pigs, the sounds of jungle fowl, and the feathers of Argus pheasants were frequent.

Bar. 29.8. Elevation to-day about ninety-five feet.

At 1.15 left our hut, and travelling along line of dip of strata 260° (W.S.W.) to find an outcrop of coal. All the way through dense forests, with tracks of red deer, wild cattle, and pigs. We struck away on the line of strike of the strata at one mile per hour.

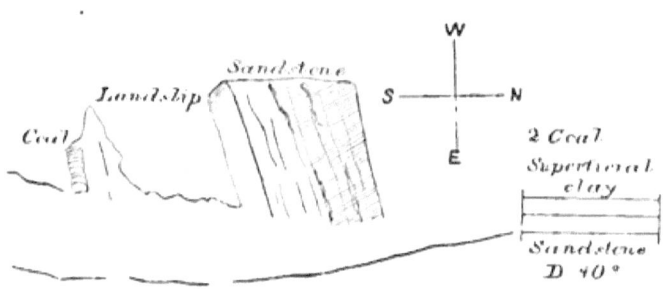

At 1.45 crossed a small stream running N.E. to the Pinungah; our course W.S.W. In the stream boulders of sandstone, but no coal, and turned off S. line of strike to the Pinungah River. Got down on the river at 2, one point above house. Sandstone, but no coal. At 2.10 took bearing of high hill, 70° (E.N.E.).

*Feb. 4th.*—At 8.10 started for a high hill. D. 110° (E.S.E.). Bar. at bottom, 29·9. At 8.30 came upon small inland lake (pace, one mile per hour) at nearly 100 feet above river, about 100 yards long. At 9.5 arrived at place near top. Elevation 490 feet. Bar. 29.23. Rocks, sandstone. *Mem.*—Remark on different character of jungle here; many palms, called by the Malays "Sardang" and "Bidang." Large canes, capital for making atap. A hill bearing 250° (W.S.W.), about 700 feet high, across the river. Left bottle on top. Continuing on in a D. E., got to elevation 650 feet at 9.45. At 11.15, 1400 feet; arrived on top of first hill. The present direction of spur N.N.E. (20°). Hills to the west of about same elevation. At 11.45, having reached an elevation of 1450 feet from the river, stopped. The hill composed of ferruginous sandstone,

Hill bearing 90° (E.) from top. Elevation about 2500 feet. Our course having been about E., 90°. The water in brooks we drank, and very pleasant it was. At 3 arrived back, having been lost since 11.45 through going S. a little away round hills and dales—a fearful thing to be lost—and eventually going W., got back at 3. Lost all my things to-day on the hill—plates, knives, &c.; but sent two men back after them, and luckily got them. C. Harean and Angang came back. Credit $2 to Salleh and Samat.

*Feb. 5th.*—Left at 7.30, D. 210° (S.W.), bar. 29.75. Rate, half a mile per hour. At 8, 190° (S.) and terrific rapid. At 8.25, 230° (S.W.).

Did not notice any coal on the "carangans," except on that one quite near the outcrop of the coal-seam above noted. This carangan is about 400 yards long, and under each boulder is a small rolled pebble of coal. At 8.50, 210° (S.W.). At 9, small houses on the left (right bank) for rattan gathering. Orang Tungara. At ——150° (S.E.); travel on foot near the banks of the river all the way. Sandstone and quartz measures.

At 9.15, 160° (S.E.). At 9.40, 170° (S.E.). Foot travel again after having eaten Sukang Durian. At 11, 160° (S.E.); and as we had got to a terrific waterfall and rapid, where it was very dangerous and almost impossible for the prahus to go up, stopped. Bar. ——; elevation, fifty feet.

We stopped at a place on the right bank (left bank), where found part of a skull of a man (and copper tobacco-box lid), whom Jabit said had been killed while swimming in the river by men of "Sepulut," who are Elangs, and cannot be far from the Sebokong. Jabit says that the day he came down the Pinungah was the day after the Sepulut men had come down to Tungara and killed ten men. The river Sepulut men are said to live on a big river whose mouth is not far from Silam, and which therefore must be either the Siboku or the Sumbakong.

*Feb. 6th.*—Bar. 28.5. At 8.20, D. 170° (S.E.), started on foot. At 8.30 travelling along river-bank, 80 to 100 feet high. Sandstone. At 8.40, 160° (S.E.). Height, 100 feet. At 9.25, 130° (S.E.), flood. Continuing our arduous way along places where a slip would have been fatal, we arrived at 9.55 on the river again, and the country to the S. and S.E. seemed more open and less hilly. Our direction 110° (S.E.). Elevation, 100 feet. Carangan composed of red and black ferruginous sandstone. At 10.30 got on some prahus, which luckily were going up the river. 110° (S.E.). Two miles per hour.

*Feb. 7th.*—Prahus came up at 9, having been upset four times. We lost several paddles, some rice, and the men a lot of other small things. At 10.40 got away up stream. . . . As we proceed the country becomes flatter and flatter. . . . At 3.30 stopped. Elevation 20 feet.

\* \* \* \* \*

*Feb. 8th.*—At 2.15 arrived at Tungara, where we nearly had a row, all through a misunderstanding with the Muruts, which, had not some traders arrived just in time, would have ended in a fight. The Tungara people took our party for people from the Upper Kinabatangan (Millian), with whom they are in feud, and who are also Muruts of Tungara. My men say they resemble the Padan people

*Feb. 9th.*—Tracing back Witti's letter to some Tungara men named Silomboks. Witti is said to have given it at Telonangoh, which is a Tungara campong, at the head of the Pinungah. From Telonangoh, Witti was going to the Sepulut, which is a five-days' journey on to the Simbokong, at the junction of that river with the Rouhab.

At 9.15, 310° (N.W.)   Bar. 29.75.

Tungara: houses, 6; men, 25; women, 36; headman, " Kawangin."

*Description:* Short hair, inclined to be frizzy; dark skins; wear chawat about two inches wide. Use spears, sumpitans, and parangs. At 9.45, 200° (S.W.).

At 10.20 stopped at a carangan and secured specimens of coal, sandstone, and clay. A high waterfall eventually stopped us. Much against will had to go back, as river much flooded. Natives know of no outcrop of coal about here, but there must be one somewhere.

At 1.25 got back to last Tumbanoi huts. Torrents of rain. The most terrible day ever spent, shooting rapids. Nearly over in one rapid; we stuck half-way down on some stones, and the prahu nearly broke in two.

At Tungara our prahus came to the bank, and, fearing nothing, we walked up to a place where several Muruts were making a new house. We entered, and I told my interpreter to buy a native bamboo-case for keeping tobacco and light (bamboo, piece of china, and touchwood). There were about seven or eight men in the house, and I noticed that, in spite of my interpreter, one by one they slipped away and went into the jungle, taking their sumpitans, spears, &c., and making as if they would shoot birds or monkeys. My men became suspicious, and they also one by one went away to get their guns and other weapons. The interpreter and myself were at last the only occupants of the house, when I heard shouting on the hills near us, and my man said, "Get down, master; quick, quick!" I lost no time in jumping down and calling for my rifle and sword. The Muruts I saw about fifteen on a hill to the right, and about twice that number on a hill in front. They were coming down on us also. Now, however, my men came up from the boats, guns full-cocked, and my boy came running with my Winchester. We grouped our little band, mounting eleven rifles, and waited. The sumpitans of the Muruts were pointed towards us, and their spears were already elevated. My men had their rifles at their shoulders, ready to fire, when who should rush up (just in time to save us, perhaps) but our friends the Tambanois, our Suluman friends of Bongoku. "Run away!" shouted (*mugidoh*) they to the Muruts, "run away!" "Wait, don't fire," they shouted to our party, and running to the headman of the Muruts they explained matters, and we learnt that seeing no faces they knew, the Muruts thought we wanted to kill them, and they thought my interpreter was merely a trap to deceive them. They also thought my camp-chair was a machine to trap men and catch them. Matters were now explained, and in the morning they were anxious to trade with us, and I bought a sumpitan and some other native things. The old man said that he and all his people would go with us to fight Sepuluts, if I would go with them; they assured me that these were the people that killed Witti, and that it was five days' journey from the head of the Pinungah.

Shooting rapids to-day was indeed a terrible business. The river flooded, and waves like those on the beach at Labuan all across the river, with the roar

"A FRIEND IN NEED."—AN INCIDENT OF THE LAST EXPEDITION.

From a drawing by W. H. Margetson.

To face page 272.

of the torrent almost deafening. Once we shot down a carangan, and right in the middle we struck on a rock, *bang!* Another bang and the prahu half filled. "Get out, get out," I roared, and down got my Sarawak men, and pulled the prahu straight just in time, and we shot into deep water safely, but at the speed of a railway-train.

*Feb.* 10*th*.—At 8 got away, and going up stream until 8.15, when got on right bank (left bank), (bar. 29.8), and in D. 280° (S.W.) went through jungle; two miles per hour. At 8.25, 200°, S.W.

At 8.30 crossed the Tepokong, a tributary of the Pinungah. About W. at 8.45, and crossed the Tepokong again, D. S.W., 220°. Crossed again, 8.50. Having crossed again, 8.55, D. 260°, W. At 9.10, 300 feet, D. 260°, W.; crossed two tributaries of the Tepokong, and at 9.20 crossed latter at 450 feet. At 9.25 D. W. At 9.40 got to top of hill, 600 feet high, and rested a few minutes. D. 260°, W. At 10.10 arrived at the place where the coal was. Height 750 feet, where in a mixture of light yellow clay found a kind of lignite in small lumps, which may be decomposed surface coal.

*Feb.* 11*th*.—After a terrible day of narrow escapes from drowning got to the place where first stopped with Ward, one day up stream from Pinungah. At one rapid to-day my prahu half filled.

*Feb.* 12*th*.—To-day a fearful upset, caused by Durahim, who did not get out of the prahu.

*Lost.*

| | |
|---|---|
| Paddles . . . | . 3 |
| Prismatic compass | 1 |
| | T |

| | |
|---|---|
| Barometer, aneroid | 1 |
| Cross-staff | 1 |
| Sword-bayonet | 1 |
| Ramrod | 1 |
| Saucepans | 2 |
| Frypan | 1 |

Durahim, 1 hat; Guntar, 1 hat; Taha, 1 hat; gunpowder. Net, 1.

Wick, 1 yard; jam, 6; frypan, 1; candles, 3 packets; matches, 12; saucepan; porter-beer, 6 bottles; vegetables, 2 tins; tea, 12 bundles; fish, 7 tins; sauce, 1 bottle; sherry, 2 bottles; biscuits, 2 tins (small); butter, 2; trading cloth, 1 piece; soap, 2 pats; whisky, 1 bottle; ———, 1; fish, 2 haddocks; and a lot of macaroni.

*Men in the prahu upset.*

| | |
|---|---|
| Durahim. | Jabit. |
| Murrim. | Mile. |
| Monup. | Limbang. |
| Guntar. | |

*Our accident.*—When starting to-day I somehow feared that the large prahu would come to grief, so I got in the smaller one. We had passed two or three bad rapids, my men being very careful, and getting out at every hard bit. The big boat came shooting down one great rapid in a gallant but rather foolhardy way, and I cautioned the men. We were not far from Pinungah when we arrived at a very swift rapid, about two fathoms high perhaps. My men all got out, and we dragged the boat over some big stones very carefully. In our rear came the big boat, making straight for the middle of the rapid. I called to them, but *bang* they went on a rock, and Durahim shot off the bow into the surging torrent. I saw him disappear, and his hat float away down stream, but he got to the side and went back to his prahu. I shouted again to them to get out and pull the boat down, and then my attention was called away by the danger to ourselves, from some large waves. I got into my boat, and we were just starting away clear of the rapid when *bang, bang*, the big prahu shot down on top of us, and nearly turned us over. Her bow went right on top of our stern. The terrific current turned her over; and one, two, three men I saw carried away like corks down stream. I rushed to the prahu up to my waist in the torrent, and we all landed out the things as quick as possible—guns, ginger, bayonets, rugs, blankets, tins, &c. Fortunately our prahu had struck on two big rocks, and so we were enabled to get some of the things out; as it is, our losses are very severe, and I am not able to think of them as yet. I will cut Durahim's and Murrim's wages if it turns out, as I think, that the prahu was turned over by their fault. All my clothes, rugs, bed, wet through, and in a very miserable state we continued our journey to Pinungah, where we arrived much discouraged and tired out.

*Feb. 13th.*—Left at 8.35 Pinungah for Lamag, with the Sulu guide for Silam. Stopped at 3.30 at the place where we shot the fowls going up. About four or five days from Pinungah, if going against the stream. Took also from Pinungah one bag Company's rice; bought one bag from Hadgi Bustan, $8; one enamelled iron pot lost in the Pinungah. We get the most terrible weather, rains every day, all up the Pinungah River, and now every day rain on the Kinabatangan. The men have pretty hard times; no fish; and Beveridge's men did not even get salt coming up.

*Feb.* 14*th*.—Left up-stream at 7; stopped at Tuan Murrim at 2 to 2.30. Last night Corporal Hassan arrived with some of my things, which Bongku had fished out of the Pinungah River. My prismatic compass, cross-staff, barometer, all got back, but the two former spoiled. We go about ten miles per hour. I was very much astonished and pleased, of course, to get my things, and told the corporal to give two pieces of panjang tuguli to Bon. At 5.10 got to Tegai.

*Feb.* 15*th*.—Left at 5.30. . . . At 4 stopped at Penglina Sarai's house. Above Lakam.

*Feb.* 16*th*.—At 7.30 left Penglima Sarai, and at 1 entered the Lamag. . . . The country up the river very like that of the Tenegang, and we shall have great difficulty in going overland. Darhu says the path will be grown over and perhaps lost. . . . At 3.5 stopped on left bank. Rain and wind had set in —a terrible night.

*Feb.* 17*th*.—Got up prahus, and at 9.20 got away; general direction E. (to E.S.E. and S.E.). At 9.40 got on to the Lamag again, and as the river was flooded, we were obliged to send back for the small prahu. At 10.55 arrived at a tributary of the Lamag called Taphar Pahti, which at 11.30, having dragged the prahu through a fearful swamp, got across the stream with awful difficulties. A hundred yards further on another swamp, and got across at 11.40.

At 1.10, Thank God, got past a fearful swamp. No water, horse-leeches. A terrible elephant swamp. Elephant dung.

At 3 we stopped, as our way led us on another

swamp. We made a hut, and slept in spite of leeches, ants, and wet. Rain as usual! Our direction to-day E. to S.E., but out of our way to avoid swamp to the E.

*Feb.* 18*th.*—We found ourselves on a hill in the midst of an impenetrable swamp. As far as the eye could see, which we got at by climbing trees, nothing but swamp, swamp; rolling grass growing twenty feet high, and as sharp as a knife. Concluded to turn back, as impossible to go forward, and at 8.30 got across the swamp of yesterday. We determined to go across the Lamag again, and try for the third time to cross to Segama. The swamp which stopped us is, no doubt, the source of several small tributaries of the Kinabatangan, and is very extensive and deep. At 10.35, having got back across the Lamag, proceeded in a D. S. to S.S.E. along right bank (left bank) of the river. Travelling along, therefore, we were obliged to go S.W. to W., until impossible to proceed further, as the stream bends round to the W. and N.W. We therefore determined to cross again, and a large tree had to be cut down in order to get across. At 12.30 we began to cut; the handle of the big axe broke, and we were obliged to cut the tree down with hand-axes and parangs. At 1.15 the tree fell. At 2.15 got back on to the river Lamag again. Travelling along elephant track, suddenly heard screams in the jungle and a rush of animals. I tore down the slope in front, in spite of thorns and spines, but the animals were too quick for me and got away. At 3.30 we went into camp for the night. No water, and we were obliged to drink the muddy water found in swamp-pools. The stench of it was rank and vile. We have gone about eight miles through trackless waste and jungle; main direction S.E. to S.

*Feb. 19th.*—At 7.40 left; D. S.E., over small hills. After travelling along a trackless forest and across a swamp covered with prickly thorns (Malay—*Salak*), and at 8.50 came across small stream running S.E., and which Darhu said was a tributary of the Segama. At 9.10 came to a river about three fathoms wide, running N., which Darhu says is the Masah, a tributary of the Segama. At 10.10 crossed another stream. At 10.15 another small stream, brown in colour, as if draining a swamp, running S.E. At 11.5 another swampy tract and creek. At 12.30 stopped and ate. Another small creek at 12.30. We went on again at 1.30, and at 2.30 got to the end of our tether—that is, we arrived at the end of a hill, swamps surrounding us on all sides. A dismal waste, swarming with horse-leeches, and rotten through and through. What could be done? Only one thing—go back.

*Feb. 20th.*—Very weak from leeches, as no less than ten fed full on each leg yesterday.

*Feb. 21st.*—Yesterday we got back to the mouth of the Lamag; a terrible day's journey; and when, tired out, we arrived, I counted no less than ten leeches on each foot. Yesterday we came across outcrop of lignite similar to that at Pinungah. Rock, sandstone.

\* \* \* \* \*

*Feb. 23rd.*—At 7 arrived at the big mouth of the Kinabatangan. Crocodiles, fish. Distance, three miles to four miles per hour. A wait from 8.30 to 9.35.

*Feb. 24th.*—We were stopped to-day preparing for sea. The monsoon blowing very strong, and the breakers white on the beach. We had to make "giroupi" all the prahus—that is, put one atap. We got away at 10.30; fearful sea. We paddled out into the night, tossing and rolling. Nearly upset, dark night, could only hear roar of breakers on the beach. At 12 put back, worn out and wretched, wet through and through.

*Feb. 25th.*—Left the mouth of the Kinabatangan at 7.30, myself, Beveridge, boy, and Bilal going on foot; the beach covered with trunks of trees and strewn with wreckage. At first we kept up well and got ahead of the four prahus, but when the sandy beach changed to mud, and we had to walk along up to our knees in the stuff, we soon fell behind. At 12 we saw the last of the prahus away out to sea. We were toiling through a swamp, the sun blazing down upon us and scorching our bodies to death. We shouted, we screamed, and fired guns, but the people in the boats never heard us, and footsore and tired out, with parched throats, we continued our weary way. At 5, having walked eighteen miles, half of which was through swamp and clay, we arrived at the Mamahman River, which is broad, and brackish water. Daku has been up for two days; no fresh water, and nothing but nipa. We crossed four rivers, the largest named Tausan Pukol. Snipe, ducks, deer, pigs, and crocodiles not a few. Yesterday we shot two deer.

*Feb. 26th.*—Our course yesterday was S. and then S.E. To-day we tried to get out, and from 8 to 11 fighting terrific waves, which threatened to swamp the boats. Then a squall came on and rain in torrents. On the shore was almost as bad as in the prahus, sinking up to one's knees all the time in the mud and clay; slippery and wet through. Mosquitoes terrible, and all night a hammering of distant gongs.

*Feb. 27th.*—Left Mamalunan at 7, walking along beach, which by-and-by became sandy, at two miles per hour. Shot at a shark several times, hit. At 9 arrived at the mouth of the Segama after a terrible voyage. The waves washed clean over the prahus more than once. River about 1000 yards wide at mouth. Pace two miles per hour.

\* \* \* \* \*

*March 1st.*—(Just one year ago left Sandakan for the Labok.) Got away at 7.30, D. 260° (W.). At 7.40, 240° (S.W.). At 7.45, 210° (S.W.). At 7.50, 200° (S.W.). At 8, 300° (N.W.). At 8.5, 250° (S.W.). At 8.7, 210° (S.W.). At 8.20, 270° (W.). At 8.25, 360° (N.). At 8.35, 270° (W.). At 8.45, 170° (S.). At 9, 260° (W.). At 9.10, 110° (S.E.). At 9.20, 130° (S.E.). At 9.30, 180° (S.). At 9.45 a small tributary on left six feet wide. At 9.45, 220° (S.W.). A 9.55, 260° (W.). At 10, 240° (W.S.W.). At 10.7, 270° (W.). At 10.15, 260° (W.). At 10.24, 100° (E.). At 10.30, 180° (S.). At 10.35, 270° (W.). At 10.40, 170° (S.). At 10.45, 270° (W.). At 11, 290° (N.W.). At 11.10, 170° (S.). At 11.20, 280° (W.). At 11.35, 180° (S.). Left tidal part. High banks, evidences of immense floods, much sand. At 11.50, 230° (W.). At 12.15, 250° (W.). At 12.20, 90° (E.). At 12.35, 200° (S.W.). Passed small tributary on the left about two fathoms wide ―― (name ――). I have now four men sick; one, Mile, left at Malapi. At 12.55, 230° (S.W.). At 1.15 a small tributary on the left three or four fathoms wide at mouth. Thunder and rain to-day. At 1.20, 240° (S.W.). At 1.55, 230°. At

## How the last Expedition ended.

2.10, 240° (N.W.). At 2.24, 280° (N.W.). At 2.30, 30° (N.E.). At 2.40, 300° (N.W.). Tracks of deer; large deposits of sand; river swift and deep. At 3.25, 160° (S.E.). At 3.40, 290° (N.W.).[1]

[1] The last day's notes are given in full, to show the character and method of the work, and the frequency of the observations which were set down in this manner from day to day, and almost up to the moment when the diarist left his boat to return to it a corpse in the arms of his followers. On the inside of the cover of the diary are several rough sketches of swords and spears, and geological or geographical diagrams. Among the latter is the following, which was probably intended as memoranda for a map of his route:—

## VI.

## HOW THE LAST EXPEDITION ENDED.

Letter from Governor Treacher—Mr. Resident Pryer's Report—Opening of the Inquest—The evidence—Adjourned for the arrival of the last expeditionary boats—Verdict of the jury.

"*Sandakan, March* 19*th*, 1883.

"Sir,—It is with the greatest possible regret that I enclose copy of a letter from Mr. Resident Pryer, in which he reports the sad intelligence of the death from the accidental discharge of his own gun of Mr. F. Hatton on the 1st instant, of which I only heard on my arrival here on the 16th instant.

"The melancholy details are carefully described in Mr. Pryer's letter; and the evidence given at the coroner's inquest, of which I enclose a copy, is conclusive that Mr. Hatton met with his death by shooting himself, by accident, in the jungle, whilst returning, after shooting at an elephant on the banks of the Segama River on the east coast, which he was engaged in prospecting for gold and other minerals.

"On the 4th instant he was buried at Elopura, being followed to the grave by the Resident, all the Europeans, and many inhabitants, Chinese and native, of Sandakan.

"In Mr. Hatton's death the Company has lost a

valuable officer, whose reports of journeys in the interior, and of metalliferous researches amidst circumstances of much difficulty, and oftentimes of personal danger, will remain as reliable records in the annals of the North Borneo Company.

"Mr. Hatton was devoted to the work he had in hand, and his scientific attainments made him enthusiastic in his interesting pursuits.

"Personally his amiability endeared him to all who came in contact with him. He was as popular amongst his brother officers as he was trusted among the natives who followed him so faithfully, to his death, in his inland journeys.

"To me he was always loyal, performing his duties with great zeal and intelligence, and I sincerely deplore the early loss of a scientific officer whose future was so full of promise, and for whom I entertained a personal feeling of friendship and esteem.

"Mr. Beveridge, who had accompanied the deceased on nearly all his travels in Borneo, and who was with him at the last, tells me that he had never seen him in better health and spirits, looking forward as he was to his approaching return to England and reunion with his family, his deep affection for whom was apparent to any one long in his company.

"I would add that the Winchester carbine which caused the fatal accident, appears to be a dangerous weapon to carry in the jungle, the trigger being so very sensitive that a sharp tap on the ground would set it off when at full cock.

"I have requested Mr. Resident Pryer to see that the deceased's personal effects are carefully collected and forwarded to the London office by the first opportunity. I am sorry that I cannot see to this myself, as my stay here is brief and every moment occupied, the steamer by which I leave for Kudat being expected here this evening.

"I beg to call your attention to the devotion of Mr. Beveridge and the men in bringing the corpse all the way by sea to Sandakan in a small gobang or canoe in a tropical climate. Some recognition of these services is called for, and on this subject I will address you in a separate letter.

"I have the honour to be, sir,
"Your obedient servant,
"W. H. TREACHER,
"Governor.

"The Chairman,
"British North Borneo Company."

"*Elopura, March 7th,* 1883.

"SIR,—It is my melancholy duty to have to report to you the death of Mr. Frank Hatton by a shot from his own gun on the 1st instant up the Segama River.

"I have the honour to enclose the report of the coroner's inquest; but in order to make the matter quite clear will give a short account of the sad occurrence.

"It appears that Mr. Hatton's expedition was composed of four boats. Mr. Hatton was in the first, Mr. Beveridge, about an hour behind, in the last. Mr. Hatton fired from his boat at an elephant, twice wounding it, apparently severely; and jumping on shore, accompanied only by his mandore, Drahman, gave chase. They very soon came up to the elephant, which had stopped, and was roaring or grumbling.

Thinking no doubt the Winchester rifle, with which alone he was armed, too light to attack the elephant, he left Drahman to watch it, and went back and called all the men who were near, armed them with Sniders, and told them to come with him. The elephant had, however, in the meantime moved off, and they all went after it; but it then being nearly dark, Mr. Hatton was at last persuaded to return to his boat. On the way back he was walking with his rifle (the Winchester) at the shoulder, and stooping down to pass underneath a vine (a creeper), put out his hand, holding the stock of the rifle in it, to lift up the vine. The stock was thus from him, the muzzle towards him, the rifle probably being on full cock (though there is no direct evidence of this); at the instant he was in this position, partially stooping, his arm extended from him, the muzzle of the gun must have slid down his shoulder, leaving it pointing at the top of his shoulder, and at this instant it went off, presumably from the trigger having been pulled by some twigs of the creeper. The ball entered at the collar-bone and came out at the back somewhat lower down. His men were round him in a moment, and seized him before he fell, but 'Oodeen, Oodeen, mati sahya, Oodeen,' was all he said. Oodeen was his boy, a Tutong lad, on whose shoulder his head was then resting. One, if not two, of the main arteries were severed, and death ensued very rapidly; but Mr Beveridge had almost arrived at the place where Mr. Hatton landed, heard the fatal shot and the cries that followed, and rushed up to the spot, arriving there within four to five minutes of the occurrence, and while Mr. Hatton was still alive; but nothing could be done, and in a moment or two more he breathed his last.

" The body was then placed in a gobang and brought down with all despatch to Elopura.

" On Sunday last, the 4th instant, the inquest was opened, and on the same day the body was buried in the Christian burial-ground here.

" This morning, the remaining three boats having arrived, the inquest was resumed, and a verdict returned with which I fully concur.

" Mr. Hatton's diary includes, as far as I have been able to see, full observations and notes of the course of the Kinabatangan up to and beyond Pinungah. They will be most valuable, and I will take care to have them worked out.

" I propose to reward the men who specially exerted themselves, and also on account of their general behaviour and feeling, with one month's extra pay, while I would propose that your Excellency sanction the payment to Mr. Beveridge of three months' extra pay on account of his great exertions on the occasion.

" In the above narrative I notice I have omitted to mention that Mr. Hatton had got back to within about 150 yards of the boats when the accident happened. I may also mention that Mr. Hatton having shot himself with his own rifle appearing almost incredible to Mr. Beveridge, he took special pains, and within a very few minutes of the occurrence, to inquire into and satisfy himself of the truth of the matter.

" I cannot refrain from expressing my sorrow, which is shared in by all those here, down to the lowest native who knew him, at this untimely close to a career which, brilliantly begun, was full of so much promise in the future. His geographical notes will, however,

MR. RESIDENT PRYER AND A GROUP OF NATIVE INHABITANTS OF SANDAKAN.

From a photograph by J. W. Robson, engraved by J. D. Cooper.

be of great value, and his name will be attached to the first correct chart of the Kinabatangan River.

"I have the honour to be, sir,

"Your most obedient servant,

"(Signed) W. B. PRYER,

"Resident.

"His Excellency,
"The Hon. W. H. Treacher,
"Governor of Sabah."

---

*Elopura, March 4th*, 1883

INQUEST INTO DEATH OF FRANK HATTON.

Messrs. Little, Cook, Sampson, Wickham, Rossell, Collinson, Pendon, McLean, Neubronner, Wait, De Lissa, Allen. Mr. Collinson agreed to as foreman.

Jury sworn in.

DR. WALKER (sworn) says:—About 1 a.m. this morning was called and told that Mr. Hatton was dead. Saw him in a gobang. Examined the body and found wound under the right collar-bone below middle of bone; in turning over body, there was one opening about half an inch from spine, opposite the lower third of shoulder-blade; the former named was evidently the entrance, the latter the exit, of a bullet. The wound was evidently that of a bullet. Seemed to be light traces of burning near former wound, as though the gun had been very close. The wound was such as might have been made by cartridge (produced). I examined gun (produced) and find it covered with mud, about one-third of an inch of dried mud stopping up muzzle. I removed cartridges; find seven all loaded; no discharged cartridge. Gun dirty, and had evidently been fired recently. Body very much decomposed. Examined coat of deceased; so much coated with blood, impossible to say whether it had been singed by the discharge or not; seems blackened, but it is impossible to say whether dried blood or not; coat had been washed at the time I examined it.

*Cross-examined by Mr. de Lissa:*—There was a hole in both coat and singlet.

*Cross-examined by Foreman :*—There was no discharged cartridge in the rifle. The rifle was loaded in the ordinary way. This (producing one) is the identical bullet that was in the discharging chamber.

*Cross-examined by Mr. Little :*—Wound was nearly horizontal position; wound slightly below.

*Cross-examined by Mr. de Lissa :*—Think it unlikely Mr. Hatton (deceased) would have used the lever for reloading the rifle. (Rifle is a Winchester repeater.)

ANDREW BEVERIDGE (sworn) states :—On the 1st of March, about 5 p.m., I was going up the Segama River, Sugoon Tukal exact name of place on the right-hand bank going up Segama. I heard report of a gun inland while still in gobang. Heard man sing out from the bank, " Lekas tuan matee." I ran as quickly as possible to the spot, and found Mr. Hatton just breathing his last. Could see that he just had breath in him and no more. Gun was on left side of him, muzzle pointing from him. Men had removed it from where it was before. Oodin was holding his head up, and Drahim had his arm round his shoulder. I at once took charge of the gun. I put him into the gobang and fetched him to Sandakan as quickly as possible, arriving here about 12, midnight, last night.

*Cross-examined by Mr. de Lissa :*—Only heard one shot fired from the time shot was fired until time I arrived on the spot ; it might be from four to five minutes.

*Cross-examined by Mr. Collinson :*—I did nothing to the gun beyond taking care of it, and having nothing taken from it. I took no cartridges out of it, and told the boy not to take any.

*Cross-examined by Mr. Cook :*—Was the hammer of the gun down ? It was. I did not inquire if any cartridges had been taken out of the gun. It was the gun he always used. There were three other guns (rifles) there.

*Cross-examined by Coroner :*—I did not notice if any of the other guns had been recently discharged. Mr. Hatton was on the best terms with his men, and there was no reason to suppose any ill-feeling between them ; they would do anything for him. It was a very open place Mr. Hatton was lying at ; not much undergrowth ; there was a vine within four feet of him ; his feet were towards it. Saw no other people for four days previously. The men told me Mr. Hatton had been pushing the vine out of his way with the rifle ; that he (deceased) had a gun in each hand. I examined the vine, and it was marked as though by a gun ; it would have impeded his progress. The abrasion on the vine was below. The men said the muzzle was on his breast as he fell. (Mr. Beveridge explains how the men said he (deceased) was carrying the rifle, viz. with it at the shoulder. He pushed up the vine from below, the muzzle being slightly free from the shoulder, and it went off at that moment. All this is possible as demonstrated.)

Dr. WALKER (recalled) states:—Thinks it quite possible that the muzzle was within a few inches of his body at the time of discharge, and thinks it quite possible the matter might have occurred as demonstrated. Also wishes to add, wound was such as to cause very sudden death, as one at least, if not two main arteries must have been severed.

Mr. BEVERIDGE states deceased was in the habit of carrying a stick with which he brushed vines out of his way as he walked. The mark on the vine was about four feet from the ground.

*Cross-examined by Mr. de Lissa:*—It was after six o'clock. I left scene of accident on the 1st of March, and arrived about 11 last night, fifty-three hours. Came down Segama, one day along sea-beach; entered main mouth of Kina Batangan, through Tuisan bahru, out of the Mumiang along the sea-shore, into the Bay of Sandakan. Had eleven men in the small gobang. Did not sleep night or day till we arrived at Sandakan. Stopped three times, for about half an hour each time, to cook rice. Should say we were sixty miles up the Segama. Paddled the whole distance. (Mr. Beveridge complimented on his conduct in the matter.)

BEELAH (sworn by Court Interpreter) states:—Were going up the Segama. I was in a small gobang behind with the cooking utensils. I was cook, general assistant, and interpreter. Was in the gobang. Heard two shots. Paddled on quickly. Mr. Hatton's boy came and said, "Tuan wants your gun." I was sick. Boy said, "You come too." Muddy ground. Was told there had been two elephants. Mr. Hatton told me to come. I said, "It's nearly dark; perhaps the elephants will hurt us." Mr. Hatton ordered lamps, and told two men to bring them, Nugong and Jabit. Went quarter of an hour into the forest. It was growing dark. I said, "Let us go back." Mr. Hatton said, "Come on; I would rather $100 than lose the elephant." Dramant said, "Come back; it's dark." Mr. Hatton said, "Very well." I went back to get hot tea and other things. The boy was behind Mr. Hatton. Mr. Hatton lifted a creeper. Rifle went off. Tuan called "Oodin." Boy, Draman and myself took hold of him. I said, " 'Lukas,' call Mr. Beveridge." Mr. Beveridge said,

U

"Who has done this, the elephant?" I said, "No, we would have died first." He ordered him (deceased) to be put in the boat. The rifle was entangled in the "akar" of the vine and "rice dua kalee." I was about ten fathoms off on Mr. Hatton's left hand. When Mr. Hatton fell, the rifle fell too. Jumat told me the rifle was entangled. I did not absolutely see it myself. Mr. Hatton was in the habit of holding the rifle in the middle. I don't know exactly who touched the rifle first. I was looking to Mr. Hatton. A lot of men came. It was about half-past five. When I got to the boat it was dark. Mr. Hatton said simply, "Oodin, Oodin, matee sayah." The boy took care of the rifle in an ordinary way. Mr. Hatton himself used to clean the rifle. I don't know exactly who carried the Winchester rifle back to the boat. No one closely examined the wound. We were all afraid to touch the gun.

(Court adjourned.)

Seven of us, and with Mr. Hatton, eight, went in search of the elephants. At the time Mr. Hatton was shot, five men were within 100 fathoms of him.

MR. BEVERIDGE :—The rifle gun had been handled before I came up, and I do not know whether anybody had not handled the lever, discharging the old cartridge and bringing up a new one. I do not think any one of the men would have touched him. Half of them were crying when he was shot. The rifles carried by the men were not loaded. Orders were not to load their rifles unless they saw something to shoot at. The Winchester rifle was loaded at the time Mr. Hatton went on shore. Don't know who loaded it.

OODIN (sworn by the Emaum) states :—I am boy to Tuan Hatton. We paddled up the Segama. Saw a deer; it ran away: saw another. Some one said, "There is a wild bull." "No," said Mr. Hatton, "it's an elephant." Twice he (deceased) fired at it. Tuan said, "The elephant's hurt to death, let us chase it, Ibrahim." I also went. We went into the forest. There was an elephant. It roared. Its leg was hit. We had no guns. We went and got men and guns, and all went after it—ten men. Tuan ordered Jabit to bring a lamp. Five men were with Mr. Hatton. Ibrahim said, 'Don't let's go,' but Mr. Hatton ordered us to go on. After a time Ibrahim again remonstrated. Mr. Hatton said he would rather $100 than not get the elephant. Ibrahim said, "What's the good of 100 elephants if we get hurt?" Several of us were with Mr. Hatton; we returned.

## How the last Expedition ended.

Mr. Hatton was pushing aside some creepers, when his gun went off. He said, "Oodin, Oodin, sahya matee." We took hold of him. Mandore said, "Call Mr. Beveridge." We called him.

*Cross-examined:* In an ordinary way I take care of the rifle. I loaded it with fourteen cartridges. Mr. Hatton fired at white birds, deer, and elephants. I didn't clean the rifle after the accident, because Mr. Beveridge ordered no one to touch it. I don't know how many cartridges were left in. I did not count how many shots were fired. The rifle fell when Mr. Hatton fell, and then the rifle got mud in it. Taha took up the rifle and rested it against the tree. (Witness here shows how Mr. Hatton got hit, using the rifle to brush aside a creeper. Mr. Hatton originally had two rifles, but afterwards put one against a stump beside the river. Beelah was on Mr. Hatton's left; I was just behind. Kumat was immediately behind him, and declared the ball passed close by him (Kumat). I saw Mr. Hatton twice trying to brush the creeper aside. I was behind Kumat. No one had ill-feelings against Mr. Hatton. There was smoke and smell of powder on Mr. Hatton's shoulder when I took his head on my knees.

IBRAHIM (sworn) states:—I am mandore to Mr. Hatton; have been with him a long time. Three days ago, towards evening, men said, "*Tambadau*" (wild cattle). "No," said Mr. Hatton, "it's an elephant." He fired and hit him twice. Elephant ran away. Mr. Hatton said, "Come and hunt him, Ibrahim." We went after him. We saw the elephant. He (deceased) went back to get rifles, and brought two; he put one down, and we went on; the elephant having gone, we went after him. It was growing late; I remonstrated. We got lamps and still pursued him; again I remonstrated, and Mr. Hatton agreed to come back. We were all close by. Mr. Hatton was not exactly in my sight when I heard a shot, and Mr. Hatton immediately called out, "Oodin, Oodin, matee sayah!" I rushed up. Mr. Hatton's head was on Oodin's shoulders. He was murmuring, "Oodin, Oodin." Mr. Beveridge was sent for. We put him in the gobang, and paddled night and day until we got to Sandakan.

*Cross-examined:*—The first time we went after the elephant— Mr. Hatton and I alone—Mr. Hatton only was armed with his Winchester, and went back to get other guns and men. Does not know how it is there is a filled cartridge in the rifle when examined this day. Six of us were armed with rifles. On the return I ordered them to take the cartridges out. All the rifles were Sniders except the one Winchester.

TAHA :—Three days ago was with Mr. Hatton in the Segama. Mr. Hatton fired at an elephant; hit it twice. Ibrahim and Mr. Hatton went after it; afterwards we all went. Came on dark; Ibrahim remonstrated, and at last Mr. Hatton returned. I myself saw Mr. Hatton stoop, brushing the creeper with his rifle; it exploded, and he (deceased) fell. Boy (Oodin) and Drahim seized him. The gun fell. Think it was Bulah took it to the boat.

*Examined* :—What became of the discharged cartridge case?—I don't know; perhaps it was some one threw it out; it was dark—all was confusion.

JUMAH relates the same tale. Was close by Mr. Hatton when he stooped to get under the creeper, raising it with his rifle. The rifleball went so close to him (Jumah) that he felt the wind of it. He does not know who touched the rifle after it fell.

POODEN was in Mr. Beveridge's boat. Heard report of a gun; went on shore, found Mr. Hatton dead. Mr. Beveridge ordered me to take the rifle back to the boat, but not to clean it. I took it to the boat. I did not extract the empty cartridge; should not know how to do it.

(Court adjourned for further evidence expected daily in three boats now on their way.)

*March 7th.*—Case resumed; boats having arrived, it is suggested that one or two of the men be called.

A piece of Mr. Hatton's singlet, showing evident signs of singing, is put in evidence.

DR. WALKER states that the piece of singlet shown is distinctly singed.

All the jury agree in this also.

DR. WALKER says, having heard a theory advanced that perhaps a man walking in front might have discharged his gun, Dr. Walker now states that he believes this to be impossible, the direction of the wound being down and not up, and all the men being shorter than Mr. Hatton, and that he, the doctor, is clearly of opinion it could only have been a gun discharged within three inches of Mr. Hatton's breast, and therefore his own.

*Cross-examined* :—Is clearly of opinion that such a wound would cause insensibility as stated.

UNGONG says he arrived on the scene behind Mr. Beveridge. Mr. Beveridge told him to assist in carrying the body, and he did so. He was very sorry. Mr. Hatton was dead when he arrived on the scene. We all cried. I was with Mr. Hatton a year. We all said, " Better we had died than this." When I arrived, the rifle was standing up against a tree close by. Always understood that it was Mr. Hatton's own rifle that killed Mr. Hatton. Doesn't know if any one took out the empty cartridge.

## JURY'S VERDICT.

Jury are of opinion that Frank Hatton came by his death from the accidental discharge of his rifle on the evening of the 1st of March, while returning from elephant shooting at Sugoon Jukol, which is situated about sixty miles up the Segama River, and about 160 miles by water from Sandakan, and whilst he was pushing aside a vine with the aid of said loaded rifle carried in his hand.

The jury much deplore the sudden death of Mr. Hatton, who, as an explorer and mineralogist, had proved himself of much value to the British North Borneo Company, and the world generally, and on account of his many excellent social qualities.

The jury also wish to express their admiration of the conduct of Mr. Beveridge, who, under the sad circumstances of the case, behaved in a most self-denying and praiseworthy manner in bringing the body to Sandakan, without either he or the natives who accompanied him taking rest night or day. They also wish to express their satisfaction of the conduct of the natives.

(Signed) G. D. COLLINSON, *Foreman*.
,, ALEX. COOK.
,, JAS. SAMPSON.
,, J. M. PARDON.
,, J. McLEAN.
,, N. B. WAIT.
,, L. E. NEUBRONNER.
,, R. McEVEN LITTLE.
,, S. W. ALLEN.
,, J. C. ROSSELL.
,, B. C. DE LISSA.
,, FRANK GORDON WICKHAM.

(Signed) W. B. PRYER, *Coroner*.

## VII.

## A POSTSCRIPT IN LONDON.

[BY JOSEPH HATTON, HERBERT WARD, AND ARTHUR HARINGTON.]

A visitor—The European who last saw Frank alive—Mr. Herbert Ward who is mentioned in the last diary—In Frank's room at Kudat—About seven hundred miles up the Kinabatangan—Frank's call at Pinungah—Talks of home—Sport—Native superstitions—Among the Tungara men—Strange pipes—Poisoned arrows—"Good-bye"—Sadness and foreboding—"His men loved him"—The boy Ooleen—"Roughing it"—Adventure and adventurers—Memorials in Borneo and at home—Experiences at Kudat—Incidents related by Col. Harington—Count Mongelas lost in the jungle—Sports and pastimes—Curious fishing excursion—Memorials in Borneo and London.

### I.

WHEN I (Joseph Hatton) was in America, during the autumn of 1882 and the spring of 1883, I received several letters from Mr. Herbert Ward, who had been a cadet in the service of the British North Borneo Company. He informed me that he was the white man who last saw Frank alive on his last expedition, that he possessed probably the latest words he ever wrote, and that he would postpone his departure from England until my return, in order that he might tell me all he knew of my son's last days, and perhaps render me some service in connection with the removal of the body from Borneo to

England. On my return, Mr. Ward called upon me. A short but compactly-built young fellow, of two or three and twenty, he was in appearance what one might fancifully describe as "a pocket Hercules." He gave me a grip of iron with a strong, large hand. His face was bronzed, and he had something of the frank yet nervous manner of a young sailor just home from long voyaging in distant seas. In the course of conversation I found that he had spent most of his early life as a sailor before the mast. He had run away from school and taken to the sea, had worked his way to the position of an A.B. seaman, had seen life in the Australian bush and in the California mines, had lived with the Maories, had roughed it in many lands; finally presenting himself to the Bornean authorities, had worked under them for some months; and on his first expedition—a mission to Pinungah—had met my son; had got back to headquarters suffering from a severe attack of fever, and thence had come to London to recuperate before "trying his fortune" at home or again "seeking it" beyond the seas. In spite of roughing it, and often under the most demoralizing circumstances, Mr. Ward was a gentleman in appearance and manners. His early training at home and at Mill Hill College in association with cultivated people had lost none of its influence upon what I should judge to be a naturally refined nature. I soon found myself taking a deep interest in the young fellow and his prospects, an interest which grew with increasing knowledge of him; and among my miscellaneous letters from many parts of the world I always now look forward with pleasure to his despatches from the Congo, where he is fighting his way, I hope, to an influential position under the auspices of the discoverer of Livingstone and the founder of the Congo Free State, Mr. H. M. Stanley. But we will now go back to my first acquaintance with Mr. Ward.

II.

"You knew my son; he has a note in his last diary referring to you. I am very glad to see you."

MR. HERBERT WARD.

"Thank you; I would have left England again before this, but for the satisfaction of seeing you, in case I might be of any service to Mr. Frank Hatton's parents, or give them any information that might interest them."

"I appreciate your thoughtful kindness. You are the second of his *Borneo* friends who have talked to me about him since his death; and if there is a bitter pang now and then in the memories you revive, there is real consolation in the tributes paid to his valour and simple virtues. Where did you meet him first?"

"On board the steamer *Borneo* on the 14th of November, 1882. We had just arrived alongside the Kudat wharf. On shore there was a motley crowd of natives, Chinamen, and Sikhs, in their varied costumes, some in very scanty attire, for it was very hot. From their midst a tall, handsome young fellow stepped out, and came aboard. He looked ill, but I noted his wiry frame and distinguished manner. Mr. Edwards introduced him to me as Mr. Frank Hatton, the company's scientific explorer. I had already heard of him at Singapore and on board the steamer. He had a great reputation for personal courage, was very popular with the officials, had made a great hit in the way of controlling natives, and his latest expedition was mentioned as a very plucky business. I was, therefore, much interested in him. When Edwards introduced me, Mr. Hatton—"

"Call him Frank," I said. "Forgive me for interrupting you."

"Frank took me aside and asked me if I knew Colonel Wilmer; and upon my answering in the affirmative, we began to talk. In a short time we found that we had both been at London colleges, and both lived in the same great city of London, and that we were both particularly familiar with Regent's Park, the Zoo, Hampstead, and all about there. He said he was ill, had been laid up since his last expedition with jungle fever, and that he was about to proceed to Singapore, and would go out on the *Borneo's* return, to restore his health, and prepare for his next journey. He spoke very modestly about his work, in reply to some questions I asked, and turned them off to give me some valuable hints as to my mode of living, in view of the danger of jungle fever, which was prevalent among Europeans whose duties took them into the interior. After breakfast Frank took me ashore, and introduced me to Mr. Treacher, the governor, who received me most kindly, and made arrangements for my accommodation at the Treasury, houses at that time being very few and far between. I spent the day with Frank, helping him to pack, and talking about London. He spoke very affectionately of you and his mother, and showed me all your pictures."

"What was his room like?"

"It was a large room, and had a very miscellaneous appearance. There were one or two tin cases, with things half packed; his revolvers hung on his bedstead; there were some shelves with bottles of chemicals on them, a few mineral specimens, some note-books, a rifle, and other things. His pistols hung on the bedpost, over which was drawn a large mosquito-net. There were letters and papers scattered around, straps, and everything that denoted overhauling things and packing. He said he was a good deal played out, but had great hopes of his next expedition, though he said the native reports of minerals were, as a rule, fables, and the difficulties of exploration great beyond description, the rivers being so often in a state of overflow. He was very kind to me, as he seemed to be to everybody, and his advice was most useful to me. The next morning everybody mustered on the wharf to say adieu to the *Boruco*. Very friendly was the leave-taking with Frank. I grasped his hand warmly, for I had already got to like as well as to admire him; and I little thought that our next meeting would be far away in the interior—in the heart, in fact, of the Sabah country, beyond the ken of white men."

"Now, I want you, if you will, to dictate to a short-hand writer the account of your second meeting with Frank, your last meeting, with all the details of it that you can remember; and then, when I have read it, we will talk again about our dear Frank—again and often, I hope."

"Yes," he said, "I will do what you suggest."

He did, and two days afterwards handed me the following interesting and touching narrative, all the more pathetic that the united ages of the two brave young fellows was not more than forty-four; Ward, a sturdy, squarely-built, thick-set youngster, about the height of Stanley, and with something of his calm expression of face; Frank, close on six feet, a head taller than any of his native followers, lithe, supple of limb, and with a far-away look in his eyes. "And I admired him so much," said Ward; "envied him, but not to desire his injury, of course; envied his acquirements, his knowledge, his skill; thought what a great man he would be some day, and wondered what would become of me; for though he was so modest and unostentatious, he had a commanding way, and talked with authority, as you may say; and what struck me was the quiet, uncomplaining style in which he took hardships, just as if he had been used to camping out and eating rice all his life."

III.

But here is the transcription of the shorthand notes:—

"Six months elapsed, and I was at Penungah—a little native settlement, hitherto, I believe, unvisited—about 700 miles up the Kinabatangan river. I was lying in my hammock about sundown, on the 29th of January, 1883, feeling sick, miserable, and lonely, and wondering how long it would be before I should again hear my own language spoken. All around was very calm and quiet; the sky was clear, and hardly a sound was to be heard. In front of my rude hut the sun was setting in all its glory behind the thickly wooded hills that intervened between Pinungah and Kimanis. To the eastward the sharp outline of the mountain of Impak stood in bold relief. My men, some fifteen Brunei Malays (dubbed Mata-matas by the Bornean officials in their youthful pride), were lying idly upon the verandah of their rough barracks. Suddenly I heard some voices coming nearer, and, looking up, I saw two Tumbunwahs approaching from the river. They came straight towards me, sat down, and looked as if they had something to say.

"I called Hassan, my sergeant, to interpret for me into Malay; and, owing to my limited knowledge of that language, I had some difficulty in understanding their mission. I at last gathered that two days down the river was an *orang-putih*, or white man, with two canoes, plenty of men, and a large flag.

"This was news indeed. I grew excited, and wondered who could possibly be the visitor. My informants, however, were totally unacquainted with details. I had to content myself with looking longingly in the distance, and wishing heartily for the time when this unknown should arrive.

"I interrogated Hassan as to the white man's name, but could get no further information than that the stranger had thirty men and two gobangs, and that he spoke Malay very fluently. I wondered what could possibly bring him away thus far into the unknown interior. I had never in my dreams even expected a visitor, and had almost come to the conclusion that I had seen a white man for the last time, so ill was I, and so far from all ideas of civilization.

"No sleep, no food could I take for the next two days. I was in feverish excitement, and towards the close of the second day I stationed myself upon the highest point, my men around me, with their guns ready to fire a salute of welcome. By-and-by, in the dim distance, I could hear shouts, and see three or four small canoes approaching rapidly against the stream. My excitement was intense, and at last I was rewarded by seeing a large prahu slowly turn the bend of the river, manned by some twenty *orang-dyang*, or paddlers, who occupied the fore-part of the canoe. Amidships a roof of leaves, and astern stood the form of my unknown visitor, bareheaded, and in white. I gave the word, "Fire!" and never was there such a row in Pinungah before. "Bang! bang!" at irregular intervals was kept up during the quarter of an hour it took for the prahu to arrive alongside the landing-place. There stepping lightly ashore was Frank Hatton once more; and again we grasped hands, this time with an indescribable feeling of thankfulness. He looked well and strong, and was in high spirits.

"We walked together up the hill, and entered my humble dwelling, which consisted of a roof and a floor of split bamboos, built on piles. Having no chairs, we sat together upon the hammock, and we each seemed to have so much to say that we found a difficulty in conversing at all.

"The rest of that evening we spent in talking over our homes and our respective relations, and conjecturing together what our friends far away at home were then doing; whether it was fine weather in the old country or not; and many other things like that. We opened a bottle of wine from my stores, and drank to each other's healths; we smoked cigarettes, and talked far into the night. Frank then ordered his hammock to be prepared, and we turned in; but not to sleep. We each had too many questions to ask of one another. We would both be silent for a few minutes, and I would ask some question about Sandakan. Then silence again, and Frank would be the interrogator. This was kept up till sunrise, when we both dozed off for half an hour.

"We then got up, had some coffee, and were busily engaged in making arrangements for a journey up the Mullykup, eating *durian* and *langsat*, smoking cigarettes, and chatting gaily about the dear old mother country. That night we managed to get more sleep, and were up at daylight, refreshed and ready for the journey upon which we were to start that morning.

"All being prepared, we got into our canoes, and started away about nine o'clock from Pinungah, paddling quietly against the stream for the remainder of the day; passing some beautiful scenery, wild in the extreme, lovely butterflies skimming everywhere, birds chirping, and the lesser hornbill trumpeting enthusiastically from the tops of the high trees on either side of the Mullykup River. Now and then we found an opportunity of having a shot at a stray deer or *palandok*, and once or twice were startled by an iguana dropping from the branches of a tree flat on its belly in the mud, and scampering into the water and disappearing. At short intervals it was necessary to alight from the canoes, which had to be carried over the rapids, whilst we wended our way over enormous rocks to rejoin them higher up.

"That night at sundown we decided to halt, and orders were given for a fire to be lit, and Frank's hammock to be fixed, I preferring to sleep in my canoe, out of the reach of the enormous ants which tormented poor Frank all night. He happened to remark in Malay to one of his attendants, '*Samut debawa, namok diatas.*' This expression, simple enough, meaning 'Ants below, mosquitoes above,' in Malay was a remarkably witty speech, and excited a deal of amusement and laughter from our Malayan followers. He told me an amusing story of his man Smith. He liked Smith, and thought his repartee in this case very smart, and laughed heartily as he related the circumstance. In one district where they were the first comers, and had no maps to guide them, Frank said, 'Smith, we must name some of these places for our charts, supposing we call this spot *Hatton Garden?*' Smith waited a little time without replying, and then said, 'Well, Mr. 'Atton, if you calls that 'Atton Garden—what do you say to calling this *Smithfield?*'

"Our meal that night was simple in the extreme, consisting of a pot of tea, hard-boiled eggs, while our men were filling themselves with rice. We had so much to talk about that we did not think of the meagreness of our fare, but, on the contrary, thoroughly enjoyed it. As it grew dark we had a large fire made, and posted sentinels for the night, it being rumoured among the natives that there was a tribe who lived in the jungle close by of a hostile and warlike character. I noticed when it was quite dark that two or three of Frank's men kept dropping a kind of powder into the fire, and asking him what it meant and what the powder was, he said his natives were very superstitious, and were afraid of ghosts. The powder which they threw into the fire was, he said, composed of bits of worsted, the bark of the upas-tree, and an occasional glass bead. This they believed pleased the deity, who in return for this attention kept watch over them through the night, to protect them from the attack of the spirits of their departed relatives. This led to Frank telling me many interesting things about the superstitious fears of the natives. The fitful firelight and the intense outer darkness made the stories all the more impressive. My visitor and fellow-countryman also taught me many Malay words, and gave me many valuable hints in regard to the language, all of which I thoroughly remember to this day. We finally retired to our respective sleeping-places and fell asleep.

"Next morning at daylight we were up again, and in half an hour were once more battling our way against the swift current. The rapids now became more frequent, and during the whole of that day we did not, I think, cover more than three miles. We shot a monkey, had one canoe upset, and were both stung very much by mosquitoes. The travelling was rough

"GOOD-BYE TILL WE MEET AGAIN IN LONDON."

Drawn by W. H. Margetson, from a sketch by Herbert Ward.

To face page 306.

and dangerous, and I was very ill, the fever still clinging to me; and Frank persuaded me to go back to Pinungah, telling me he would return again in a few days. I took an affectionate leave of him, and warned him to be careful of his head, reminding him that he was going close to the tribe who massacred and decapitated poor Witti. 'Keep your powder dry,' I said. He replied with a smile that he would be all right, and so we parted. I started on my homeward journey. Things went smoothly with me till we approached the biggest of the rapids, which had a fall of about seven feet, and there my boat came to grief, and I had a narrow escape of being drowned, but got back eventually to Raigson house and slept there; the next day, in one of his canoes, and with Usof's help as navigator, reached Pinungah once more, and was laid up once more, my immersion in the river proving an additional obstruction to my recovery.

"Frank's mission among the Tungara people was I think in furtherance of his search for minerals. On this subject, however, he was reticent, not evidently caring to talk about his discoveries or his hopes in that direction, though he once or twice mentioned the tremendous difficulties in the way of exploration that he encountered in the dense jungle, the constant rains, and the swollen rivers. He brought from the Tungara people a collection of strange, diminutive opium pipes, with red stems and quaint carvings, the work of the Tungara men; to me one of the greatest curiosities was a 'peluru sumpitan,' or poisoned arrow case, used by the very tribe of Subluts that murdered and beheaded Witti.

"Unfortunately on his return to me one of his gobangs had been smashed up on the very same bit of rock or snag where I had come to grief, and he was a good deal worried at the loss of his azimuth, compasses, aneroids, and other instruments. He stayed four days with me, during which time, when he was not busy with his diary and his boats, we arranged pleasant little excursions to be made together on our return home to England, which we expected would be in about six months. Frank ate durian the whole day, and showed me during that time all his little curiosities, his note-books and portraits, one of which was the picture of a young lady (not one of his two sisters), of whom, however, he said nothing.

"At last, Frank's arrangements being quite completed, the date was fixed for his departure, to investigate the Segama River on the 14th of February. He collected a few things together, which he said he would not require upon that journey, and asked me to take care of them and send them down to Sandakan at the first opportunity. Then came the time for our parting, and we walked together sadly down the hill to the boats, and stood for some minutes grasping hands and wishing each other good-bye. His last words to me were, 'Good-bye, old chap, till we meet again in London! We'll have jolly times then.' His boat pushed off, and he glided slowly with the stream.

"As I stood there, watching him disappear round the bend in the distance, a feeling of sadness and a strange foreboding came over me, such a feeling that I had never had before, and I wondered how long it would be before I once again would see him. I was very sad as I walked up the hill to the hut. I rested many times, and felt a choking sensation in my throat. I,

OVERLOOKING SANDAKAN BAY.

Drawn by E. J. Meeker, from a photograph by Mr. Robson.

To face page 87.

however, lay down in my hammock and spent the remainder of that night gazing listlessly at the sky, feeling down-hearted and thoroughly miserable; till, all at once, I heard the splash of a canoe, and, jumping up, found that Bongsu had just arrived with his two sons. They approached me in an agitated manner, and told me in Malay that they had dived in the river where Frank's canoe was upset, and they showed me a prismatic compass and a flat compass, and an aneroid which they had recovered from the bottom of the river. I immediately whistled up my men, and gave orders to Hassan, my corporal, to immediately start off, and try and overtake Frank and give him these things, which I knew were a serious loss to him. Half an hour afterwards all was quiet again, and Hassan was well on his way down the river.

"On the third day Hassan returned, and brought me a note, upon which was written, '4 a.m.—Dear Ward,—Thanks for the things, but I fear they are sadly damaged.' I took this note, folded it carefully, and stowed it away. Everything was miserable for the next week. I was sad, ill, and down-hearted. I wanted to return to Sandakan, but feared to leave the place on account of rumours of a band of desperadoes from a neighbouring tribe coming up and docking off our heads.

"Whilst in this uncertain state of mind, a man arrived at Pinungah, whom I recognized, and who proved afterwards to have been one of Frank's followers. He was in a terrible state of excitement, and spoke so quickly I was unable to understand a single word he said. At last by the aid of Hassan,[1] I was told that

[1] This Sergeant Hassan (who is again mentioned in the succeed-

poor Frank was dead, and was made acquainted with the sad details of his sad accident. I then made up my mind, at all hazards, to try and return as soon as possible, and about a month afterwards I was on my way down the river to Sandakan, prostrated with the jungle fever. I then found that the tale was only too true."

ing chapter) has since been murdered. The story is told in the *North Borneo Herald* of September 1st, 1884:—

"While a party, including the Governor, the Resident and others was being hospitably entertained at dinner by Captain Hamlin on board the s.s. *Amatista* of Hongkong, a sudden check was given to the prevailing gaiety by the arrival on board of one of the crew of a boat which had, a few weeks before, left Sandakan, taking Sergeant Hassan back to his post at Pinungah in the Upper Kinabatangan. The lad reported that Sergeant Hassan had found fault with and struck one of the men, called Tali, who cried and merely said, 'Trima kasih, Bapa Hassan.'—'Thank you, father Hassan.' During the night, however, he seized his rifle, and aided by two others of the crew, shot Hassan and Limbang, who had gone to his assistance, and decamped, the narrator of the sad incident having secured his own safety by taking to the water and making for the jungle. It is known that Sergeant Hassan had $300 of his own with him besides other property, and it is probable, therefore, that cupidity was added to the thirst for revenge so often found in Malays and caused the perpetration of the crime. None of the men concerned are natives of the river, nor indeed of North Borneo, so that the sad event has no political significance whatever. Sergeant Hassan had been for many months in charge of the Upper Kinabatangan district and had acquired most valuable information concerning the resources of that rich province, especially as to certain valuable birds'-nests caves. Unfortunately, as he could not write, this is all lost with him, and this loss will be much felt by Mr. D. D. Daly, who is leading an expedition of exploration, and who has relied to a great extent on the co-operation of the sergeant, who was a man of very considerable intelligence. A reward of $100 has been offered by the Government for the apprehension of the murderers. [The assassins were eventually captured and punished.]

IV.

"You said Frank was reticent as to his mission on the Segama?"

"Yes, but hopeful, evidently."

"Did he speak of a possible gold find?"

"He did not talk much of the business of his expedition; he examined the banks of the river and the bed whenever he could with great care, and regretted that it was the rainy season. He spoke once of the great mineral promise of the Kina Balu and Kinoram country. He talked more of London than of Borneo, though he spoke of an intended visit to Java and Siam. I heard from others more of his expeditions than from himself; but he said a little opium-pipe that he bought from the Tungara men nearly cost him his life. He was remarkably cool-headed, I thought, and brave, and his men loved him. Passing one of the rapids, I saw his boat slue round towards a jutting rock. I saw him bend down and speak to one of his men, the strongest and biggest of them. The man leaped from the boat, clung to the rock, and received the shock of the collision with his feet, and saved the boat. He had been upset himself more than once or twice on his river expeditions. You see, nobody knew what there was to encounter in the way of currents, cataracts, floating timber, snags."

"How was he dressed?"

"In the boat he wore a light shirt, trousers, and boots. Occasionally when resting he wore only a sarong; but he rarely rested; he worked too hard. He had an English cricketing cap on his head; but when I caught my first glimpse of him coming down the river he was bareheaded, and all in white, so

far as I could see, and it was a figure that impressed
me. He was tall, and seemed even taller than he
was, no doubt because the natives, as a rule, are
short. His boy, Oodeen, was very devoted to him.
He remained in my service for some time after Frank's
death, and would cry and moan whenever Tuan Hatton
was mentioned. He was little better than a wild boy
of the woods when Frank had him first, and used to
sleep up in trees. He had been a slave; had sought and
obtained Frank's protection, and had been with him for
more than a year. I heard of him last in service at
Singapore, but about to return to Borneo. So far as
I could understand from him and others, Frank trod
upon a tree stump, when his rifle exploded; the tree
was quite rotten, and crumbled under his foot, which
made him stumble at the moment he was pushing
through the vines or rattans that obstruct you all the
time in the forest jungle. It was a brave thing to
follow up the elephant as he did, but he had great
confidence in his Winchester, and was a capital
shot. He was most careful in the management of his
weapon, and seemed very thoughtful in all he did,
having, as it seemed to me, a high sense of his responsibility; and what he did was done as if he had had
years of experience, and, indeed, as if he were a man
in years and knowledge, and yet I never met any one
so modest with it all, so unassuming and so cheerful,
and so willing to give another the benefit of his experience. I had roughed it since I was fifteen, on sea
and on land, and under all sorts of circumstances, and
without friends, and therefore was accustomed to
tinned food, to no food at all, and to sleeping out in
all weathers, more especially when I was in Australia;

but Frank had, I knew, until he went to Borneo, been accustomed to the luxuries of life, and if he had scampered through Europe, it had been with money in his pocket and all paths made easy; therefore I was astonished that he should take this new life of roughing it with perfect content, as if he had been accustomed to it as I had. He took the hardships of it calmly, and was never ruffled, made the best of everything, and was always in a good temper. He seemed to be looking ahead, and I think he expected great things of this trip, notwithstanding that, as I said before, the rainy season put such great obstacles in his way."

"Let us for a moment get back to Pinungah," I said, "his notes about it are so brief."

"He wrote an account of Pinungah and made some rough sketches."

"Had he more than one note-book then?"

"Yes, a small one and a larger one."

"Did he look well and strong?"

"When I first saw him he was ill from fever and hard work, and looked ill; therefore to me, when I saw him next, he seemed very well indeed, and looked strong and healthy. He was far better in that respect than I was, a great deal more cheerful and contented. As I said before, nothing came amiss to him, either in the way of bad food or personal hardships. I can see him now, for instance, eating durian—a filthy fruit to my taste. He would sit down and make a meal of it, flinging the rind around him, he sitting in a ring of it and laughing when any one tried to approach him, because when we did so, we had to dodge the spikes and prickles of the rind or husks."

## V.

Among Frank's other friends (including Mr. Everett, late Resident at Pappar, and now working on his own account an important mineral concession from the Company) I have had some interesting conversations with Lieut.-Colonel Harington, of the Egyptian gendarmerie at Cairo.

COL. ARTHUR HARINGTON.

"I first met Frank," he writes, "at the Company's offices in Old Broad Street, before he started for Borneo. He and Dr. Walker were then arranging for their departure. I thought Frank very young for the work. I next heard of him at Singapore as an enthusiastic billiard-player. He was one of those young fellows who would go in earnestly for anything that interested them. I expect he and Walker were glad to stretch their legs around a billiard-table after their confinement on board ship. I renewed my acquaintance with Frank later at Labuan. We shared rooms in a crazy old bungalow. Mr. Cook, the Company's treasurer, lived in the same house. Frank was what we old Indians call 'a griffin,' and accepted what we considered wretched accommodation as first-rate; though I think in his heart he was a little disappointed. I was naturally drawn more towards him than to the other members of our society; we had more in common to talk about—England, London, and the world—and, above all things, our mutual taste for music. We used to discuss the plays and the operas we had seen and heard. Frank used to rave about Irving, and we had many a discussion about acting. I remember making him laugh very much at my experience of *The Bells*, and how I was so horrified at the terrible reality of the acting that I had to go to my club and imbibe a strong drink before I ventured to go to bed. The play I liked best was *The Lyons Mail*. We often went to Dr. Leys', the British Governor's, and we would play the piano at Government House and sing. One particularly favourite piece of mine that Frank played was a march in F.—I think Mendelssohn— Like all youngsters, Frank was burning for sport. We paid a visit to Coal Point, and in the evening went to shoot grunters. Frank turned out very much *à la chasseur*—brown canvas trousers, and a long hunting-knife in his belt. I named him that night 'the bushranger,' a name which stuck to him a good deal. Frank, I remember, shot during his rambles several fine specimens of kingfishers. There are, I believe, thirteen specimens of the kingfisher tribe in Borneo—some really gorgeous in plumage. Frank and I made many sporting expeditions about the island, and had some good shooting. I remember cautioning him about his Winchester—a rifle that is an awkward customer at times. You do not always know when it is loaded or not. A useful weapon in a tight place, no doubt. Witti carried a Winchester. I liked Witti. He was a gentleman—a little odd, perhaps, but a fine fellow. He and Frank got along well.

"You ask me to give you some details of our life at Kudat, and any special incidents of travel or sport. Of the many incidents in our life at Kudat, one of the most amusing—though at one time it seemed very serious—was the loss in the bush of Count Montgelas. He had come out to Borneo 'globe-trotting,' and was staying at Kudat, preparatory to a trip to Sandakan and elsewhere. We were a large party at Kudat at that time, as the Company's yacht, *Leila*, was in harbour with Mr. Treacher, Governor of Sabah, Major Papillon, R.E. (a friend of his), and Mr. Du Boulay, private secretary, on board. We had all been bidden to a feast on board the *Leila* that evening. During the afternoon several of us had gone out in different directions for the evening 'crawl.' Montgelas was one who went out 'gunning.' We all assembled to dress for dinner, and ordered our boat to be in readiness to take us off to the yacht, which was anchored some quarter of a mile off in the bay. On calling the roll before dinner, Montgelas was reported absent—his servant saying the 'Tuan' hadn't come in. Just then we heard a report of a gun in the bush near, and some one said, 'There he is.' So we decided to go on board, and to send the boat back for him, telling his servant to make him 'hurry up.' On arriving on board, Mr. Treacher waited a while and then decided to sit down to dinner. To our surprise Montgelas, after some time, didn't appear, and on sending off to the shore we were told he hadn't come in. This sounded serious— so finishing dinner as rapidly as possible, we all went on shore, and learning that no signs of him were to be found, we organized a search expedition. I selected a party of Sikhs, picking out all the *shikarries* (men that knew the bush), dividing it into two parties: one to go along the jungle-path that runs to the point at the coast from Kudat, and the other to go along the sea-beach to the point, where the parties were to meet for further action; with the Sikhs I also told off some of the Malay police. Gueritz and some others went with one party by the jungle-path, Frank Hatton and I by the sea-beach with the other. We arranged a few signals, viz. by firing a certain number of shots from a rifle. Off went the two parties, and after a sharp walk, stopping every now and then to yell in concert, 'Montgelas!' we, the beach party, heard three shots fired, signifying that a trail or news had been found. We doubled on, rounded the point, and entered the bush by the jungle-path, and soon came to the spot where Gueritz had fired the three signal shots. Here we found that a reply had been heard from the bush on their left to their shouts. Taking the trail from the right, we all shouted 'Montgelas,' and to our joy heard a faint answering shout. 'He's moved,' they said, as the voice sounded further off than the first answer. I then fired a single shot, which was answered from the direction in the bush in which the shout had come. On this we divided again and skirmished through the bush—Gueritz going to the left, Frank Hatton and I to the right. It was pitch dark, and I cautioned every one not to lose themselves. Frank and I at last got through the bush and emerged on the sea-shore beyond the point. We again shouted and heard a faint reply. Then I divided our little party, sending Frank into the bush by a path used by the wood-cutters, while I went further up the coast to another path I knew of. Here I entered the bush, penetrating so far in that I made sure of coming up with Montgelas, as I had had an answering shout, when to my disgust I came on an impassable swamp. After several in-effectual attempts to cross, and finding it impossible to get round it, I decided to return and try another place, when I found that what I had cautioned the others about had happened to me. *I was lost.* In trying to cross the swamp we had left our pathway and could not find it. The bush in Borneo is not only extremely dense, but the trees grow so high that the sky is hidden from view in many places, and just where we were lost the trees were gigantic. As ill-luck would have it, there was no moon, and we had nothing to guide us. *Of course* in our hurry we had left our compasses behind, though I had one fastened to the belt I always wore in the bush, but to-night I had come out in a pair of white trowsers, straight from dinner, and had forgotten my belt. I had only one thing to guide me by—the *swamp*, which I knew lay towards the west; at least it did as I approached it from the sea-shore, but in my attempts at trying to get round it, I had probably changed my position, and it might only serve to mislead me. I, however, determined to try, and assuming that it *was* to the west, and therefore by keeping my *right* hand towards it I should have my head turned *south*, a direction which would take me towards the beach. I extended my few Sikhs *from the right*, ordering each man to keep within speaking distance of the man on his right, and to keep a bright look-out. We had brought several lanterns and a supply of candles. I gave the word 'march,' and on we plunged. Fortune favoured us, for after a desperate scramble through the bush I came on a tree that looked familiar, and found we had struck a path that led to the beach. I was pretty well familiar with the bush, having walked round it and through it in my evening and morning walks many a weary time. It was then close on 2 a.m. On returning to the beach, I marched round to the point, entering the bush by the large jungle-path, and from there returned to Kudat, as I could hear nothing of the other parties, both myself and men being quite done up, having been on foot for over four hours. On getting back to the station I found all the others had come in, but without finding any trace of Montgelas. Frank had had an adventure much the same as mine, having missed his way and been lost for some little time; however, he was nearer the main bush-path, and soon got himself and men extricated. We decided to go out at dawn, and gave orders for a general parade of all hands to regularly beat out the bush, as we began to think Montgelas must be wounded. Accordingly at dawn we marshalled our forces and entered the bush, but had hardly gone a hundred yards when a loud hurrah and 'Here he is!' announced the lost one's return. A grinning, dancing *mata-mata* of the Kudat police proclaimed himself his *discoverer*—the facts being that as soon as it was light enough Montgelas had headed for the south, and would have been back at the station in a few minutes when we met him. It appears that he had wounded a deer shortly before sunset, and forgetting the time, had followed it across the swamp. Darkness came on in the rapid way it does in the tropics, and before he could get back across the swamp it was pitch dark, and he was done. The shot we heard before dinner was not fired by him.

"He could hear us distinctly when we were searching for him, but could not reach us in the darkness and the thick bush. The more he tried to reach us the further he seemed to get away from us, and finally he made up his mind to wait for daylight. He passed a miserable night—devoured by mosquitoes.

"We gave him a jorum of quinine and some champagne, and after a sleep and a tub he was none the worse for his night's adventure.

"It was a lesson to all of us not to go too far into the bush in the late afternoon, also 'the *wise man taketh a compass into the bush.*'

"The *mata-mata* who met the count was for days a hero in our small community at Kudat, and we often saw and heard him relating and describing 'how *he* found MONTGELAS.'"

"During our stay at Kudat we organized a fishing trip up the Bongon River, which runs into the Bay of Kudat in Marudu Bay. H.M.S. *Fly* was in harbour at Kudat, and her captain and several of her officers took part in the sport. The arrangements for the fishing were all carried out under the orders of Mr. Gueritz, Assistant Resident at Kudat, who had had experience of this sort of fishing when he was in Sarawak, in the service of Rajah Brooke.

"The plan of operations is as follows:—A certain number of natives collect a sufficient quantity of *tabah* root, a shrub that grows in the jungle. This root on being beaten emits a thick milky juice, highly poisonous and stupefying. On the day fixed for the fishing, at about half an hour before full high water, the river to be fished is staked across a short distance from its mouth with the close-made fishing-stakes used by the natives. These stakes entirely prevent any fish passing. The fish having gone up stream with the tide are thus cooped up in the river and cannot get out into the sea. A couple of canoes, each with a native on board, go up stream as far as is considered the proper place for placing the poison in the stream. The two canoes are pretty full of 'tabah' juice, having had it beaten out ready beforehand. In the meantime the sportsmen assemble on the stream some couple of hundred yards or so below the two canoes containing the tabah juice—each sportsman armed with a fish-spear in his canoe. The canoes are steered and propelled by a native in the stern. Two or three spare fish-spears are placed in each canoe in case of need. All being ready, the signal to commence is given, and the natives in the two canoes begin swaying sideways, rolling the canoes from side to side, singing a kind of chant, the other natives joining in. By degrees the canoes gradually fill with water, and at last turn over, sending the tabah juice into the stream, the natives recovering their canoes when the juice has all disappeared. Then every one is on the look-out. The *tabah juice* soon takes effect, and fish of all sorts and sizes are seen struggling on the surface of the water, half stupefied by the tabah poison. Then it is a case of every man for himself—helped by his paddler, who, under his directions, steers for the fish, which are speared in succession with the sharp-pointed fish-spears. To a beginner it is no easy job to stand up in the little canoe, direct its movements, and finally strike the fish. Many a time, in his eagerness, a man topples over into the stream amidst the laughter of the others, and to the huge delight of the natives at seeing a TUAN go floundering into the stream. The Malay is a laughter-loving, jovial soul, and a day's tabah fishing to him is an endless amusement.

"We started away at daylight. Besides the officers of the *Fly* and two of her boats with blue jackets, and tiffin, our party consisted of Mr. Gueritz, Mr. Hewitt, Frank Hatton, and myself. We sent on canoes for the different sportsmen. Arriving at the river's mouth, we found that it was close on high water, and the closing in of the river with stakes just commencing. The stakes are beautifully made, resembling the 'chick blind' of India in appearance and material. Hewett, Frank, and I had had a little practice at fish-spearing in the shoal waters at Kudat. One has to strike very straight, otherwise the spear glides off the slippery hard skin of the fish, and unless the spear is very sharp it takes a sharp stroke to *prong* the fish.

"All being ready, and each man on board his canoe, the signal was given to let out the tabah. The Malays were quite as eager and excited as we were, and soon the fishing chant commenced, and after a few minutes a louder shout announced the capsizing of the poison-laden canoes, and the commencement of the sport.

"The river, unfortunately, wound about a good deal, and we were unable to see the ceremony of poisoning the river, which took place above the bend of the river which closed the reach we were in.

"Presently a shout announced the appearance of the first 'drunken' fish, and in a moment everything was wild excitement. Right and left and everywhere the fish rose to the surface, floundering about, unable to keep below, and being speared on all sides. Sometimes a larger fish than usual would attract three or four canoes, the spearmen all striking for the fish, and the native paddlers urging them on and thrusting their canoes forward so as to drive the other canoes out of the line. For over a couple of hours the sport went on, until we had worked our way down to the stakes. Here a regular *battue* took place, as lots of fish had got down only to be stopped by the stakes. It was a regular *hot corner*, reminding one of covert shooting at home without the smoke. It was grilling hot work, for by now the sun was high above the jungle trees, which at first had shaded us, and we were not sorry to leave off for the welcome cry of *breakfast*. So, leaving the natives to collect the fish, we got under the shade of the boats' awnings and enjoyed our well-earned meal. Gueritz, I think, took the top score, his experience in Sarawak helping him greatly. No one enjoyed it more than Frank Hatton. To him the whole thing had even a greater charm of freshness than it had to me.

"We returned to Kudat about noon, after a most enjoyable morning's sport and picnic.

"The scenery of the Bongon River is extremely pretty, and we made several excursions up it for hunting and for amusement. On one occasion Captain Hope, H.M.S. *Fly*, and I took a long walk through the jungle, having gone up the river some distance. He is an authority on ferns, and was greatly delighted at the lavish display in the jungle of Borneo. The foliage is lovely and rich, the ever-varying colour and tints impossible to describe. If anything the extreme luxuriance *palls* on one, exciting at times a longing for the grim leafless aspect of the trees in Old England at winter time."

### VI.

In Frank's trunks and cases which eventually reached England there were some examples of native arms and implements. They included the head of the spear given to Frank by the Dusun chief (one of his blood-brothers), the pipe referred to by Mr. Ward at page 309, and other trophies and mementoes of Frank's expeditions. Examples of these are illustrated in succeeding pages. The Bornean parang (1) and Malay kris (2) are interesting specimens of these weapons. The parang is used as much for agricultural purposes as in warfare. The sheath is made of hard polished and unpolished wood, decorated with human hair, and bound together with ornamental rattan. The blade is of Kayan manufacture, made from native iron, and tempered by a process pretty generally known in Borneo, but concerning which no traveller has yet been able to give any information. No European blade is more finely tempered than these Kayan weapons. " I have seen some of them that will

BORNEAN PARANG (in sheath) AND MALAY KRIS.
(*Drawn by W. H. Margetson.*)

cut a strong nail in two, without turning the edge," says Mr. Crocker; "and I don't know that any writer has pointed out the peculiar and ingenious method of their form. Take for example the blade sent home by Frank. It is concave on one side, convex on the other; the tree or other object attacked with it is struck with the concave side, which prevents the weapon glancing off, and the convex side assists by a curving action the force of penetration." It is a damaskeen blade beautifully inlaid with brass. It is fastened by a band round the waist, secured by a large button made of mother-of-pearl. The Malay kris (2) is a long wavy steel blade, the handle made of what is called *kumnium* wood, which takes a fine polish. The kris is peculiarly a weapon of war, and is made in Brunei, where the native artificers in metal are remarkably clever. While the parang has only one cutting edge, the kris is a two-edged sword. Mr. Carl Bock tried to investigate the manufacture of similar weapons in that part of Borneo which he visited under the protection of the Dutch. "The process of grinding and sharpening," he says, "is very slow, and to polish and put a proper edge on a plain blade occupies more than a fortnight. Many of the blades are beautifully inlaid with brass along the sides and near the back, while others have open scroll patterns cut right through the blade. How this work is done I could not ascertain, as both Dyaks and Malays were very wary of giving any information, and very unwilling to show me any of their tools. Regular workshops do not seem to exist, each man being apparently, to a great extent, his own cutler." Many blades, however, are imported into the interior of Borneo from native Brunei traders.

This second group of arms and implements (page 325) represents (1) the blade of a parang, the handle of bone, the lower part bound with brass wire; (2) head of Dusun spear; (3) small parang and sheath, the handle of the blade made of deer horn, the sheath being two pieces of light wood bound together with plaited rattan; (4) a paddy cutter, or reaping-hook, as old in form and manufacture as the biblical days of Ruth. The handle is made of a specially hard Bornean wood bound both for ornament and use with bamboo cane. The implement is small. Only the heads of the rice are reaped. It would be interesting if it were possible to trace the history of this almost universal implement to the savage tribes of Borneo. The method of rice cultivation is curious. A clearing being made, the undergrowth is fired. The ashes are an excellent manure. Meanwhile the cultivators construct rafts, cover them with earth, sow them with seed, and place them in the river, where they are kept moist. Very quickly the rafts become green floating islands. Then the women transplant the grain into the newly cleared ground, which has to be constantly weeded. Rats are often as troublesome as weeds, and the natives have a cleverly constructed trap which does great execution among them.

The third group of implements, parangs and reaper sheaths (page 326),

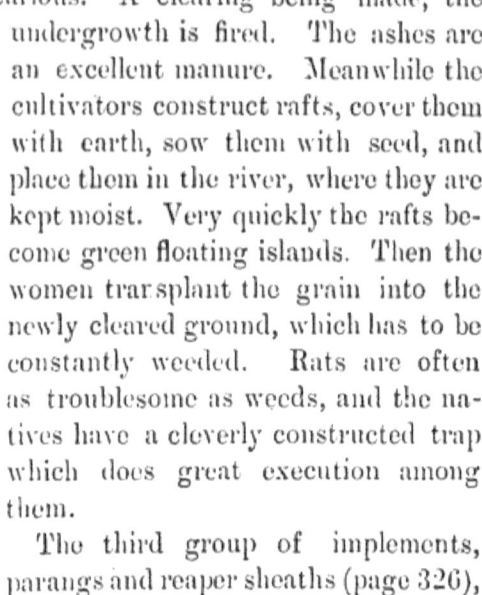

GROUP OF BORNEAN ARMS AND IMPLEMENTS.
(*Drawn by Helen H. Hatton.*)

exhibits in a marked degree the primitive and civilized methods of Bornean workmanship. These sheaths are of the most ordinary and primitive character—two roughly fashioned pieces of wood bound together with rattan and ornamental plaitings of bam-

boo, while the blades they contain are worthy of a
Sheffield cutler. (1) A parang; (2) the rough, clumsy
sheath of the rice-reaper; (3) the sheath of the handsome, straight, beautifully balanced parang blade in the
previous group; and (4) the last is a parang sheath
with a suggestion of artistic instinct which finds expression in a little scroll cut with a knife at the end of

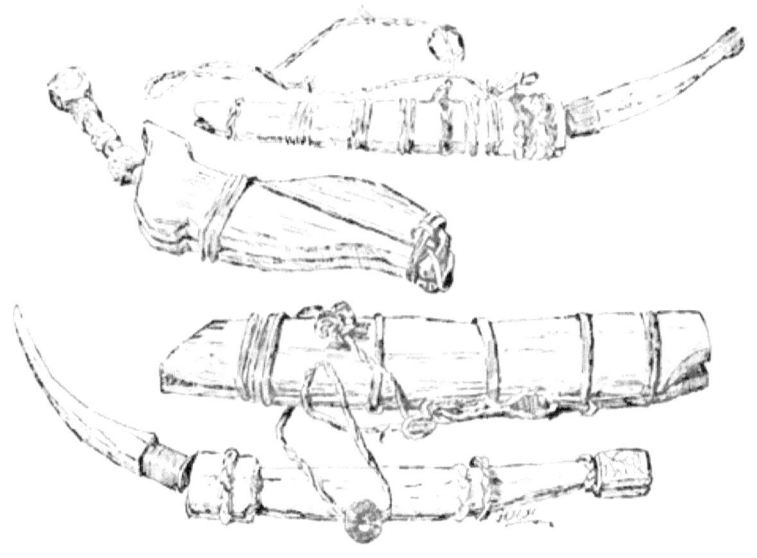

PARANGS AND REAPER-SHEATHS.
(*Drawn by Helen H. Hatton.*)

the scabbard, and in the dainty twisting of the rattan
bands. The parang is used for every purpose that a
knife can be put to, including the carving of blade
handles, raft-making, cutting up of game, and as a
weapon of warfare.

The following illustration (page 327) represents a
bamboo case, and examples of its poisoned arrows. It
is bound and deftly ornamented with rattan work, and

## A Postscript in London.

has a rattan fixture for slipping into the sarong girdle, previously described. The arrows are small shafts of light wood sharpened at one end, a knob being left at the other to fit the blow-pipe. This latter is called a sumpitan. It is formed of bamboo, and the length and use of it is illustrated in the drawing on page 272. The arrows are both plain and barbed, and they are anointed with a deadly poison. Frank's cases contain several examples of them, set apart for analysis,

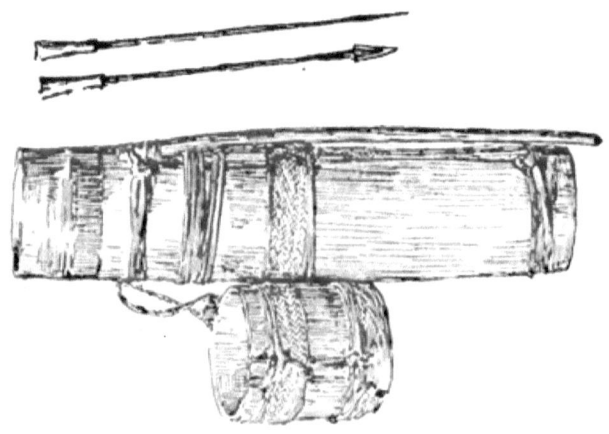

POISONED ARROW-CASE AND ARROWS.
(*Drawn by W. H. Margetson.*)

one packet being forwarded to him by Mr. Witti. Mr. Crocker says, "The poison is understood to be a compound of the milk of two different trees. It is very deadly, will kill a man in a few minutes, and yet animals or birds killed with it are edible. In some parts of Borneo the sumpitan is the only weapon of defence and offence, and the natives depend upon it as hunters for their subsistence."

"The pipes (page 328) which Frank obtained from

the Tungara people are unique," says Mr. Crocker. "I have never seen nor heard of any Bornean tribes who smoke pipes. These two examples were evidently highly valued by Frank. Ward says Frank risked his life in obtaining them. Coming from the far interior, they are all the more curious and interesting. They must be peculiar to that one tribe, the Tungara people. All the natives of Borneo smoke, almost from the moment they leave their mothers' arms. They roll the tobacco in a palm leaf to smoke it, and it has a very fine flavour. But pipes: this is the first time anybody

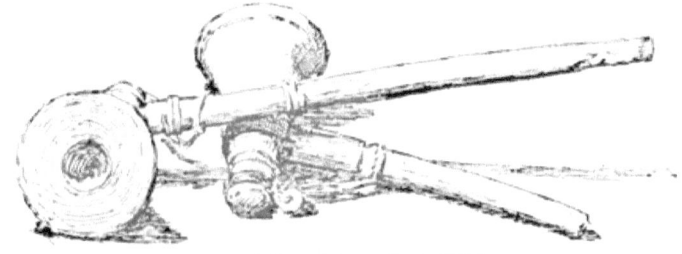

PIPES FROM THE TUNGARA COUNTRY.
(*Drawn by Helen H. Hatton.*)

has ever heard of pipes in Borneo. These two pipe-relics of Frank's last expedition, are made of hard red wood, and have bamboo stems. They are much the same kind of pipe as that used by the Chinese, who only put in a pinch of tobacco. The discovery of these pipes suggests another piece of evidence favourable to the belief that at some very remote period Borneo was partially settled and occupied by China." The small orifices of the large bowls contain the remains of half-smoked tobacco. In Sulu and in Brunei the sultans and great officers smoke pipes, imported from Java and Singapore, of a large and elaborate character, and

*A Postscript in London.* 329

Mr. Carl Bock describes a Dyak pipe of this kind in Dutch Borneo.

The accompanying musical instrument, which I venture to call a mouth-organ, is, Mr. Crocker tells me, "peculiar to the Kayan tribe, which has, I believe, offshoots in the centre of Borneo. This specimen picked up by Frank shows that it is so, and indeed I think it will eventually be found that the tribes of Sarawak, with which of course I am most intimately acquainted, have branches or off-shoots throughout the entire island. This Kayan instrument gives forth a soft and soothing kind of music. I have often heard it

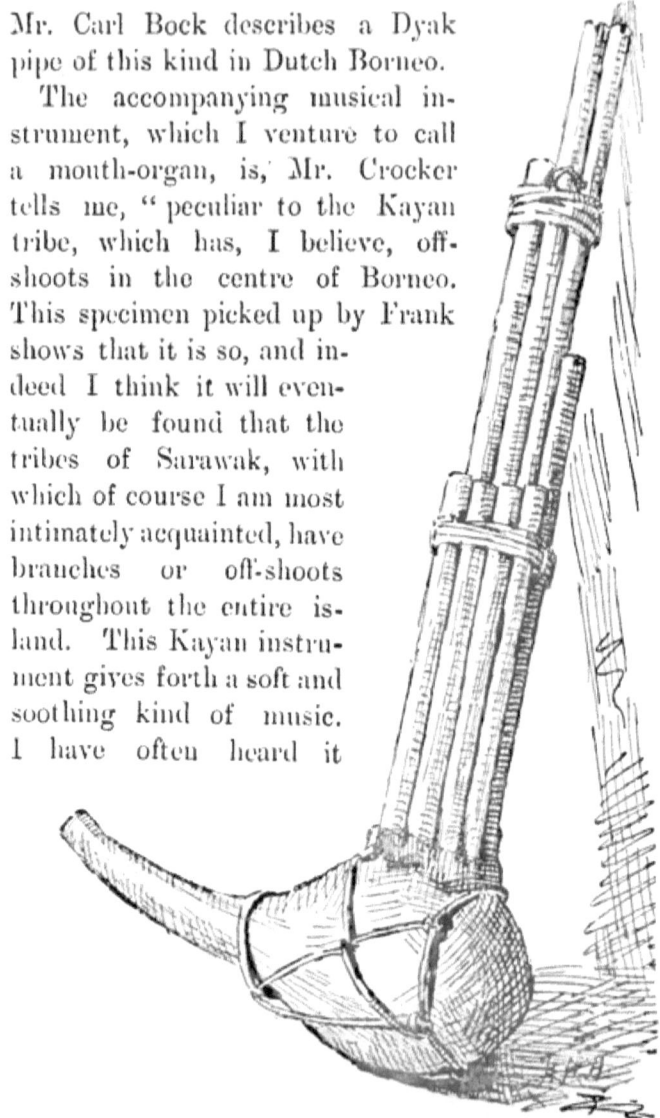

BORNEAN MOUTH-ORGAN.
(*Drawn by Helen H. Hatton.*)

played. It is made of bamboo reeds, and a gourd. The reeds are eight in number. They are fastened into a gourd, the stalk of which is the mouth-piece The pipes are from twelve to twenty inches in length, and the fingers play upon the tops, like keys. I have seen some with orifices in the sides of the pipes. I

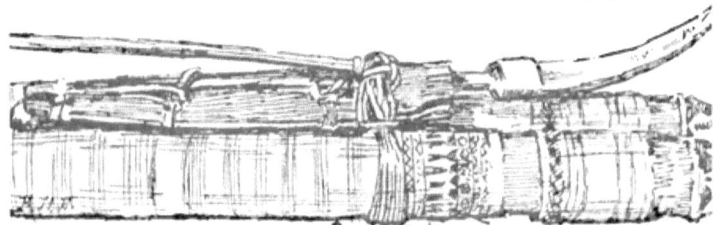

notice only one in this instrument." Mr. Carl Bock, who found a similar instrument among the tribes of Dutch Borneo, says, "Mr. Augustus Franks, of the British Museum, has a Chinese book in which there is figured an instrument made in a very similar manner." The one which I engrave is a far more artistic and ela-

SIRIH-BOX, KNIFE, AND DETAIL OF DECORATION.
(*Drawn by Helen H. Hatton.*)

borate specimen than that which Mr. Bock exhibits among his fine collection of Dyak utensils in his "Head Hunters of Borneo."

The last of these illustrations of Frank's small but interesting collection, is a remarkable example of barbaric art. It is a double sirih-box and knife or parang. The lids are ornamented with cowrie shells and gold and brass grouted into a composition which is as hard as cement. The cases are carved with circular lines, and at the top with ornamental bands, conspicuous in the design being a row of human heads. The cases still contain lime, a very fine white powder.

"The natives," says Mr. Crocker, "mix the sirih leaf in the lime, and also betel-nut, sometimes gambier, and chew the mixture. When they are old and lose their teeth they have a kind of pestle with which they beat it up into a paste. The effect of this sirih-chewing is very stimulating. Europeans often become confirmed sirih-eaters. On a novice the first effects are startling, producing a deadly feeling of drunkenness, sometimes of sickness. Perseverance in the habit, as in the case of other narcotics, often establishes a confirmed and regular use of it. On a long march it is often useful in its effects. The first token of welcome in a Dyak house is the handing round of the sirih-box. The Malays are great *intriguantes*, and they have quite a language of sirih leaves, a regular lover's dictionary."

Frank's specimens of natural history, mostly birds, were said to be "not in a fit condition to send home." A box of beetles and moths are represented in an early chapter. His latest work at South Kensington, before he left England, was to fill a number of jars with fruits and vegetables, with a view to investigation on his return, in connection with his bacteria researches, and also with a view to the possible discovery of new chemical bodies in the decayed matter. It was his intention to supplement these investigations with experiments upon Bornean fruits, vegetables, and other natural products of the country. His latest correspondence referred to the possibilities of obtaining a grant from the Royal Society in connection with these researches. Among his papers were several photographs which I am inclined to think were not taken by himself, and as there is no clue to their origin, I have not had them engraved. Some of them may possibly have been obtained at Jahore (which he visited during one of his Singapore vacations) or at Sarawak. There is one, however, which is an imperfect and evidently hurried production. "This," says Mr. Alfred Dent, "is, I should say, one of Frank's own. It is a group of native Dyak women, taken in the interior and near a stockade. It is a remarkable illustration, not only as giving a real picture of the best class of Dyak women, but showing their mode of dress, or the absence of it, and the fashion of wearing brass wire around the arms, legs, and neck. The photograph is also proof of the confidence shown in the European who made it, the Dyaks being exceedingly jealous of their women." Frank in his letters mentions several photographs which have not reached England. The most serious loss is of course his diaries. Not one of them came home among his effects, which were ordered to be carefully collected and despatched to England. A portion of the first, and the whole of the last one, came home long after his clothes and other property. "His roving life," as his friend Dr. Walker writes, "made the collecting together of his things a difficult business." Every possible inquiry and investigation into the matter has, I know, been made by the Governor and Mr. Resident Pryer, whose

uniform kindness and sympathy, with that of the rest of the officers and Company, I cannot sufficiently acknowledge.[1] At the same time I know that the

[1] Among Frank's papers there were friendly letters from most of the officers of the Company, from the Governor downwards, all of which he had carefully preserved. They were folded and packed away with so much care, as were the whole of my letters to him, that, to quote a letter which I lately received from Mr. Resident Pryer, it does seem all the more "strange about the missing diaries. I hardly think Frank would have taken them with him, to be exposed to all the possible dangers of a scrambling journey in small canoes, and through the forest in this wet season. So it seems reasonable to suppose they must have been put away carefully somewhere in Kudat; in the laboratory seems most likely." I select from among the papers that came home, a letter from Mr. Witti. It was written to me, and sent by me to Frank, as evidencing the feeling which Witti entertained towards him. I had had reason to fear there might be a little jealousy in their relationship; and I had written to Witti commending Frank to him, and trusting that Frank's youth and worthy ambition would command his sympathy, and that whenever Witti came to London he would give me the opportunity of thanking him in person for the kindly courtesy that I felt sure he would extend to my son. His reply may be quoted now, not only as a tribute to his young colleague, but as an indication of the generosity of his own disposition :—

Kimanis, N.W. Borneo.
1st March, 1882.

DEAR SIR,—The encouraging remarks in your kind letter I may thankfully accept, but as to your anticipating any merits of mine about your son, I could scarcely be happier in acting up to your opinion, than what I am by stating that he prospers in the new field without any other aid from part of his brother-officers than knowing himself liked by each of them. In as far as I lost my own chance of a more intimate fellowship with your son through the Governor's orders, I feel inclined to grumble; but at the same time I admit that the arrangement offers your son a fairer field and more liberty of action than what had, apparently, been the case otherwise. The present situation is illustrative of what became of the original idea of allowing me to co-operate with your son: he himself is by this time

diaries existed, and it is possible they may yet be discovered. If the stimulus of a reward could unearth them, the Company, as well as myself, would be only too glad to recompense the finder of the missing books and other lost property, of little or no account in Borneo, but of inestimable value to me.

A few friends and fellow-workers of the late Frank Hatton have created, in honour of his memory, an Annual Prize, to be held by the Students of the Royal School of Mines and Normal College of Science, South Kensington, and to be called "The Frank Hatton Memorial Prize." The Council, in a special order, signifying their approval of the project, recommended that the prize be given for Organic Chemistry, in which important branch of science the late Mr. Frank Hatton more especially distinguished himself at South Kensington. "The intention of the founders of this memorial is twofold. While perpetuating the memory of a student whose useful and brilliant career was cut short almost at its commencement, and during a notable scientific expedition in the interior of Borneo, it is hoped that this Memorial Prize will encourage others of the same College and School to special exertion in chemical research."

An obelisk to the memory of Frank Hatton and Franz

---

following up traces of antimony in the Labuk, and I am going upland here to try and tame the Dalit-men, who delight in now and then killing some traders. I may safely predict, I shall miss your son's supporting company at my business, while he will scarcely notice my absence at his.

I am, dear sir, very sincerely yours,
F. WITTI.

To Joseph Hatton, Esq.,
London.

Xavier Witti [2] is being placed in front of the Government Buildings at Elopura, the result of a subscription on the spot. Neither of these officers named after

[2] Since these closing notes were written, and before this memorial column is finished, the subscribing officials of the Company have ordered three other names to be engraven upon the pedestal, namely, Dr. D. Manson Fraser, Captain A. M. de Fontaine, and Jemadhar Asa Singh, who were treacherously killed in a fray with Bajous on the 12th of May, 1885, while on an expedition with a party of native constabulary to capture a notorious head-hunter and cattle-raiding chief, one Kandurong. Captain de Fontaine had charge of the expedition, the two other Europeans accompanied him in no official capacity, but Asa Singh was a member of his staff. At the village of Kawang on the west coast, while making their arrangements for baggage-carriers and other assistance, they were unexpectedly attacked, one of the natives (Bajous), while talking to Dr. Fraser in an apparently friendly way, suddenly discharging his musket at him and killing him on the spot. Two other natives (who turned out to be well-known cattle thieves) at once *amoked* and fatally speared Jemadhar Asa Singh, and private Jeudah Singh, and then rushed off for the jungle. Captain de Fontaine dashed after them. Before the rest had time to support him, he stumbled and fell, whereupon the Bajous turned back to the attack. He shot three of them with his revolver, but was speared in nine places, and eventually died of his wounds. His little constabulary force fell upon the remainder of the retreating Bajous and dispersed them, killing several, and sustaining some severe casualties themselves. None of the villagers took part in the affair, the assailants turning out to be part of a roving band of marauders who are as hostile to the settled peaceful natives of the villages as to the Company. Captain de Fontaine, the head of the constabulary force (first organized by Colonel Harington), was very popular in the service, as were Dr. Manson Fraser and the native officer, Jemadhar Asa Singh. While these calamities are very lamentable, it is worthy of note that, considering they cover a period of six or seven years of government, deaths from violence have been remarkably few. Dr. Fraser's death is peculiarly sad. He went to Borneo a newly married man, some two years ago. His wife had died with her first child, a few months prior to his assassination. They lie together in the little cemetery at Sandakan.

themselves or their friends any part of the countries they explored. Frank Hatton, in a private letter, amused himself with a reference to "Hattonville;" and in one of his private diaries makes a memorandum in respect of a possible new discovery of a chemical body, to call it "Hattonite;" but whenever it fell to his lot to name any stream or tract of country, he used a native designation. The identification of portions of the newly-explored lands with his name comes therefore with a special grace from his successors and superior officers. "Mount Hatton" will keep his memory green in the territory where he fell; and "The Witti River" might well hand down to posterity the name and fame of his brave and unfortunate colleague.

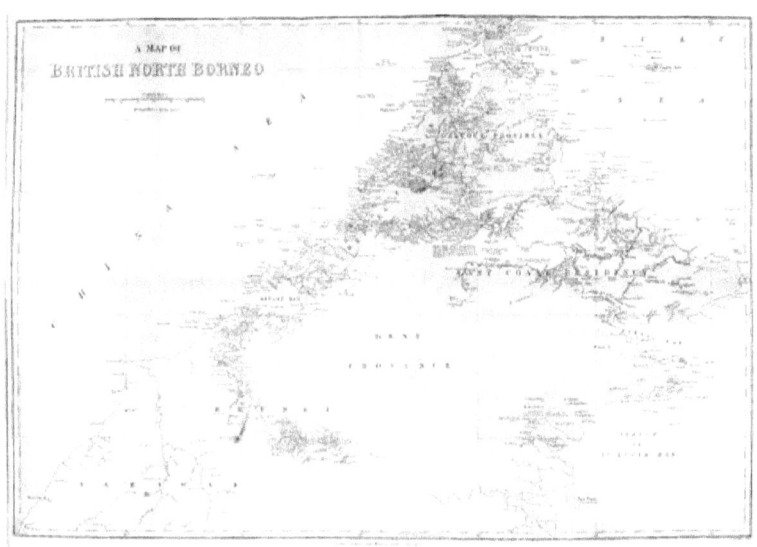

# INDEX.

ABAI, 137 (note); harbour, 167.
A'Beckett, Mr. Gilbert, 101 (note).
"Action of Bacteria on Various Gases," 53.
"A Drop of Thames Water," 17, 40.
Ague, Attack of, 260.
Alabaster, Mr. H., death of, 68 (note).
Ali, Sheriff, 167.
Alligators, 261.
Alowakie river, 248.
"Analysis of Thames Water where *Princess Alice* went down," 46 (note).
Antimony, *see* "Geological Notes."
Arms, Native, 322—327.
Armstrong, Dr. H. E., 59.
"Arrak," 209.
Arrows, Poisoned, *see* "Sumpitan."
Attacked by Muruts, 272.

BAJOUS, The, 335 (note).
Balambangan, Garrison at, assaulted by pirates, 4 (note).
Barker, Dr. Fordyce, 31.
Beelah, Evidence of, at inquest, 289.
Bendowen, 292.
Beveridge, Mr., 99, 100 (note), 105, 106, 110, 113, 226—232, 279, 283; evidence of, at inquest, 288, 290.
Bukoka district, Geology of, 172.
"Bintang-marrow" station, 186 (note).
*Biograph*, 39.
Birds'-nests, Edible, 247.

Blood-brother Ceremonies, 196, 203.
Boa constrictor, A, 132.
Bock, Mr. Carl, 190 (note), 324, 329, 330.
Bongon, 169, 172, 236.
Bongon river, 73, 168, 318—322.
Borneo, Dutch and English in, 4 (note); Sir Jas. Brooke in, 4 (note); Missionary work in, 80.
Bradshaw, Mrs., 101 (note).
*Bradstreets*, 39, 40, 48.
Brass cannon, Chinese, 238.
British North Borneo Company, 5 (note), 20, 24, 25, 61, 85, 96, 97, 110, 136 (note), 283, 334 (note).
Brooke, (Rajah) Sir Jas., 4 (note); founded Sarawak, 5 (note); 6 (note).
Brunei, 324, 328.
Brunei, Sultan of, 5 (note).
Buffalo-riding, 169.
Buli Dupie, Story of, 257.
Bungalow life in Labuan, 70, 124.
Byag, 205.

CARPENTER bees, 126.
*Chemical News*, 54.
*Chemical Society's Journal*, 60.
Clearing, An ancient, 255.
Coal, 73, 128, 144, 145, 155, 173, 266—273; *see also* "Geological Notes."
Coal-beds, Future, 262.
Coal Point (Tanjong Kubong), 69, 128, 130, 313.

z

Copper, Exploring for, 82, 91 (note), 92 (note), 94, 221, 246, 250—252.
Crocker, Mr. W. M., 26, 61, 96, 266 (note), 323, 327, 331.
Crossman, Col., 139 (note).

*Daily News*, 108 (note).
Dalit-men, 333 (note).
Daly, Mr. D. D., 308 (note).
Danao houses, 213.
Danao plain, 208, 214.
Datu Malunad, 169, 173.
Datu Ower, 171.
Datu Serikaya, 179.
Dead, Treatment of, 214, 266.
Dead man's ghost, Talking to, 204.
De Crespigny, C. E., 205 (note).
De Fontaine, Capt. A. M., 335 (note).
Degadong, 169, 212.
De Lissa, Mr., 108 (note).
Dent, Mr. Alfred, 26, 100, 332.
Dilke, Mr. A. W., M.P., 17.
Durahim, Evidence of, at inquest, 291.
Durian, Fruit of the, 263 (note).
Dusuns, The, 114, 152, 158, 164, 169, 193, 199, 218, 223 (note), 233, 264.
Dyaks, The, 258, 324, 330, 332.

East India Company, 4.
Elephant-hunting, 284.
Elephant swamp, 276.
Elk's-horn fern, 147.
Elopura, 7, 8, 109, 111, 284; inquest at, 287, 335.
Elphinstone, Lord, 98.
Empty tins better than cloth, 211.
*English Illustrated Magazine*, 115.
Everett, Mr. A. H., 70, 72.
Expeditions: Bongon river, 73; Timbong Batu, 73; Labuk to Kinoram, 76; Kina Balu to Tumboyonkon, 82; up the Segama and round Silam and Sibokon, 90, 94; Labuk river to Kudat, 108, 174—221; Sandakan to Labuk, 114; Marudu Bay, 114; on the Sequati and Kurina rivers; 135—173; four months in Kinoram and the Marudu, 222—253; last expedition, 254—281.

Ferns, 322.
Fever, To avoid, 257; attacks of, 257, 260.
Fishing, Mode of, 318—321.
Floods, 74, 171, 210, 214, 231, 263, 272.
Frankland, Prof., 3, 16, 54, 56, 58.
Franks, Mr. A., 330.
Fraser, Dr. D. M., Assassination of, 335 (note).

Garass hill, 217.
Garfield, President, 68.
Gensalong (chief), 235.
Geological Notes, 73, 76, 82, 91 (note), 113, 114, 141—145, 148, 153, 155—157, 161, 168, 169, 172—174, 179, 180, 183—185, 192, 200, 206, 215, 223 (note), 225, 229, 235, 245, 256—252, 261—273.
Ghanaghana, 209.
Gilbert, Dr., 58.
Goat-sucker, 131.
Gold, Discovery of, 266 (note); see also "Geological notes."
Gueritz, Mr., 219 (note), 321.

Habalu, 209.
Hamilton, Hon. A., 71, 121 (note).
Harington, Col., Notes by, 120—131; 135, 137, 219 (note); his acquaintance with Frank Hatton, 312—322; fishing trip up the Bongon, 319—322; 335 (note).
Hassan, Sergeant, 276; murder of, 308 (note)
Hatton, Frank: Boyhood, 8; birthplace, 10; school life, 11; at College of Marcq, Lille, 12; at King's College, 13; Oxford and Cambridge Examinations, 14; at the Royal School of Mines, 15; at Jermyn Street and South Kensington, 15, 331; geological tours, 15; visit to Derbyshire, 15 (note); commendations of eminent scientific men, and of the Chemical Society, 16, 56, 58—60; his admiration for Darwin and Huxley, 16; literary work, 17, 32; travels on the Continent, 17; portrait in *Graphic*, 17; personal

appearance, 19; Fellow of the Chemical Society, 23; engagement by the Company, 24; essays, 40; papers read before the Chemical Society, 53; arrangements for leaving England, 60; letters *en route*, 63—68; in Paris, 63; memoranda for proposed book, 66 (note), 115, 135 (note); invitation to Bangkok, Siam, 68; at Government House, Labuan, 69, 71; expeditions in the interior, 73—94; knowledge of Malay and Dusun, 78, 82, 90; dinner in the bush, 78; ascent of Kina Balu, 80; last exploration, 90; telegraphic news of his death, 96, 97; sympathy of Court of Directors, 97 (note); letters of condolence, 97—101; the fatal accident, 105, 113; the last journey, 107; inquest and verdict, 109, 110, 287—293, interred at Elopura, 111; eloquent tribute to, in *North Borneo Herald*, 112; Governor Treacher's letter to the Company, 284; Mr. Beveridge's devotion, 284; Mr. Pryer's account of the accident, 284—287; Mr. Herbert Ward's narrative, 300—308; incidents of life in Borneo related by Col. Harington, 312—322; loss of diaries, 332; "Frank Hatton Memorial Prize," 334; memorial obelisk, 334; "Mount Hatton," 336.

"Hattonville," 75, 336.

"Head-Hunters of Borneo," 190 (note), 330.

Head-hunting, 77, 88, 189, 212.

Hodgkinson, Dr., 16, 61, 91.

Hooker, Sir Joseph, 16.

Hope, Capt., 322.

Houses, Floating, 262.

Huxley, Prof., 3.

"INFLUENCE of Intermittent Filtration," &c., 53.

Inland lakes, 256, 268.

Inquest, The, 287—293.

JACKSON, Father, 71.

Jahore, Visit to, 332.

Java, Earthquake in, 93 (note).

Johnston, Mr. H. H., 105 (note).

Jumah, Evidence of, at inquest, 292.

Jungle, Tropical, 146, 149, 170, 243, 322.

KAGIBANGAN, 194.

Kaladi, 158.

Kaliga Point, 148.

Kambigging (chief), 224, 232.

Kandurong (chief), 335 (note).

Kaponakan river, 218, 248.

Kawang, 335 (note).

Kayan tribe, 329.

Kayan weapons, 322.

Keppel, Admiral, 5 (note).

Khoribson river, 243.

Kias, 226, 236, 246.

Kimauis, 335 (note).

Kina Balu, 3, 5, 79, 109, 120, 137 (note), 198, 221.

Kinabatangan cave, Story of, 257.

Kinabatangan river, 111, 113, 184, 186 (note), 254, 278.

Kinarringan (god), 161, 201, 233.

King-fisher, The, 131 (note).

Kinoram, 76, 77, 82, 90, 91 (note), 219, 222—253.

Kion Gendokod, 241.

Klings, The, 123.

Knox, Col., 28.

Koetei, Sultan of, 190 (note).

Koligan, 214; baggage-bearers, 215.

Kondorikan river, 249.

Kris, Malay, 322—324.

Kudat, 73, 77, 81, 91 (note), 108, 114, 166, 173, 174—221, 314.

Kuching, 76.

Kurina river, 143—173.

LABUAN, Purchase of, by English Government, 5 (note); 69, 70, 72, 76; life at, 119—134, 313; deserted colliery works, 129.

Labuan Coal Company, 73.

Labuk hills, 178, 180.

Labuk river, 109, 114, 174, 221.

Lamag river, 276.

Lasas, 216.

Leeches ("limatungs"), 185 (note), 262, 278.

Leys, Governor, 70, 72.
Liborreu, 175.
Lilompatie, 206.
Lobah, 224.
Lomantic, 176.
Longat, 205.
Luru, 160.
Luru river, 153, 161.

Madalon mountain, 225, 234.
Madanao, 237.
Malays, The North Bornean, 71, 121, 324.
Mamahunan river, 279.
Maran-Parang, 216.
Marudu (Toaran) river, 232—253.
Mason wasp, 127.
Medhurst, Sir W., 96, 97.
Meerschaum, Specimen of, 256.
Mentapok, 192, 197.
Mentapom mountain, 193.
Mentapose mountain, 172.
"Men with tails," 190.
Merrisinsing, 172.
Meteorological Notes, 38, 67, 70, 126, 139, 152, 201, 208, 251, 256, 257—273.
Minerals, see "Geological Notes," &c.
Mint, Visit to the, 48.
Miruru country, 192.
Missionary work, 89.
Montgelas, Count, 80; lost in the bush, 314—318.
Moroli in the vale, 247.
Mosquitoes, 127, 131, 255, 279.
Moths, 128.
Mouth-organ, Bornean, 329.
Mundy, Capt., 241 (note).
Mullykup river, 302.
Mumus, 224, 226.
Munnus, 219.
Murray, Capt., 28.
Muruts, The, 88, 204, 213, 270, 272.
Muruyan river, 254.
Musical instruments, 133, 163, 329, 330.

Nabalu mountain, 234, 241, 245.
Narrow escapes, 265, 305.
Native cloth, 151.

Natural history Notes, 126—128, 131—133, 146, 185 (note), 199, 228, 229, 262, 267, 276, 279, 303, 314, 331.
"New Ceylon," 6, 87, 93.
Niasaune, 207.
Nonoban-t-agaioh mountain, 224, 227.
*North Borneo Herald*, 112, 308 (note).

Oodeen (Udin), 106, 110, 113, 285; evidence of, at inquest, 290; 310.
Oriental Coal Company, 128.
Overbeck, Baron, 85.

Paddy-cutter, 324.
Page, Mr. F. J. M., 56.
Palu-palu ravine, 250.
Pampang, 235, 239; house at, 253.
Panataran river, 244, 245.
Pangeran Brunei, 148—152, 159, 161.
Parang, Bornean, 322—326, 330.
Paris, A day in, 63.
Passir, Sultan of, 190 (note).
Pengopuyan mountains, 225, 236.
Petroleum, 137 (note), 139—146, 153—157.
Pigeon-shooting, 264.
Pigs, Mode of killing, 214.
Pinowanter, 248.
Pinungah, 300, 311.
Pinungah river, 268, 275.
Pipes, Curious, 305, 327—329.
Pirates, Sulu, 141.
Poduss, 244.
Pomodanyoun, 185.
Pontianak, 4 (note).
Port Said, 66 (note).
Prahu accident, 273—275.
Prize, The Frank Hatton Memorial, 334.
Pryer, Mr. (Resident), 87, 111, 112, 186 (note), 282, 332, 333 (note).
Pudi, 225.
Pungoh, 182.

Quamut, 259, 262.

# Index.

"Rajah Brooke's Journal," 241 (note).
Rapid, Fearful, 265.
Read, Mr., 26, 67.
Regent's Canal explosion, 12.
Roscoe, Prof., 53, 54, 58.
Rothschild's, Visit to, 48.
Royal Geographical Society, 28.
Royal School of Mines, 15, 334.
Rumalow river, 241.

Sambar, English expedition against, 4 (note).
Sandakan, 69, 92, 94, 109, 115, 282.
Sarong, The, 158 (note).
Segama, 8, 90, 94, 336.
"Semungup" custom, 186 (note).
Senendan, 202.
Sepulut men, 269.
Shooting rapids, 272.
Silam hills, 109.
Sin-Dyaks, 187, 258.
Singapore, 66, 75, 91.
Singat vale, 109.
Singh, Jemadhar Asa, 335 (note).
Sinoront, 212.
Siquati, Oil and coal at, 73.
Siquati river, 135—173.
Sirih-box, A, 330, 331.
Sirih-leaves, Language of, 331.
Slave, Killing a, 212.
Smith at Siquati, 73; and Labuk, 194.
Sogolitan, 189.
Spear, Dusun, 324.
St. John, Mr., 121.
Succadana, 4 (note).
Suez Canal, 66 (note).
Sugut rivers, 215.
Sulu men, 180.
Sumpitan, Description of the, 89, 326, 327; 212 (note), 305.
Sun-birds, 126.
Sunsets, 134, 137 (note), 197.
Superstitions, 193, 233, 263, 304.
Swallows' nests, 228.
Swamp, An impenetrable, 277.

Tara root, 319.
Taba, Evidence of, at inquest, 292.
Tale, Hill of, 184.

Tampassuk river, 241.
Tampias, 194.
Tanah Dupas (Tampolon), 183.
Tander Batu, 177.
Tanjong Sugut, 175.
Telupid river, 184.
Temperature, see "Meteorological Notes."
Tenegang, 255.
Tertipan, 172.
Tertipan river, 167, 168.
Thames water, 17, 40, 46 (note).
Thomson, Mr. J., 105 (note).
Tidy, Prof.: Paper on "River Water," 58; oratorical manner, 59.
Timbong Batu, 73, 169.
Tinggaluns, The, 256.
Toadilah, 198.
Tobacco, Use of, 328.
Tonaran river, 234.
Traveller's tree, 67.
Treacher, Mr. (Governor), 27, 70—72, 105 (note), 110, 112, 223 (note), 284.
Treacher, Mrs., 99.
Tree fern, 67.
Trentidan, 242.
Tuan Murrim, 276.
Tumboyonkon mountain, 225, 250.
Tungara, 270; people of, 305, 328.
Tuntoul, 211.
Tyndall, Prof., 37.

Upas juice, Collecting, 198.

Van Moort, Oliver, 4 (note).
Victoria, Labuan, 120.
"Visit to Rothschild's, and to the British Mint," 40, 48.
Von Donnop, Mr., 238, 246.

Walker, Dr., 61, 109, 185 (note); evidence of, at inquest, 287, 289, 292, 332.
Walker, Mr., 266 (note).
Wallace, "Malay Archipelago," 264 (note).

Ward, Mr. Herbert, 294, reminiscences of Frank Hatton, 296—311; 322, 328.
Watts, Mr. H., 60.
Wild-cattle shooting, 153.
Wild-pig shooting, 130.
Witti, Mr. Franz Xavier, 20, 26, 72, 81; assassination of, 83; sketch of his career, 84—90; 135, 137 (note), 155, 182, 211 (note), 212, 217, 259, 270, 305, 327; letter from, 333 (note); obelisk in memory of, 334.

LONDON:
PRINTED BY GILBERT AND RIVINGTON, LIMITED
ST. JOHN'S SQUARE.

www.ingramcontent.com/pod-product-compliance
Lightning Source LLC
Chambersburg PA
CBHW030428300426
44112CB00009B/902